Instructor's Manual

to accompany

Deux mondes

A COMMUNICATIVE APPROACH

Fifth Edition

Tracy D. Terrell

Mary B. Rogers

Betsy J. Kerr

Guy Spielmann

Boston   Burr Ridge, IL   Dubuque, IA   New York
San Francisco   St. Louis   Bangkok   Bogotá   Caracas   Kuala Lumpur
Lisbon   London   Madrid   Mexico City   Milan   Montreal   New Delhi
Santiago   Seoul   Singapore   Sydney   Taipei   Toronto

Higher Education

This is an  book.

Instructor's Manual to accompany
Deux mondes: A Communicative Approach

Published by McGraw-Hill, an imprint of The McGraw-Hill Companies, Inc., 1221 Avenue of the Americas, New York, NY 10020. Copyright © 2005, 2002, 1997, 1993, 1989 by The McGraw-Hill Companies, Inc. All rights reserved. No part of this publication may be reproduced or distributed in any form or by any means, or stored in a database or retrieval system, without the prior written consent of The McGraw-Hill Companies, Inc., including, but not limited to, in any network or other electronic storage or transmission, or broadcast for distance learning.

This book is printed on acid-free paper.

1 2 3 4 5 6 7 8 9 0 QSR QSR 0 9 8 7 6 5 4

ISBN 0-07-295935-5

Editor-in-chief: *Emily G. Barrosse*
Publisher: *William R. Glass*
Development editor: *Michelle-Noelle Magallanez*
Director of development: *Susan Blatty*
Executive marketing manager: *Nick Agnew*
Lead project manager: *David M. Staloch*
Senior supplements producer: *Louis Swaim*
Compositor: *Eisner/Martin Typographics*
Typeface: *10/12 Palatino*
Printer and Binder: *Quebecor World, Dubuque*

www.mhhe.com

Contents

How to Teach with *Deux mondes*: An Illustrated Walkthrough

Deux mondes is designed for a course in which students, interacting with the instructor and their class-mates, develop the ability to communicate their thoughts and ideas in French. It is based on the philoso-phy and approach to teaching second languages known as the Natural Approach (NA). Although we believe that *Deux mondes* is used most effectively according to the principles of the Natural Approach, it is a flexible and extremely "user friendly" program that has produced excellent results in a variety of classroom situations.

In addition to achieving functional proficiency through their language study, students should learn how to acquire a language, gain some insight into the acquisition process itself, and enjoy the experience. We hope to lay a good foundation for continued acquisition so that students will want to continue with French or to repeat the process with another language in their lives.

The "To the Instructor" preface in the main text presents the basic principles of the Natural Approach. You may wish to assign the "To the Student" preface to your class, since, in our experience, students learn best when they are active, informed participants in the instructional process. Later in this Instruc-tor's Manual, we outline in detail the theories and principles underlying the Natural Approach, suggest instructional goals for the various language uses, and describe how to use the activities provided in *Deux mondes*. In this section, we provide a clear introduction to both the Natural Approach and *Deux mondes* through a narrative description of the pages found in the early chapters of the book. The introductory Walkthrough includes reproductions of the student pages of the **Première étape** and **Chapitre 1,** together with an annotated discussion of the Natural Approach as its features are seen in these pages.

If you wish to learn more about the Natural Approach after reading the Walkthrough and the other information in this Instructor's Manual, you may be interested in the following items, newly available from McGraw-Hill:

- *Natural Approach Training Video,* ISBN 0-07-063873-X. The nearly two-hour video combines a discussion of the theoretical underpinnings of the Natural Approach with classroom footage demonstrating the method in action.
- *The Natural Approach from Theory to Practice,* ISBN 0-07-079620-3. This two-hour video focuses on both theory and practice of the Natural Approach. The panel of master instructors includes Stephen D. Krashen and *Deux mondes* author Mary Rogers.
- *Studies in Language Learning and Spanish Linguistics in Honor of Tracy D. Terrell,* ISBN 0-07-064488-8. One section of this Festschrift for Tracy D. Terrell is devoted to the Natural Approach and includes essays by Stephen D. Krashen, Bill VanPatten, Wilga Rivers, and other leading scholars.

These and related items in the McGraw-Hill Professional Series are available only for purchase. For further information, please call 1.800.338.3987, or visit the McGraw-Hill College Division's website at **http://www.mhhe.com.**

This Walkthrough illustrates certain Natural Approach principles that underlie the initial stages of language learning. *Deux mondes* allows for three stages of language development.

- Stage 1: Comprehension (**Première étape**)
- Stage 2: Comprehension and Early Speech (**Deuxième étape**)
- Stage 3: Comprehension, Early Speech, and Speech Emergence (**Chapitres 1–14**)

The activities in the **Première étape** are designed to give students a chance to develop initial comprehension abilities without being required to produce a significant amount of French. The activities in the **Deuxième étape** (not illustrated here) encourage the transition from comprehension to an ability to respond naturally in single words or short phrases. By the end of these two preliminary chapters and at the beginning of the regular chapters, students are making the transition from short answers to longer phrases and more complex sentences. Students will pass through these same three stages with the new material of each chapter.

We find that Natural Approach students talk significantly more than the students in most traditional classes. We hope that this introductory Walkthrough of *Deux mondes* will help you understand why.

The *Première étape:* Comprehension Phase

We believe that to acquire a language the learner must begin to comprehend that language before being called on to use it in speech. In other words, comprehension must precede production. The **Première étape** is designed so that students can hear and begin understanding a basic vocabulary in French.

In this first comprehensive stage (Stage 1), language learners concentrate on meaning and on understanding the new language they are hearing. The **Première étape** provides a variety of Stage 1 activities that do not require students to produce speech. Instead, students have an opportunity to absorb, to bind meaning to the words they hear. Our experience as classroom teachers has taught us that learners comprehend much faster when, at the earliest stages, they are asked to show only that they understand what is being said.

PREMIÈRE ÉTAPE

Des étudiantes à l'université de Paris

Premières rencontres

OBJECTIFS IN THE PREMIÈRE ÉTAPE, *you will learn to understand a good deal of spoken French and get to know your classmates. The listening skills you develop will enhance your ability to understand and speak French.*

Activités
La communication en classe
Qui est-ce? Les camarades de classe
Comment sont-ils? La description des personnes
Les vêtements et les couleurs
Les nombres (0-34)
Rencontres

Grammaire
A.1 Giving instructions: Commands with vous
A.2 Identifying people: C'est... , je m'appelle...
A.3 Gender and articles
A.4 Describing people: Être, subject pronouns, and ne... pas
A.5 Plural nouns and articles
A.6 Addressing others: Tu and vous

Pre-Text Oral Activities

Our approach to acquiring French is easy to understand. Students first begin to comprehend new language through oral input ("teacher-talk") that is accompanied by aids such as visuals and gestures. Initially, their only task is to show that they understand what they hear. Before students open their books, the instructor should use the **Mise en train** (Pre-Text Oral) activities to begin the acquisition process. The **Mise en train** activities ask students to verify their comprehension by following commands requiring physical movements, by answering **oui/non** to questions, and by saying someone's name. Through these activities, students discover that they can understand when the instructor speaks French. They begin establishing a basic vocabulary, and they start to develop listening skills essential to proficiency. Many instructors find that during the first few days of class, they do not need to use the book at all.

Early TPR (Total Physical Response)

The first **Mise en train** activity outlined in the Instructor's Edition is a TPR activity that asks students to follow a number of simple commands. We recommend that the instructor begin each class with commands for a number of days, adding new ones each day. In a short time, the students come to understand imperative forms of a large number of verbs. The focus is on the meaning of the verbs, so there is no need to make grammatical distinctions as to infinitive types or imperative forms when selecting verbs for the activity. TPR done by a whole class participating simultaneously creates an informal atmosphere in which students acquire proficiency quickly. TPR also allows the instructor to introduce instructions necessary for class routine: **Prenez votre livre, ouvrez-le à la page 10, fermez la porte,** and so on. The Instructor's Manual outlines in clear detail how to begin and develop TPR activities. See the Instructor's Resource Kit (IRK) for detailed TPR sequences.

The Vocabulary Display

Each topical section in every chapter begins with an illustrated display that introduces key vocabulary. In the display for **La communication en classe,** the topic is taken from the pre-text TPR activities recommended in the **Mise en train** activities found in the Instructor's Edition. If the instructor has already done the **Mise en train** activities, students will be seeing familiar words as they look at this page for the first time. The characters here will recur often throughout the textbook, the *Cahier d'exercices,* and the Audio Program.

Using the *Activités*

Activité 1 is a Comprehension (Stage 1) activity that asks students to associate the TPR commands they have been hearing in pre-text activities with the drawings. Students need only to point to the appropriate drawing as they listen to the instructor read the commands.

Activités

La communication en classe

Attention! Étudier Grammaire A.1

écrivez asseyez-vous
écoutez levez-vous
lisez

Daniel Jacqueline Louis Albert Barbara
Madame Martin

Activité 1: Associations: Les ordres

a. Tournez la page!
b. Ouvrez le livre!
c. Fermez le livre!
d. Regardez le tableau!
e. Écrivez votre nom!
f. Levez la main!
g. Prenez un stylo!

2

Grammar References

Grammar study is separated from the acquisition activities in *Deux mondes,* and all components of the grammar are designed to be done by students as homework. Depending on the instructor's emphasis, students may be asked to read and study grammar at home as a means of complementing language activities introduced and used in the classroom. The instructor may choose to assign grammar before, during, or after any particular section. Each section of communication activities contains references (**Attention!**) to the explanations and exercises that correspond to that particular section.

Introducing Vocabulary with Visuals

Many **Mise en train** activities suggest the use of visuals, especially pictures from magazines. Before students look at the display on page 3, we recommend that the instructor ask about photos of well-known people: **Qui est-ce? (Bill Cosby) Oui, c'est Bill Cosby. Et sur cette photo? Est-ce que c'est (Uma Thurman)? (non) Ce n'est pas Uma Thurman? Est-ce que c'est Gwyneth Paltrow? (oui) Et cette personne? Est-ce qu'elle s'appelle (Céline Dion ou Brittany Spears)? (Céline Dion)** The instructor might then ask these same questions about members of the class.

Responding with Names of People

Activité 2 is another type of Stage 1, or Comprehension Phase, activity. Rather than using gestures to show they understand, students are asked to use **oui/non** or the names of people. The instructor should provide lots of input that uses the target vocabulary while students look at the drawings: **Comment s'appelle l'amie de Denise? (Barbara) Est-ce que l'amie de Barbara s'appelle Jacqueline ou Denise? (Denise)**

Using a Picture File (PF)

Magazine pictures and ads provide an excellent variety of contexts for oral input activities. The Instructor's Manual includes a topical listing of pictures for each section of each chapter, as well as suggestions for how to create a Picture File. In the **Première étape,** we recommend that the instructor use photos to teach words for naming and describing people (for example, **petit garçon, homme, enfant, ami, cheveux blonds,** adjectives, names of clothing, and colors): **Voici la photo d'une femme. Elle est très célèbre. C'est une star de télévision. Elle est brune, elle est grande et elle est mince** (point to illustrate adjectives). **Très mince! Qui est-ce? (Calista Flockhart) Bravo! C'est Calista. Et voici une autre femme. Comment s'appelle cette femme? (Rosie O'Donnell) Oui, c'est Rosie. Calista est très mince.** (photo again) **Est-ce que Rosie est mince aussi?**

Input and the Vocabulary Display

The vocabulary displays allow the instructor to review or to present key vocabulary using the techniques from the **Mise en train** activities mentioned earlier. For example, the instructor might describe one of the characters and ask students to touch the drawing of the person to show they understand (TPR) or could ask questions requiring **oui/non** or names as responses: **Qui est petite et belle? Est-ce c'est Marise ou Claudine? (Marise) Est-ce que Marie Lasalle est jeune? (non)**

Discussion Activities

Activités 3 and **4** are **Discussion** activities. This means that they are designed to allow the instructor to lead a group discussion. In the early chapters, students need only comprehend and reply with names or short answers in the **Discussion** activities. Here are some examples from **Activités 3** and **4: Qui dans la classe a une moustache? (Robert) Comment est Catherine Deneuve? Est-ce qu'elle est jeune? (non) Est-ce qu'elle est brune ou blonde? (blonde)**

Despite the limited vocabulary, the focus is on meaningful reality, and students think in French without needing to translate.

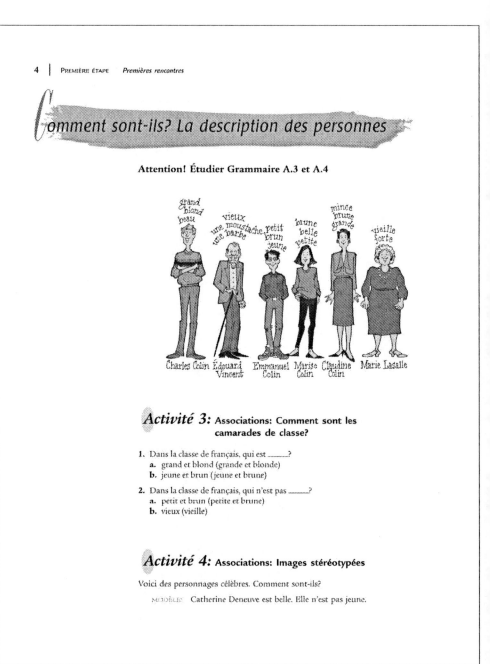

Comment sont-ils? La description des personnes

Attention! Étudier Grammaire A.3 et A.4

grand
blond
beau
vieux
une moustache
une barbe
petit
brun
jeune
brune
belle
petite
mince
brune
grande
vieille
forte

Charles Colin   Edouard Vincent   Emmanuel Colin   Marise Colin   Claudine Colin   Marie Lasalle

Activité 3: **Associations: Comment sont les camarades de classe?**

1. Dans la classe de français, qui est _____?
   a. grand et blond (grande et blonde)
   b. jeune et brun (jeune et brune)

2. Dans la classe de français, qui n'est pas _____?
   a. petit et brun (petite et brune)
   b. vieux (vieille)

Activité 4: **Associations: Images stéréotypées**

Voici des personnages célèbres. Comment sont-ils?

MODÈLE: Catherine Deneuve est belle. Elle n'est pas jeune.

Student-Centered Input

An interesting variation on using PF photos to introduce vocabulary is to describe members of the class and have the other students guess who is being described. This context is very appealing since it draws on the students' own classroom reality. It also helps both instructor and students to quickly learn the names of everyone in class. There is no need to restrict descriptions to using only words from the chapter, providing the students can follow the gist of the unfamiliar language. It is, however, important that the instructor use the key words many times during input. Here is an example: **Bonjour, je m'appelle (Henri Brulot). Et vous, comment vous appelez-vous? (Alex) Bonjour, Alex. Alors la classe, cet étudiant s'appelle Alex. Regardez-le, s'il vous plaît. Comment est-il? Il est blond. Il est grand.** (point out clothing) **Il porte un short bleu et un tee-shirt vert. Et** (point) **il porte des lunettes.** Describe two or three students; then ask questions. **Qui est grand et blond et porte des lunettes?**

Oui, c'est Alex. Comment s'appelle la personne qui porte une robe longue?

Recurring Characters

Deux mondes has a small cast of recurring characters who are particularly prominent in the early chapters. They gradually develop personality traits, tastes, and so forth, and are often useful as a point of reference to make a contrast or to introduce delicate terms such as **mince** and **fort(e)**. The characters are described in some detail in the Student Introduction of the book.

Associations

Deux mondes has many types of **Associations.** These are matching activities intended to be done with the whole class with ample teacher input before and during the activity. In **Activité 5,** as is usually the case for **Associations,** there is more than one correct answer for most items, so students are encouraged to begin thinking flexibly in class.

Activités | 5

1. Nicole Kidman
2. Brad Pitt
3. Cléopâtre
4. Juliette Binoche
5. Céline Dion
6. Gérard Depardieu

a. laid/laide ≠ beau/belle
b. vieux/vieille ≠ jeune
c. fort/forte ≠ mince
d. grand/grande ≠ petit/petite
e. ?

es vêtements et les couleurs

Attention! Étudier Grammaire A.5

une chemise blanche
← un chapeau noir
une cravate verte
une veste grise
un costume gris
des chaussures noires
Victor Colin

un blouson vert
un pantalon bleu
des tennis blancs
Joël Colin

un chemisier jaune
un pull-over orange
une jupe marron
des bottes marron
Clarisse Colin

une robe rose
un manteau violet
une rose rouge
Claudine Colin

Activité 5: Associations: Les couleurs

De quelle couleur est... ?

1. un pingouin
2. un éléphant
3. un tigre
4. une plante
5. une tragédie
6. un jean
7. une banane
8. une tomate
9. une carotte
10. le chocolat

a. vert/verte
b. noir/noire
c. gris/grise
d. brun/brune
e. orange
f. blanc/blanche
g. rouge
h. jaune
i. bleu/bleue

Dans le monde francophone

The activities labeled **Dans le monde francophone** are based on authentic materials. Students should be taught to use the realia to get information they need to do the accompanying activity, but they should not be held accountable for the vocabulary in the realia. Instead, we suggest that instructors use these unedited materials to help students develop basic reading skills such as skimming a piece for facts or learning to recognize cognates and word relationships to determine meaning. The authentic materials usually bring new cultural information or reveal another approach to a common human situation. In **Activité 6,** for example, students use the ad to apply their knowledge of words for colors and clothing. At the same time, however, they see a Haitian marketplace and find out or are reminded that French is an official language in Haiti.

Using Numbers

We suggest that the instructor provide input with numbers by counting students in class.

At first, have students listen. Then they may respond with **oui/non** as you give them statements with counts of different groups in the classroom: **Il y a deux hommes avec une moustache dans notre classe? Y a-t-il quatre femmes blondes?** As students grow accustomed to hearing the numbers, they will gradually join in as the instructor counts **les femmes, les hommes, les femmes aux cheveux bruns, les hommes qui portent une barbe, les étudiant(e)s qui portent un jean,** and so on.

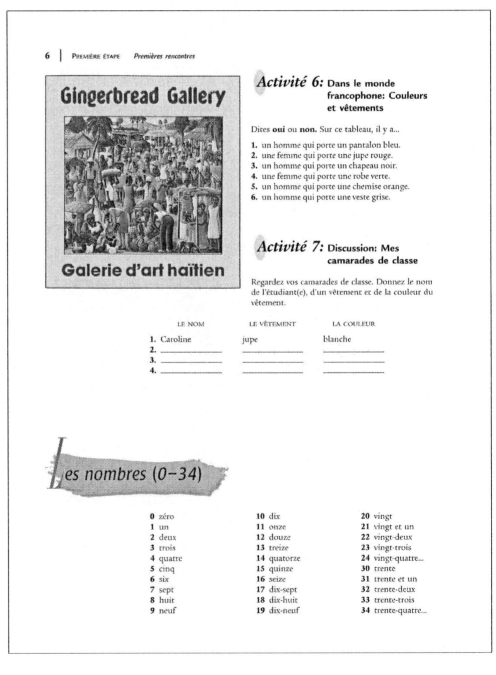

Gingerbread Gallery

Galerie d'art haïtien

Activité 6: **Dans le monde francophone: Couleurs et vêtements**

Dites **oui** ou **non**. Sur ce tableau, il y a...

1. un homme qui porte un pantalon bleu.
2. une femme qui porte une jupe rouge.
3. un homme qui porte un chapeau noir.
4. une femme qui porte une robe verte.
5. un homme qui porte une chemise orange.
6. un homme qui porte une veste grise.

Activité 7: **Discussion: Mes camarades de classe**

Regardez vos camarades de classe. Donnez le nom de l'étudiant(e), d'un vêtement et de la couleur du vêtement.

LE NOM	LE VÊTEMENT	LA COULEUR
1. Caroline	jupe	blanche
2.		
3.		
4.		

Les nombres (0–34)

0 zéro	**10** dix	**20** vingt
1 un	**11** onze	**21** vingt et un
2 deux	**12** douze	**22** vingt-deux
3 trois	**13** treize	**23** vingt-trois
4 quatre	**14** quatorze	**24** vingt-quatre...
5 cinq	**15** quinze	**30** trente
6 six	**16** seize	**31** trente et un
7 sept	**17** dix-sept	**32** trente-deux
8 huit	**18** dix-huit	**33** trente-trois
9 neuf	**19** dix-neuf	**34** trente-quatre...

TPR: Beginning the Transition to Early Speech

We recommend that the instructor include TPR activities daily at least throughout the **Première étape,** gradually bringing in new verbs and useful expressions such as **allez au tableau, fermez votre livre,** or **tournez à gauche / à droite.** TPR is a good way to introduce students to speaking with one another. As an example, after a series of commands, include other commands such as **Dites «bonjour», Dites «Comment allez-vous?»** and then give commands such as **Regardez la personne à votre gauche et dites «bonjour». Maintenant, dites-lui «Comment allez-vous?». Et maintenant, répondez «Très bien, merci».** The instructor may choose to illustrate with gestures as needed and to introduce other commands such as **serrez-vous la main** and **embrassez-le/la.**

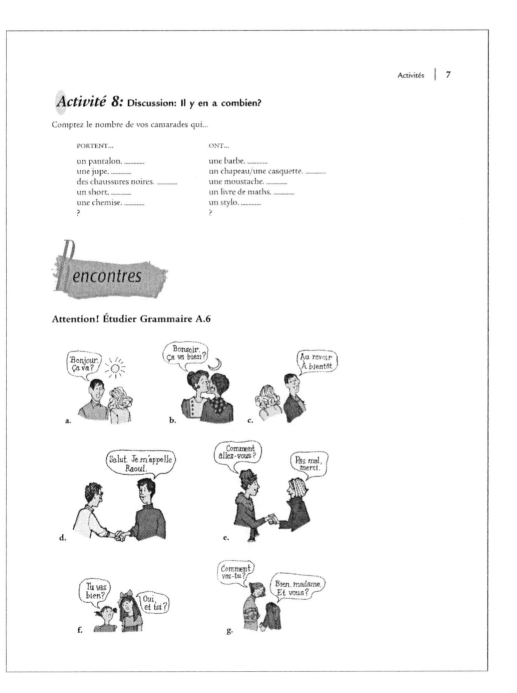

Activité 8: Discussion: Il y en a combien?

Comptez le nombre de vos camarades qui...

PORTENT...	ONT...
un pantalon.	une barbe. ....
une jupe.	un chapeau/une casquette. ....
des chaussures noires.	une moustache. ....
un short.	un livre de maths. ....
une chemise.	un stylo. ....
?	?

Rencontres

Attention! Étudier Grammaire A.6

Dialogues

There are two types of **Dialogues** activities in *Deux mondes,* open dialogues (see **Activité 2**) and model dialogues (**Activité 9**). Open dialogues require students to do little more than fill in names, because the script is provided. This engenders a realistic exchange without making students produce the sentences. The model dialogues in **Activité 9** are short and are intended as models for conversation. Students should not be asked to memorize them.

   We suggest that the instructor read each model dialogue aloud at least two times, with as natural an intonation as possible, while the class follows along in the book. Students may identify (in English if necessary) any words or phrases they do not understand so that the instructor can explain them. After the meaning is clear, the instructor may read one of the roles aloud, with the class all together taking the other. The practice is then repeated with the next dialogue. Finally, the

instructor may choose to put students in pairs to practice together. In such practice, they should exchange roles, so that each student plays each role. The "read, look up, and say" technique may be useful here: Students read a line silently to themselves, then look at their partner and say the line as meaningfully as possible without looking at the text. After doing the model dialogues, the instructor may wish to have students change partners to do the open dialogue at the end of the activity.

Activité 9: Dialogue: Les salutations

1. Victor Colin parle au directeur du bureau.
   —Bonjour, monsieur. Comment allez-vous?
   —Très bien, merci. Et vous?
   —Bien, merci.
2. Après le match de foot, Charles Colin parle avec sa cousine Camille.
   —Salut, Camille. Ça va?
   —Je suis très fatiguée! Et toi?
   —Moi, ça va.
3. Louis présente Barbara à Raoul Durand, un étudiant canadien.
   —Raoul, je te présente une camarade de classe, Barbara.
   —Enchanté, mademoiselle.
   —Enchantée.
4. Claudine Colin parle au téléphone avec son père, Francis Lasalle.
   —Bonsoir, papa. Tu vas bien?
   —Comme ci, comme ça. Un peu fatigué.
   —Et maman? Elle va bien?
   —Elle va très bien.
5. Vous parlez avec un/une camarade de classe.
   É₁*: Bonjour. Je m'appelle ....
   É₂: Enchanté(e). Je ....
   É₁: Salut, ... Ça va bien?
   É₂: ...., et toi?
   É₁: ...., merci.

---

*É1 et É2 = Étudiant(e) 1 et Étudiant(e) 2

Vocabulaire **Sections**

The **Vocabulaire** sections contain the new words in each chapter. Natural Approach classes develop proficiency in listening and speaking by exposing students to a wide and "real" vocabulary that recurs often in many different contexts. Students should be able to recognize the words in the **Vocabulaire,** but many instructors opt not to have students memorize all the words in the lists. Students should be encouraged to skim through the

Vocabulaire regularly before coming to class and also as part of their home preparation. Insofar as possible, all new vocabulary terms are grouped by topic in the **Vocabulaire** to facilitate acquisition through association with themes and ideas.

The notes in the Instructor's Edition for each vocabulary display and oral activity in the **Activités** section include a listing of all new vocabulary that has not yet been included in the text or in our suggested Pre-Text Oral Activities.

Vocabulaire

See the *Lexique* for a key to the abbreviations used in *Vocabulaire* lists.

Dans la classe de français

In French class

un/une camarade de classe	classmate
un crayon	pencil
un étudiant / une étudiante	student
un livre	book
un stylo	(ballpoint) pen
un tableau	(black)board

Mots apparentés: **une activité, une conversation, la grammaire, une page, un professeur,* une table, le vocabulaire**

Asseyez-vous.	Sit down.
Attention!	Pay attention!
Écoutez.	Listen.
Écrivez votre nom.	Write your name.
Fermez le livre.	Close the book.
Levez la main.	Raise your hand.
Levez-vous.	Stand up. (Get up.)
Lisez.	Read.
Ouvrez le livre.	Open the book.
Prenez un stylo.	Get a pen.
Regardez le tableau.	Look at the (black)board.
Tournez la page.	Turn the page.

Les personnes

People

un ami / une amie	friend
une femme	woman
un homme	man

La description des personnes

Describing people

Qui est... ?	Who is . . . ?
Qui n'est pas... ?	Who isn't . . . ?
beau/belle	handsome/beautiful
blond/blonde	blond

*For the purpose of this edition, **un professeur** *is presented as an invariable masculine noun. See p. 22 for more information.*

brun/brune	dark-haired
fort/forte	heavy, plump
grand/grande	tall
jeune	young
laid/laide	ugly
mince	thin
moyen/moyenne	average
petit/petite	small, little, short
vieux/vieille	old, elderly
Qui a... ?	Who has . . . ?
une barbe	a beard
une moustache	a moustache
Qui n'a pas... ?	Who doesn't have . . . ?
les cheveux courts/ longs	short/long hair
les yeux bleus	blue eyes

Les couleurs

Colors

blanc/blanche	white
bleu/bleue	blue
gris/grise	gray
jaune	yellow
marron *(inv.)*	brown
noir/noire	black
rose	pink
rouge	red
vert/verte	green

Mots apparentés: **orange** *(inv.),* **violet/violette**

Les vêtements

Clothing

Qui dans la classe porte... ?	Who in class is wearing . . . ?
Il/Elle porte...	He's/She's wearing . . .
Ils/Elles portent...	They're wearing . . .
un blouson	a jacket, windbreaker
des bottes *(f.)*	boots
un chapeau	a hat
des chaussures *(f.)*	shoes
une chemise	a man's shirt
un chemisier	a woman's blouse
un costume	a man's suit
une cravate	a necktie
une jupe	a skirt
un manteau	a coat

9

Teaching Vocabulary

An important goal of *Deux mondes* is to help students acquire enough vocabulary to become proficient listeners and speakers who can function in a wide variety of contexts. We believe that students are capable of acquiring a very large vocabulary if they are given frequent opportunities to hear the words in meaningful contexts. This is particularly true for students of French because of the rich vocabulary of cognate words that exists between English and French.

Our approach to vocabulary derives from our belief that speech emerges in stages. We expect students to show they understand words used frequently in communicative situations. However, students should not be required to memorize and mechanically produce the words in a list. The end-of-chapter vocabulary in *Deux mondes* is intended primarily for reference. These and other words in *Deux mondes* will recur many times throughout the book and in class activities. As students acquire more language, they will be able to produce and write them.

---

un pantalon	a pair of pants
une robe	a dress
une veste	a sportcoat, suitcoat
un vêtement	a piece of clothing

Mots apparentés: un jean, un pull-over, des tennis (*m.*)

Mots et expressions utiles
Useful words and expressions

l'ami/l'amie de Daniel	Daniel's friend
aussi	too, also
bien	well
dans	in
mais	but
moi aussi	me too
ne... pas	not
non	no
oui	yes
s'il vous plaît (s'il te plaît)	please
tout le monde	everybody
tu	you (*fam.*)
vous	you (*form. or pl.*)

Les ordres
Commands

Chantez.	Sing.
Courez.	Run.
Dites *bonjour*.	Say *hello*. (Say *good morning*.)
Marchez.	Walk.
Sautez.	Jump.
Tournez à droite (à gauche).	Turn right (left).

Salutations et formules de politesse
Greetings and polite expressions

À bientôt.	See you soon.
aujourd'hui	today
Au revoir.	Good-bye.
Bonjour.	Hello; Good morning/ afternoon/day.
Bonsoir.	Good evening; Good-bye. (*in the evening*).
Ça va?	How's it going?
Moi, ça va. Et toi?	Fine. How about you?

Comment allez-vous?	How are you? (*form.*)
Très bien, merci. Et vous?	Fine, thanks. And you?
Pas mal, merci.	Not bad, thanks
Je suis un peu fatigué/fatiguée.	I'm a little tired.
Comment vas-tu?	How are you? (*fam.*)
Bien. Et toi?	Fine. And you? (*fam.*)
Je vous (te) présente...	I want you to meet . . .
Enchanté/Enchantée.	Delighted.
madame	madam, ma'am; Mrs.
mademoiselle	miss
monsieur	sir; Mr.
Salut!	Hi!; Good-bye. (*fam.*)

Questions
Questions

Combien de... ?	How many . . . ?
Comment est-il/elle?	What's he/she/it like?
Comment s'appelle... ?	What is . . . 's name?
Il/Elle s'appelle...	His/Her name is . . .
Comment sont-ils?	What are they like?
Comment va... ?	How is . . . ?
Il/Elle va bien/mal.	He's/She's fine / not well.
Comment vous appelez-vous?	What's your name? (*form. or pl.*)
Comment t'appelles-tu?	What's your name? (*fam.*)
Je m'appelle...	My name is . . .
De quelle couleur est... ?	What color is . . . ?
Est-ce que c'est un/une... ?	Is this a . . . ?
Oui, c'est un/une...	Yes, it's a . . .
Non, ce n'est pas un/une...	No, it's not a . . .
n'est-ce pas?	isn't it?, right?
Où est... ?	Where's . . . ?
Qui est-ce?	Who's that? (Who is it?)
C'est...	It's . . .
Y a-t-il... ? / Il y a...	Is/Are there . . . ? / There is/are . . .

Mots apparentés
Cognates

une banane, une carotte, le chocolat, un éléphant, un général, une image, un pingouin, une plante, un tigre, une tomate, une tragédie

---

The Role of Grammar in *Deux mondes*

The organization of *Deux mondes* derives from our belief that grammar is secondary to vocabulary in expressing meaning until students reach an advanced level. As students move beyond the comprehension and early speech stages, they develop an emerging ability to express their thoughts (stage 3, Speech Emergence). At this point of early self-expression, however, they do so with a reduced and simplified language that will gradually improve and become more "grammatical" as they progress through the course. We believe that this improvement occurs because of their increasing ability to understand and to attend more carefully to input.

However, many Natural Approach students report that the study of grammar is helpful in improving their speech. Grammar study serves to improve comprehension by providing advance organizers that focus attention on specific grammatical markers. Grammar study, then, has a useful part in the acquisition process but is not the primary focus of *Deux mondes*. As in previous editions, grammar pages are tinted blue for ease of reference.

Grammar Topics

Grammar topics in each chapter of *Deux mondes* are selected to enhance the primary language of the chapter. Since students have encountered commands in TPR activities from the **Mise en train** activities and in the textbook itself, commands are the logical first subject in the **Grammaire et exercices**. This is an introduction to the topic; a fuller explanation of commands is given later in the book.

Definitions

Since many students are not familiar with basic grammatical terms or may have forgotten their meaning, we define the terms when they first occur in the text with examples in English.

Grammaire et exercices

Introduction

The **Grammaire et exercices** section of each chapter presents grammar points used in the preceding **Activités** section.

The **Attention!** notes that begin each new topic in the **Activités** section tell you which grammar point(s) you should study at that time. Study the grammar point(s) carefully, reading the examples out loud. Then do the exercises, both orally and in writing, and check your answers in the Appendix. Your instructor may choose not to discuss grammar in class because it is explained in nontechnical language in the book and because answers to the exercises are provided.

Keep in mind that successful completion of a grammar exercise indicates that you have understood the explanation. However, you are not immediately expected to use that grammar without error. As you listen to your instructor, your fellow students, and the audio program, and as you talk with others, you will gradually assimilate that grammar point into your own speech and writing.

If you have trouble with an exercise or with a particular point, ask your instructor for assistance. In difficult cases, your instructor may want to go over the material in class to be sure that everyone understands. However, class time is best used for real experience in communicating in French.

A.1 Giving instructions: Commands with **vous**

A. Commands are verb forms used without a subject pronoun to tell or ask someone to do something.

> Raise your hand.   Open your book, please.

B. The commands in the **Première étape** are all verb forms that end in **-ez.** This ending is associated with the pronoun **vous** and can refer to a single person or to a group of people.

> Louis, **ouvrez** la fenêtre, s'il vous plaît.   Louis, open the window, please.
>
> Barbara et Denise, **regardez** le tableau.   Barbara and Denise, look at the board.

C. Notice that some commands have the word **vous** attached to the verb, whereas others do not.

> **Asseyez-vous**, s'il vous plaît!   Sit down, please!

Definition: A verb conveys an action or a state: sit, raise, be.

Definitions: A subject performs the action or exists in the state conveyed by the verb. A noun represents a person or thing. A subject pronoun substitutes for a subject noun: Joël sits. He sits.

*✷ You will learn more about the pronoun **vous** in **Grammaire A.6**.*

11

Grammar Explanations

Grammar explanations in *Deux mondes* are written in English, for successful at-home study and review. They are clear, straightforward, and brief to increase students' comprehension of essential information. We try to provide only as much grammatical information in the explanations as students need at that particular point. All grammar points are presented in numerical order in each chapter for easy reference and are listed on chapter-opening pages along with the chapter themes.

Grammar Exercises

The grammar exercises are intended to verify students' understanding of the grammar explanations. They check the students' ability to recognize or supply correct forms in a controlled, form-focused context. Answers to the exercises are printed in Appendix D of the textbook so that students can check their work at home. You may wish to reserve some class time to answer questions and for brief presentations or review of the more complex grammar points. Many grammar exercises (particularly in **Chapitres 1–14**) also lend themselves to in-class oral practice, since they often incorporate a question/answer format and relate to students' real-life contexts. These exercises

provide more structured input with grammatical forms than do the **Activités**.

Cross-Reference Pointers

The cross-reference annotations in the margins, highlighted by an arrow, allow students to locate both earlier and later lessons related to the same topic. They are designed to make the "blue pages" an even handier reference and are especially useful for at-home study and review.

---

12 | PREMIÈRE ÉTAPE *Premières rencontres*

✳ *You will learn more about verb endings in* **Grammaire A.4** *and in following chapters.*

Verbs of this sort are called reflexive verbs and are presented in **Chapitre 2**. At this point, you need only understand the meaning of these commands.

Pronunciation Hint

Most final consonants are not pronounced in French. For example: **ouvre/, français/, asseye/, vou/, e/, écoute/.** In these hints, a slash through a letter indicates when a letter is not pronounced.

Exercice 1: Écoutez!

Are these commands given in a logical order? Answer **oui** or **non**.

1. Ouvrez le livre! → Lisez!
2. Asseyez-vous! → Courez!
3. Écrivez! → Prenez un stylo!
4. Tournez la page! → Regardez!
5. Levez-vous! → Marchez!
6. Regardez le tableau! → Écoutez!
7. Levez-vous! → Asseyez-vous!
8. Fermez le livre! → Regardez la page!

A.2 Identifying people: C'est... , je m'appelle...

A. To ask who someone is, use the interrogative (question) expression **Qui est-ce?** The usual reply is **C'est** and the name of a person, or simply the name of a person.

—**Qui est-ce?**	*Who's that?*
—**C'est** Denise.	*It's Denise.*

B. If you are not sure of someone's identity, you can use the expression **Est-ce que c'est... ?** with the name of a person. The reply is **oui** or **non**.

—**Est-ce que c'est** Jacqueline?	*Is that Jacqueline?*
—**Non,** c'est Barbara.	*No, it's Barbara.*

C. When you ask someone's name or give your own, use these patterns:

—Comment t'appelles-tu?	*What's your name?*
—Je m'appelle Barbara.	*My name is Barbara.*
—Comment vous appelez-vous?	*What's your name?*
—Je m'appelle Raoul Durand.	*My name is Raoul Durand.*
—Comment s'appelle-t-il?	*What's his name?*
—Il s'appelle Daniel.	*His name is Daniel.*
—Comment s'appelle-t-elle?	*What's her name?*
—Elle s'appelle Denise.	*Her name is Denise.*

Pronunciation Hints

Pronunciation Hints occur in conjunction with new forms in the grammar explanations that are likely to present some difficulty. They help students working independently at home to more closely approximate the oral forms.

Functional Grammar Explanations

Whenever possible, grammar is approached from a functional rather than a formal point of view; that is, the starting point is how the structure is naturally used in everyday speech. For example, in **A.1** on page 13 of this Walkthrough, a variety of **vous**-form commands are presented for comprehension only. They are addressed here because of their frequency in TPR activities. We do not discuss their grammatical classifications at this early stage. The purpose of the explanation is to focus attention on the association between the **-ez** verb form and the imperative meaning. It also alerts students to the fact that some commands have the reflexive pronoun **vous** attached to the verb form. This awareness should help students make sense of both reflexive and nonreflexive commands that are present in the input they have been hearing, and it should also serve as an advance organizer for understanding reflexive verb constructions when they are formally presented in later chapters.

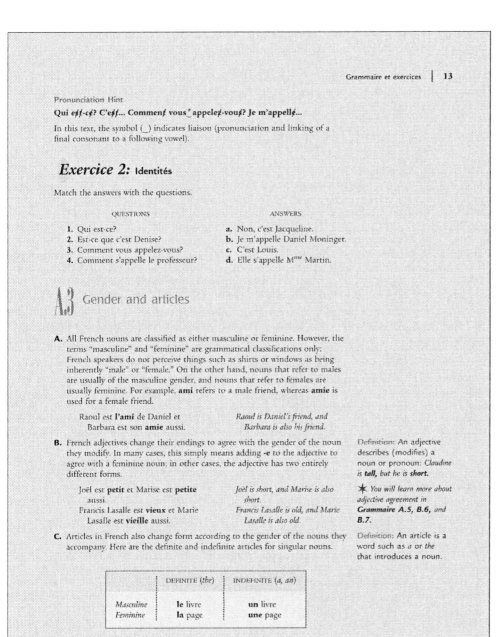

Grammaire et exercices | 13

Pronunciation Hint

Qui est-ce? C'est... Comment vous_appelez-vous? Je m'appelle...

In this text, the symbol (_) indicates liaison (pronunciation and linking of a final consonant to a following vowel).

Exercice 2: Identités

Match the answers with the questions.

QUESTIONS	ANSWERS
1. Qui est-ce?	a. Non, c'est Jacqueline.
2. Est-ce que c'est Denise?	b. Je m'appelle Daniel Moninger.
3. Comment vous appelez-vous?	c. C'est Louis.
4. Comment s'appelle le professeur?	d. Elle s'appelle Mme Martin.

A.3 Gender and articles

A. All French nouns are classified as either masculine or feminine. However, the terms "masculine" and "feminine" are grammatical classifications only: French speakers do not perceive things such as shirts or windows as being inherently "male" or "female." On the other hand, nouns that refer to males are usually of the masculine gender, and nouns that refer to females are usually feminine. For example, **ami** refers to a male friend, whereas **amie** is used for a female friend.

| Raoul est **l'ami** de Daniel et Barbara est son **amie** aussi. | *Raoul is Daniel's friend, and Barbara is also his friend.* |

B. French adjectives change their endings to agree with the gender of the noun they modify. In many cases, this simply means adding **-e** to the adjective to agree with a feminine noun; in other cases, the adjective has two entirely different forms.

| Joël est **petit** et Marise est **petite** aussi. | *Joël is short, and Marise is also short.* |
| Francis Lasalle est **vieux** et Marie Lasalle est **vieille** aussi. | *Francis Lasalle is old, and Marie Lasalle is also old.* |

Definition: An adjective describes (modifies) a noun or pronoun: *Claudine is **tall**, but he is **short**.*

★ *You will learn more about adjective agreement in* **Grammaire A.5, B.6,** *and* **B.7.**

C. Articles in French also change form according to the gender of the nouns they accompany. Here are the definite and indefinite articles for singular nouns.

Definition: An article is a word such as *a* or *the* that introduces a noun.

	DEFINITE (*the*)	INDEFINITE (*a, an*)
Masculine	**le** livre	**un** livre
Feminine	**la** page	**une** page

Spiraling

Through spiraling, complex or difficult grammar topics are treated in a number of small and manageable "chunks" that are introduced progressively throughout the course. This means that a particular point is first presented in an initial section, then reintroduced and expanded on in later sections as the communicative need arises. Each time the point is re-entered, there is a cross-reference note in the margin.

The treatment of grammatical gender and noun-adjective agreement in **A.3** (see Walkthrough, page 15) is an example of the spiraling technique used in *Deux mondes*. This section only introduces the concept of grammatical gender, serving to help students understand the variation in adjective forms that they hear in teacher talk and other input. Variant forms of common adjectives are presented in **B.6** of the **Deuxième étape,** and adjective placement plus pre-nominal adjectives such as **beau** are treated in **4.1.**

D. The definite articles **le** and **la** become **l'** before a word that starts with a vowel (a, e, i, o, u) or a mute **h;** this includes most words that begin with the letter **h.** You will learn more about mute **h** in the **Cahier d'exercices (Prononciation et orthographe).**

l'étudiant(e)	*the student*
l'homme	*the man*
l'autre classe	*the other class*

Exercice 3: Descriptions

Complete these sentences with the correct adjective.

1. Louis est _____ et Jacqueline est _____ aussi. (petit/petite)
2. Barbara est _____ et Albert est _____ aussi. (grand/grande)
3. Mme Martin n'est pas _____. Elle est jeune. (vieux/vieille)
4. Mon acteur favori est très _____. (beau/belle)
5. Albert est _____ (noir/noire)
6. Daniel n'est pas grand. Il est _____. (moyen/moyenne)

Exercice 4: Les photos de Mme Martin

Today, Madame Martin's class is identifying people and things. Complete the sentences with **un, le,** or **l'.**

1. Regardez la photo. C'est _____ tigre. _____ tigre est beau, non?
2. Et voilà la photo d'_____ autre tigre. _____ autre tigre est très grand!
3. Regardez bien! Est-ce _____ livre ou _____ stylo? Oui, c'est _____ livre. C'est _____ livre de Daniel.

Complete the following sentences with **une, la,** or **l'.**

4. Est-ce _____ moustache ou _____ barbe? Bravo, c'est _____ barbe!
5. Est-ce que c'est _____ table? Oui, c'est _____ table de Mme Martin.
6. C'est _____ cathédrale. C'est _____ cathédrale Notre-Dame de Paris. Elle est très belle et très vieille, n'est-ce pas?

A.4 Describing people: Être, subject pronouns, and ne... pas

A. To describe yourself and others, use the verb **être.**

Using *Grammaire et exercices*

The Natural Approach distinguishes between form-focused exercises and communicative activities. Most class time will be devoted to student interactions and teacher talk. We do not consider excessive study and memorization of grammar rules to be helpful since they cause students to focus on uncontextualized discrete forms rather than on developing functional proficiency. Only real communicative experiences result in acquisition of grammatical forms and structures. Thus, we offer grammar explanations primarily as an introduction and as a reference. The way instructors use **Grammaire et exercices** will depend on teaching styles and on students' needs. Many instructors assign the **Grammaire et exercices** while working on a section of **Activités**; others prefer to assign them before they begin the corresponding section of **Activités et lectures**.

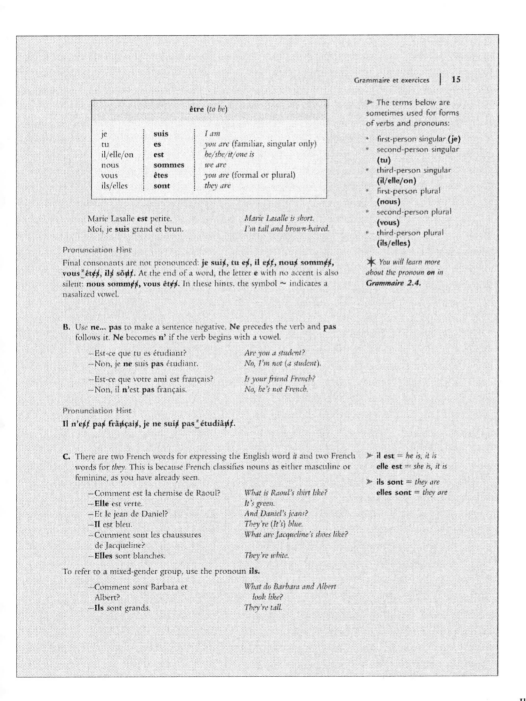

Grammaire et exercices | 15

être *(to be)*		
je	**suis**	*I am*
tu	**es**	*you are* (familiar, singular only)
il/elle/on	**est**	*he/she/it/one is*
nous	**sommes**	*we are*
vous	**êtes**	*you are* (formal or plural)
ils/elles	**sont**	*they are*

Marie Lasalle **est** petite.　　*Marie Lasalle is short.*
Moi, je **suis** grand et brun.　　*I'm tall and brown-haired.*

Pronunciation Hint

Final consonants are not pronounced: **je suis, tu es, il est, nous sommes, vous êtes, ils sont.** At the end of a word, the letter **e** with no accent is also silent: **nous sommes, vous êtes.** In these hints, the symbol ~ indicates a nasalized vowel.

> The terms below are sometimes used for forms of verbs and pronouns:

* first-person singular (**je**)
* second-person singular (**tu**)
* third-person singular (**il/elle/on**)
* first-person plural (**nous**)
* second-person plural (**vous**)
* third-person plural (**ils/elles**)

✳ *You will learn more about the pronoun* **on** *in* **Grammaire 2.4.**

B. Use **ne... pas** to make a sentence negative. **Ne** precedes the verb and **pas** follows it. **Ne** becomes **n'** if the verb begins with a vowel.

—Est-ce que tu es étudiant?　　*Are you a student?*
—Non, je **ne** suis **pas** étudiant.　　*No, I'm not (a student).*

—Est-ce que votre ami est français?　　*Is your friend French?*
—Non, il **n'est pas** français.　　*No, he's not French.*

Pronunciation Hint

Il n'est pas français, je ne suis pas étudiant.

C. There are two French words for expressing the English word *it* and two French words for *they*. This is because French classifies nouns as either masculine or feminine, as you have already seen.

—Comment est la chemise de Raoul?　　*What is Raoul's shirt like?*
—**Elle** est verte.　　*It's green.*
—Et le jean de Daniel?　　*And Daniel's jeans?*
—**Il** est bleu.　　*They're (It's) blue.*
—Comment sont les chaussures de Jacqueline?　　*What are Jacqueline's shoes like?*
—**Elles** sont blanches.　　*They're white.*

> **il est** = *he is, it is*
> **elle est** = *she is, it is*

> **ils sont** = *they are*
> **elles sont** = *they are*

To refer to a mixed-gender group, use the pronoun **ils.**

—Comment sont Barbara et Albert?　　*What do Barbara and Albert look like?*
—**Ils** sont grands.　　*They're tall.*

The Exercises

The grammar exercises are predicated on the expectation that students will already have heard the new form in teacher-talk, particularly in the Pre-Text Oral Activities and in other classroom input. The exercises are generally contextualized in relation to the chapter's theme and, although usually requiring discrete answers, always allow for the processing of meaning. They are intended to call attention to specific grammatical markers and structures that help students understand input.

Since the exercises' purpose is to help students verify that they have understood the explanations, in some cases students are provided with the set of possible forms and asked to select the appropriate one for a given context rather than produce structures and forms. This is the case in **Exercises 5** and **6**, where students do not have to produce subject pronouns or verb forms but instead are asked to show that they understand subject-verb agreement, first by inserting the correct subject, then by selecting and writing the appropriate verb form.

✷ *You will learn more about* **tu** *and* **vous** *in* **Grammaire A.6.**

D. French has two words to express the English word *you.* **Tu** always refers to only one person, but **vous** can be both singular and plural. The choice of **tu** or **vous** for the singular depends on your relationship with the person to whom you are speaking.

Exercice 5: La classe de français

Daniel is telling you about his French teacher and classmates. Complete his sentences with **je, tu, il, elle, nous, vous, ils,** or **elles.**

1. _____ m'appelle Daniel et _____ suis américain.
2. Et Louis? _____ est américain aussi.
3. Le professeur s'appelle Mme Martin. _____ est canadienne. Beaucoup de* Canadiens parlent† anglais et français. _____ sont bilingues.
4. Denise et moi, _____ sommes dans le même‡ cours de maths.
5. Barbara et Jacqueline? _____ sont absentes aujourd'hui.
6. Et toi? _____ es aussi étudiant(e)?

Exercice 6: La famille Colin

Marise Colin is describing her family in a letter to Barbara, her new American correspondent. Choose the correct form of the verb **être: suis, es, est, sommes, êtes,** or **sont** to complete each sentence.

1. Moi, je _____ petite et brune.
2. Clarisse _____ petite et brune.
3. Clarisse et moi, nous _____ étudiantes à l'université.
4. Charles et Emmanuel _____ grands.
5. Et toi? Est-ce que tu _____ grande ou petite, brune ou blonde?
6. Combien _____-vous dans la famille?

Exercice 7: Discussions dans la classe de français

Complete the following statements made by students in Madame Martin's French class while they were practicing descriptions. Use **ne... pas** and the verb **être.**

MODÈLE Les roses sont rouges. Elles _____ orange! →
Les roses sont rouges. Elles *ne sont pas* orange!

*Beaucoup... *Many*
†*speak*
‡*same*

Quick Summaries in the Margins

Besides definitions and cross-references, the **Grammaire** margin notes also contain brief summary statements about the main points in many explanations. Each of these is highlighted with a red arrowhead. Their highly condensed form makes them useful for quick review and can also help students verify that they have understood the point.

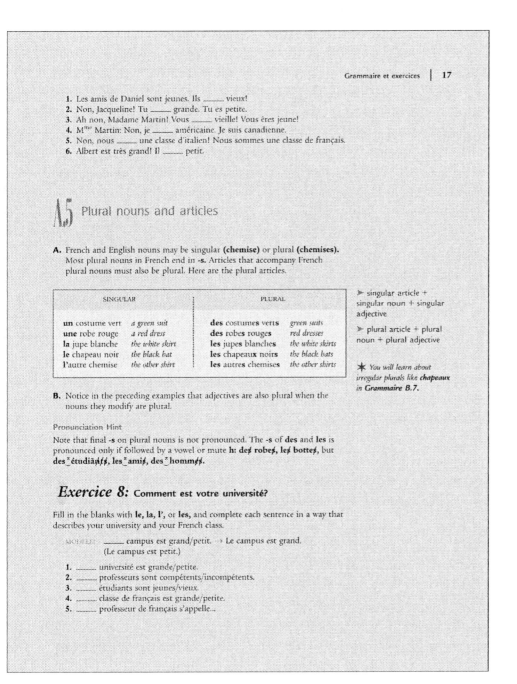

1. Les amis de Daniel sont jeunes. Ils _____ vieux!
2. Non, Jacqueline! Tu _____ grande. Tu es petite.
3. Ah non, Madame Martin! Vous _____ vieille! Vous êtes jeune!
4. Mᵐᵉ Martin: Non, je _____ américaine. Je suis canadienne.
5. Non, nous _____ une classe d'italien! Nous sommes une classe de français.
6. Albert est très grand! Il _____ petit.

A.5 Plural nouns and articles

A. French and English nouns may be singular **(chemise)** or plural **(chemises)**. Most plural nouns in French end in **-s.** Articles that accompany French plural nouns must also be plural. Here are the plural articles.

SINGULAR		PLURAL	
un costume vert	*a green suit*	**des** costumes verts	*green suits*
une robe rouge	*a red dress*	**des** robes rouges	*red dresses*
la jupe blanche	*the white skirt*	**les** jupes blanches	*the white skirts*
le chapeau noir	*the black hat*	**les** chapeaux noirs	*the black hats*
l'autre chemise	*the other shirt*	**les** autres chemises	*the other shirts*

➤ singular article + singular noun + singular adjective

➤ plural article + plural noun + plural adjective

★ You will learn about irregular plurals like **chapeaux** in *Grammaire B.7.*

B. Notice in the preceding examples that adjectives are also plural when the nouns they modify are plural.

Pronunciation Hint

Note that final **-s** on plural nouns is not pronounced. The **-s** of **des** and **les** is pronounced only if followed by a vowel or mute **h: de**s **robe**s, **le**s **botte**s, but **des ˣétudiàn**t**s, les ˣami**s, **des ˣhomm**e**s.**

Exercice 8: Comment est votre université?

Fill in the blanks with **le, la, l',** or **les,** and complete each sentence in a way that describes your university and your French class.

MODÈLE: _____ campus est grand/petit. → Le campus est grand. (Le campus est petit.)

1. _____ université est grande/petite.
2. _____ professeurs sont compétents/incompétents.
3. _____ étudiants sont jeunes/vieux.
4. _____ classe de français est grande/petite.
5. _____ professeur de français s'appelle...

Semantic and Sociolinguistic Items

In a few cases, we have chosen to include items that are not, strictly speaking, grammatical in nature. The use of **tu** and **vous** (**A.6**) is an example of such a section. Although students have been exposed to their usage in input, and the Instructor's Edition notes have suggested that the instructor provide explanations, we believe that this particular item is important enough to merit home study and specific practice since it is strikingly different from English usage. It is our experience that, from time to time, the use of contrastive analysis and analogies with English helps to make some explanations clearer.

Exercice 9: Test de mémoire

Louis has been blindfolded and must try to remember what his classmates are wearing. Fill in the blanks with **un, une,** or **des.**

1. —Est-ce que Barbara porte _____ jupe noire?
   —Non, elle porte _____ robe jaune.
2. —Est-ce qu'Albert porte _____ chemise blanche et _____ pantalon noir?
   —Non, il porte _____ pull-over bleu et _____ pantalon gris.
3. —Est-ce que Denise porte _____ bottes noires?
   —Oui, elle porte _____ bottes noires.
4. —Est-ce que Daniel porte _____ blouson vert et _____ chaussures noires?
   —Non, il porte _____ blouson violet et _____ chaussures blanches.
5. —Est-ce que Mme Martin porte _____ robe rose et _____ manteau violet?
   —Oui, elle porte _____ robe rose et _____ manteau violet.

A.6 Addressing others: Tu and vous

A. In French, there are two pronouns that correspond to English *you:* **tu** and **vous**. In general, **tu** is used among peers, that is, with friends and other students and, in most cases, with family members. **Vous** is used with those older than you and with people you don't know well or with whom you wish to keep a certain distance. In general, **vous** is used in public with clerks, taxi drivers, waiters, and so on.

—Albert, **tu** vas bien?	*Albert, are you doing well?*
—Oui, très bien, merci.	*Yes, great, thanks.*
—Bonjour, madame. Comment allez-**vous?**	*Good morning (ma'am). How are you?*
—Très bien. Et vous?	*Fine. And you?*

Note that in French, the usual and polite practice is to follow **Bonjour** with one of the terms of address: **madame, monsieur,** or **mademoiselle.**

B. **Vous** is used for speaking to more than one person regardless of the nature of the relationship between the speakers.

Joël et Emmanuel, êtes-**vous** fatigués?	*Joël and Emmanuel, are you tired?*

C. The use of **tu** and **vous** varies somewhat from country to country and even within a country. It is best to use **vous** with people you do not know personally or who are older than you. With other students or friends your own age, it is customary to use **tu.**

Chapter 1
Speech Emergence

As students begin **Chapitre 1,** most are able to comprehend an increasing amount of spoken French. In other words, in terms of the acquisition process, they have reached the Natural Approach Stage 3 (Speech Emergence). They will still use single words and short phrases to show they understand, but they will also begin producing some longer utterances, to participate more fully in dialogues, and even to produce some connected narration.

Chapitres 1–14 are designed to accommodate the Natural Approach views about the acquisition process. At the start of each section, students are given appropriate comprehension and early speech activities for new material, so that they use this new language in controlled situations. At the end of each section, they work with activities that draw on old material and that foster their emerging ability to use French spontaneously. Throughout the book, in every section of a chapter, the same progression can occur: (1) The instructor uses Stage 1 **Mise en train** activities followed by vocabulary displays to introduce new material; (2) students participate in guided Stage 2 activities in the text that allow them to express personal meaning in pair and group situations without having to produce much language on their own; (3) students talk spontaneously with classmates in Stage 3 activities appropriate for their developmental level. This continuous three-step process will take less time as students develop good listening skills and have acquired a larger store of language from previous chapters. Nonetheless, it will always be important to provide sufficient input before students engage in interactive activities or begin to write.

CHAPITRE 1

Vacances en famille sur la côte Atlantique

Ma famille et moi

OBJECTIFS IN CHAPITRE 1, you will discuss your family and favorite activities. You will learn how to give your address and phone number, and more ways to describe people.

Activités
La famille
Goûts personnels
Origines et renseignements personnels
La vie de famille

Lectures
Info: Société   Portrait de famille
Info: Société   Qui sont les Français?
Les francophones sur le vif
   Marie-Claire Schmitt
Lecture   Familles d'aujourd'hui

Grammaire
1.1 Expressing relationships: Possessive adjectives
1.2 Expressing likes and dislikes: Aimer + infinitive
1.3 Talking about dates and personal data: Numbers beyond 100
1.4 Stating origin: The verb venir
1.5 Talking about actions: Present of -er verbs
1.6 Expressing relationship and possession: Contractions of de

Pre-Text Oral Activities

The **Mise en train** activities continue to be necessary for providing comprehensible input for new semantic areas. Since **Chapitre 1** introduces verbs and other language that permit students to talk more extensively about themselves and others, pre-text input can become more complex and its content more interesting than in the **Étapes**. We find that **Association** activities work very well for introducing material at this point, since they allow instructors to present new language in rich input that involves students. (See **Chapitre 1, Mise en train, Act.1.**)

Association activities are extra-text input activities that are often done during presentations with visuals. While introducing new vocabulary such as **(il) aime voyager,** the instructor asks students if they like to do the activity, where and with whom, and so on. **Qui dans cette classe aime faire la fête? Vous aimez faire la fête, Marion? Où aimez-vous aller? Avec qui aimez-vous allez au Club Med?** If someone dislikes the activity, the instructor asks what that individual likes to do. **Vous n'aimez pas faire la fête, Paul? Qu'est-ce que vous aimez faire, alors?** Since these activities depend on personal information, students will need help with vocabulary. This can be done without intrusion: **Qu'est-ce que vous préférez faire?** (read) **Ah, vous aimez lire! Vous préférez lire de la fiction?** The instructor writes any new words on the board.

Vocabulary Displays

The vocabulary displays of each section contain key words and structures used in the corresponding sections. We assume that students will have been exposed to all or most of these during daily **Mise en train** activities. Thus, when they look at a display for the first time,

most of the language there is already familiar to them. The displays often carry cultural messages and are excellent points of departure for further input and review. Margin notes in the Instructor's Edition provide suggestions for teaching and expansion of the displays. We recommend that the instructor do a **Mise en train** activity that includes the language in a particular display before doing the vocabulary display with the class. This is an excellent opportunity to recycle past language and often to initiate a discussion of cultural matters.

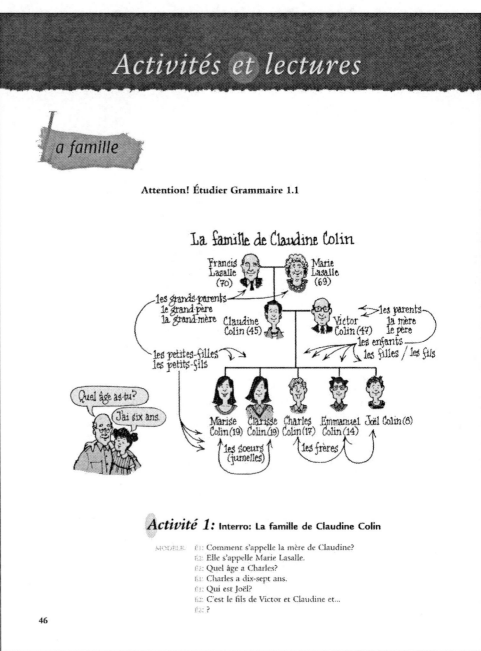

Art-Based *Interro* Activities

Interros are based on art or on information in a chart. These are early speech activities that allow students to interact in a guided way and that are also useful for oral input. Here, **Activité 1** is based on the information and art in the vocabulary display. It is intended to be assigned to partners after the instructor has discussed the display with the class. Students use the questions and answers in the **Modèle** as patterns and can add others if they wish.

Expansion of Activities

We recommend that each **Activité** be seen as an opportunity to provide teacher input. Besides doing an activity in class, the instructor can ask questions about its content, make personal remarks, or create new items of the same type as those in the activity. In **Activité 1,** for example, the instructor might ask for a show of hands to see which students have siblings, ask their names and ages, talk about their appearance and personalities. The class will find a discussion about your own family or the family members of classmates more interesting than the families we have created in *Deux mondes*. If new words arise, write them on the board for students to copy in their Vocabulary notebooks.

Vocabulaire utile

Supplementary vocabulary accompanies partner activities and is intended to help students express their own ideas or situations. In **Activité 2,** for example, we supply more family terms to facilitate the expression of relationships arising from blended families or second marriages.

Échanges

Activité 3 is an example of a typical **Échanges** activity. These are Stage 2 activities in which students can use French that is above their current level of productive ability. Most of the vocabulary is provided, as are models, so that students can read the words if needed. Because students focus on the topic, however, the final effect is that they are participating in a real discussion.

Activité 2: Dialogue: Ma famille

Vocabulaire utile

mon beau-père (beau-frère)	mon demi-frère
ma belle-mère (belle-sœur)	ma demi-sœur

É1: Combien de personnes y a-t-il dans ta famille?
É2: Il y a _____ personnes dans ma famille.
É1: Comment s'appellent les membres de la famille?
É2: Mes _____ s'appellent _____ et _____, mon/ma _____ s'appelle _____ et mon/ma _____ s'appelle _____.
É1: Quel âge ont-ils?
É2: Mon/ma _____ a _____, mes _____ ont _____ et _____.
É1: Comment est ta famille?
É2: Nous sommes _____ et _____. Nous ne sommes pas _____.
É1: Est-ce que ta famille a une maison ou un appartement?
É2: Nous avons _____. Il/Elle est _____.

Activité 3: Échanges: Ma famille et mes amis

Quelles sont les qualités importantes des membres de la famille?

Vocabulaire utile

égoïste	flexible
raisonnable	généreux/généreuse
poli(e)	sportif/sportive
intéressant(e)	réservé(e)
sympathique	décisif/décisive
strict(e)	compréhensif/compréhensive
patient(e)	réaliste
sérieux/sérieuse	

MODÈLE: le petit frère
É1: Pour toi, comment est le petit frère idéal?
É2: Pour moi, le petit frère idéal est affectueux et amusant. En général, il est calme et pas trop difficile. (Je ne sais pas. Je n'ai pas de petit frère.)

1. la sœur
2. le frère aîné
3. la mère
4. l'ami(e)
5. le fiancé / la fiancée
6. le professeur
7. le père
8. ?

Infos

Several **Info** boxes appear in each chapter accompanied by a visual that illustrates or expands the message. These are short, factual culture notes that can be used both as readings and as springboards for classroom discussion. They contain information about contemporary France and French-speaking countries and are integrated thematically with the **Activités**. The **Infos** provide a context for using French in the classroom that most closely approximates that in which native usage occurs. The **Info: Vie quotidienne** boxes describe routine daily life, whereas those titled **Info: Société** reveal the way in which society is organized and how it deals with its needs. The **Info: Arts et lettres** boxes provide information on people in the arts and, occasionally, a poem.

Vocabulary Displays in Stage 3

In the two introductory **étapes**, vocabulary displays mostly present lists of words illustrated with art. Beginning in **Chapitre 1**, however, the displays often contain complete statements, so that key words and structures for a particular section are presented in the context established by the drawings. The display for **Goûts personnels** (page 48) can be taught as photo-supported input. The instructor talks about each drawing: **Comment s'appellent ces deux jeunes filles? Est-ce qu'elles portent une jupe ou un short? En quelle couleur? Montrez-moi une raquette de tennis.** Next, the instructor reads the statement aloud, indicates some personal feeling such as **«Moi, j'adore/déteste jouer au tennis»** and then asks which students enjoy doing the same thing as the character in the drawing. This allows the display to serve as a springboard to the use of other forms and broader input: **Charles Colin aime lire un bon livre, n'est-ce pas? Et vous, Robert? Non? Vous n'aimez pas lire? Vous aimez regarder la télévision? Quel dommage! Claire et moi, nous aimons lire des magazines, des journaux...**

Info: Société

Portrait de famille

Les statistiques indiquent que la famille française a entre un et deux enfants. C'est une situation normale en Europe du nord. De plus, un tiers (1/3) des Français reste célibataire.[1] À Paris et dans les grandes villes, la proportion est beaucoup plus grande. Un couple sur dix vit en «union libre»,[2] mais la proportion double chez les 18–25 ans.

La famille reste une valeur solide. Neuf Français sur dix dînent en famille et quatre sur cinq déjeunent à la maison tous les jours. Les aspects positifs de la famille selon les Français? Les fêtes,[3] les enfants, la joie d'être ensemble[4] et la solidarité.

[1] ≠ marié
[2] vit... habite ensemble, mais n'est pas marié
[3] célébrations
[4] en groupe

Grands-parents et leurs petits-enfants dans un jardin public

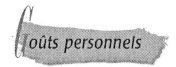
oûts personnels

Attention! Étudier Grammaire 1.2

Moi, j'aime beaucoup jouer au tennis! Et toi?

Je n'aime pas étudier le vendredi soir.

A New Look at Lexical Items

Just as students learned to understand a large number of imperative forms without grammatical explanations during TPR activities, in the second topical section of **Chapitre 1** they learn many infinitives with forms of **aimer.** As we saw previously, there is no need either to explain this structural pattern or to categorize the verbs (regular **-er,** irregular, and so on). Students will acquire the forms of **aimer** quickly because the structure permits them a greater range of self-expression. The infinitives are only vocabulary items at this point and will serve as advance organizers for subsequent chapters where different conjugation patterns are introduced.

Using French in Class

We believe that conducting class in French and exposing students to a wide vocabulary that recurs frequently in teacher input and oral activities is the best way to help students acquire French and to attain true functional proficiency. When the French spoken in class is made comprehensible by use of visual aids, gestures, cognates, and background knowledge, students not only become comfortable with it but find satisfaction in being able to comprehend and use the language. To aid this process, we make maximum use of association techniques, cognates, and art-supported activities so that students can quickly acquire a large vocabulary.

Many Natural Approach instructors conduct their classes almost completely in French, including any discussion of grammar. Others permit English when students need to ask for a word to express their personal reality or when asking a question about grammar. The important thing is that students should become accustomed to hearing French and feel confident when speaking.

Claudine Colin aime faire des courses.

Joël et ses amis aiment jouer au football.

J'adore conduire ma voiture de sport.

Charles aime lire un bon livre.

Emmanuel aime nager à la piscine municipale.

Marie Lasalle aime travailler dans le jardin.

More on *Discussions*

Discussions are Stage 2 input activities, so they are usually placed early in a topical section. We recommend that the instructor discuss the drawings one at a time, including students in the discussion. Here's an example from **Activité 4: Dans ma famille, nous ne sommes pas très sportifs. Nous sommes un peu sédentaires! Est-ce que votre famille est sportive, Ross? (oui) Ah bon! Quels sports aimez-vous? Le tennis... ?** Later, during recall of previous answers: **Qui vient d'une famille très sportive? (Ross) Oui, la famille de Ross est sportive. Qui joue au golf? (père) Oui, son père... Et sa mère, qu'est-ce qu'elle aime faire?**

Discussion activities work well for partner or small group exchanges. **Activité 4** is in a typical format, with the **Modèle** placed so that partner exchanges occur after the instructor-led input activity. Little speech production is required, so the activity allows students to speak meaningfully in a way that is probably beyond their current ability to produce.

Exprime-toi!

This optional feature exists to help students express their thoughts or reactions during conversational exchanges. As a rule, students become interested in what their partners say and want to react to or extend the conversation. Before assigning a **Discussion** to partners, the instructor should be sure that everyone is aware of the purpose of **Exprime-toi!** and has heard the words used (and pronounced) in context.

Activities for Pair Work

Students should be restricted neither to the models that are printed with paired activities, as in **Activités 5** and **6** nor to the suggested vocabulary for these activities. Instead, they should be encouraged to ask more questions or supply further information insofar as their speaking ability permits. Each partner should play both roles.

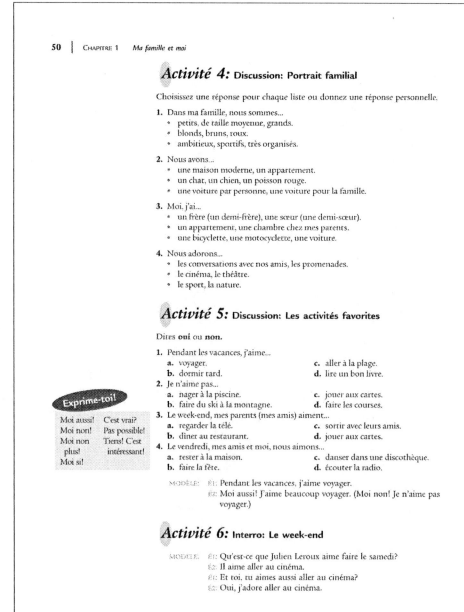

50 | CHAPITRE 1   *Ma famille et moi*

Activité 4: Discussion: Portrait familial

Choisissez une réponse pour chaque liste ou donnez une réponse personnelle.

1. Dans ma famille, nous sommes...
   * petits, de taille moyenne, grands.
   * blonds, bruns, roux.
   * ambitieux, sportifs, très organisés.

2. Nous avons...
   * une maison moderne, un appartement.
   * un chat, un chien, un poisson rouge.
   * une voiture par personne, une voiture pour la famille.

3. Moi, j'ai...
   * un frère (un demi-frère), une sœur (une demi-sœur).
   * un appartement, une chambre chez mes parents.
   * une bicyclette, une motocyclette, une voiture.

4. Nous adorons...
   * les conversations avec nos amis, les promenades.
   * le cinéma, le théâtre.
   * le sport, la nature.

Activité 5: Discussion: Les activités favorites

Dites **oui** ou **non**.

1. Pendant les vacances, j'aime...
   a. voyager.   **c.** aller à la plage.
   b. dormir tard.   **d.** lire un bon livre.
2. Je n'aime pas...
   a. nager à la piscine.   **c.** jouer aux cartes.
   b. faire du ski à la montagne.   **d.** faire les courses.
3. Le week-end, mes parents (mes amis) aiment...
   a. regarder la télé.   **c.** sortir avec leurs amis.
   b. dîner au restaurant.   **d.** jouer aux cartes.
4. Le vendredi, mes amis et moi, nous aimons...
   a. rester à la maison.   **c.** danser dans une discothèque.
   b. faire la fête.   **d.** écouter la radio.

MODÈLE: É1: Pendant les vacances, j'aime voyager.
         É2: Moi aussi! J'aime beaucoup voyager. (Moi non! Je n'aime pas voyager.)

Exprime-toi!

Moi aussi!   C'est vrai?
Moi non!   Pas possible!
Moi non   Tiens! C'est
plus!   intéressant!
Moi si!

Activité 6: Interro: Le week-end

MODÈLE: É1: Qu'est-ce que Julien Leroux aime faire le samedi?
         É2: Il aime aller au cinéma.
         É1: Et toi, tu aimes aussi aller au cinéma?
         É2: Oui, j'adore aller au cinéma.

Chart-Based *Interro* Activities

Most **Interro** activities are based on charts, as in **Activité 6.** Like those based on art, these activities provide practice in formulating and answering simple factual questions and are useful for oral input using target vocabulary. First, the instructor asks the class many simple questions about the information in the chart. This allows students to hear the pronunciation and to grasp the meaning of any new words. The instructor writes example questions on the board as they occur in the input for students to use as needed during the partner exchanges. Next, the instructor reads the **Modèle** aloud, repeats it at least once with the help of a volunteer, and assigns partners to do the activity.

Drop-In Realia

You will find several pieces of realia in every chapter of *Deux mondes*. The pieces are selected to supplement an activity or add a new dimension when you are discussing a theme. To introduce «**Tous pour la lecture,**» we suggest that the instructor show a photo of someone reading and show an equivalence on the board: **faire la lecture = lire.** This is an opportunity for more cognate use: **Aimez-vous la lecture? Qu'est-ce que vous aimez lire? Qui préfère la fiction? La biographie?**

Dans le monde francophone

As students work with realia such as **Activité 8,** they encounter authentic language occurring in authentic contexts. Since realia will almost certainly contain unfamiliar words and structures, we suggest that it be used to help teach reading strategies. After doing the activity, follow up by asking students to identify cognates and related words, to make intelligent guesses at meaning, or to practice other effective reading techniques.

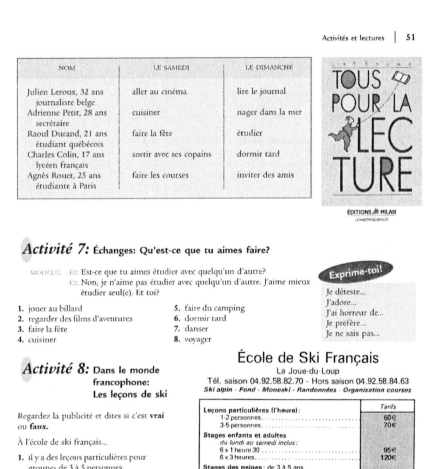

Group Work

In Stage 3, many activities are designed for student interactions. We assume that group work encourages interaction and is essential in a communicative class. Group work refers to pair work as well as to small-group work. For activities such as **Échanges, Interros,** and **Entretiens,** pairs work best. For activities in **Allons plus loin!** and **Situations,** small groups of 3–4 can work well. The Instructor's Edition notes provide suggestions for the group size appropriate to each activity and for successful facilitation of pair/group work. We find that the grouping of students happens much more smoothly if the instructor chooses the group makeup; in this way, everyone is assured a partner and students get to know many other classmates. **Activité 9,** for example, is best done with partners asking each other questions. Most students enjoy talking with their peers and feel freer to express themselves than they would if called on to speak before the whole class. Group work also frees the instructor to move around the classroom to make sure the activity is going well, to answer questions, and to provide additional input.

Language and Culture

Many displays and **Activités** in *Deux mondes* encourage the addition of cultural information. These are supported by the notes in the Instructor's Edition. Here is an example using **Activité 11:** (1) The instructor begins with PF photos of familiar people from several countries, allowing students to hear the names of the countries and nationalities during the input. (2) Next, the instructor does an input activity in which students locate the countries in the activity using the maps in the front of the textbook. (3) The instructor begins the **Activité** with more input; students look at the flags on the page while the instructor describes them and asks questions: **Ce drapeau est bleu, blanc et rouge. Il n'est pas rouge, blanc et bleu. De quel pays vient ce drapeau?** (4) Before assigning the activity, the instructor uses its vocabulary intensively so that students hear the words often: **D'où viennent les Algériens? Est-ce qu'ils viennent de Turquie ou d'Algérie? Qu'est-ce qu'on parle en Algérie? Est-ce qu'on parle espagnol? (non) Français? (oui) Arabe? (oui),** and so on.

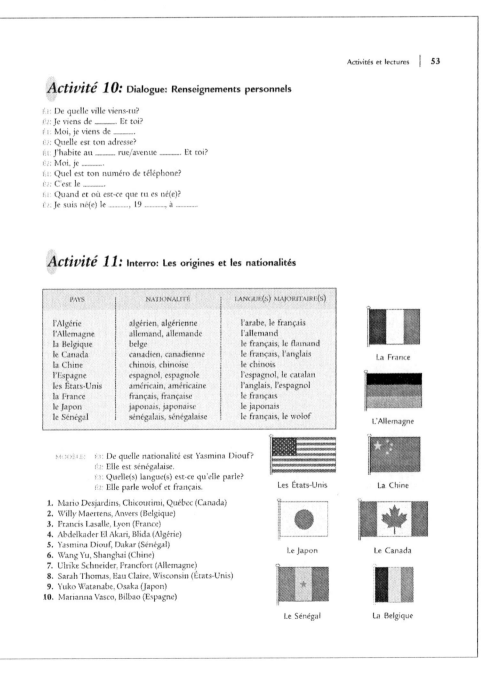

Activités et lectures | 53

Activité 10: Dialogue: Renseignements personnels

É1: De quelle ville viens-tu?
É2: Je viens de _____. Et toi?
É1: Moi, je viens de _____.
É2: Quelle est ton adresse?
É1: J'habite au _____ rue/avenue _____. Et toi?
É2: Moi, je _____.
É1: Quel est ton numéro de téléphone?
É2: C'est le _____.
É1: Quand et où est-ce que tu es né(e)?
É2: Je suis né(e) le _____, 19 _____, à _____.

Activité 11: Interro: Les origines et les nationalités

PAYS	NATIONALITÉ	LANGUE(S) MAJORITAIRE(S)
l'Algérie	algérien, algérienne	l'arabe, le français
l'Allemagne	allemand, allemande	l'allemand
la Belgique	belge	le français, le flamand
le Canada	canadien, canadienne	le français, l'anglais
la Chine	chinois, chinoise	le chinois
l'Espagne	espagnol, espagnole	l'espagnol, le catalan
les États-Unis	américain, américaine	l'anglais, l'espagnol
la France	français, française	le français
le Japon	japonais, japonaise	le japonais
le Sénégal	sénégalais, sénégalaise	le français, le wolof

La France

L'Allemagne

MODÈLE: É1: De quelle nationalité est Yasmina Diouf?
É2: Elle est sénégalaise.
É1: Quelle(s) langue(s) est-ce qu'elle parle?
É2: Elle parle wolof et français.

Les États-Unis

La Chine

1. Mario Desjardins, Chicoutimi, Québec (Canada)
2. Willy Maertens, Anvers (Belgique)
3. Francis Lasalle, Lyon (France)
4. Abdelkader El Akari, Blida (Algérie)
5. Yasmina Diouf, Dakar (Sénégal)
6. Wang Yu, Shanghai (Chine)
7. Ulrike Schneider, Francfort (Allemagne)
8. Sarah Thomas, Eau Claire, Wisconsin (États-Unis)
9. Yuko Watanabe, Osaka (Japon)
10. Marianna Vasco, Bilbao (Espagne)

Le Japon

Le Canada

Le Sénégal

La Belgique

Photographs

Take a few minutes to discuss each photograph in *Deux mondes*. Photographs generally suggest input that contains cultural information that leads students toward recognition of non-linguistic cultural patterns.

Content in Vocabulary Displays in Stage 3

Many Stage 3 displays present cultural information through the depiction of individual lifestyles and behavior or through a series of drawings that narrate one coherent situation. Such displays invite discussion that includes both the target vocabulary and comparison of how people in different societies deal with everyday life. The display for **La vie de famille** is a good example, since it introduces students to the Lasalle-Colin extended family and also provides insight into typical family life in France. At first, the instructor should do input using old and new terms for family relationships, age, and present tense forms, which are introduced here. The input should gradually expand to include descriptions of the people and places. Finally, the instructor should ask students to supply similar personal information. This in turn leads to comparing their lives with those of the French characters. **La famille de Bernard Lasalle aime passer le mois d'août à la plage, n'est-ce pas? Ça, c'est typiquement français. Le mois d'août, c'est le mois traditionnel des vacances en France. Est-ce que les Américains ont un mois de vacances tous les ans? Est-ce qu'ils partent en famille? Et vous, est-ce que votre famille... ?**

Les jeunes de la banlieue parisienne

Info: Société

Qui sont les Français?

Jason Wang est un étudiant américain d'origine asiatique. Il passe une année en France, à l'université Louis Lumière de Lyon. Il pose des questions à son professeur d'histoire M. Gondrand sur la question de l'identité des Français.

Jason: On dit que le «Français typique» est un descendant des Gaulois.[1] C'est vrai?
M. Gondrand: Pas exactement... En réalité, la population de la France est très diverse: les Bretons sont celtiques, les Alsaciens, germaniques, les gens du Midi,[2] méditerranéens comme les Italiens et les Grecs. Et, naturellement, les Français des DOM-TOM[3] représentent une grande variété de races et de cultures.
Jason: Et les immigrés?
M. Gondrand: Sur une population totale de presque 60 millions, il y a, en France, à peu près[4] 4 millions d'immigrés, en majorité du Maghreb: l'Algérie, le Maroc et la Tunisie, anciennes[5] colonies françaises.
Jason: Et tous ces gens-là sont des «Français typiques»!

[1] groupe de 90 peuples celtiques installés sur le territoire actuel de la France
[2] sud de la France
[3] Départements et Territoires d'Outre-Mer: territoires administrativement français, mais situés à l'extérieur de l'Europe
[4] à... approximativement
[5] du passé

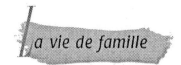

a vie de famille

Attention! Étudier Grammaire 1.5 et 1.6

La famille de Bernard Lasalle

Voilà Bernard Lasalle avec sa femme Christine. Elle est infirmière dans un hôpital à Lyon.

Effective Instructor Input

Good instructor input allows for spontaneous and innovative student responses without being threatening. It is simplified speech, which is essential to learners and should be interesting to students. Ideally, it is varied and natural, never artificial or over controlled. If the instructor reacts naturally to students' responses (for example, **Vous avez sept cours, Paul? Mon Dieu! C'est beaucoup. Quels cours avez-vous?**), new situations arise that provide additional information for discussion, thus allowing plenty of re-entry of past vocabulary and structures without a plan for specific review. It is also essential that the Natural Approach concept of comprehensible input be kept in mind. This means that the instructor talks with the class at a level that students can understand, even as some new language material that has not been previously introduced is also included. Such input is slightly above the students' current level of competence. However, it contains enough key words and structures so that they can interpret new vocabulary and structures by using what they do understand and by using the context.

We find that students acquire most rapidly when they believe that the instructor is taking a personal interest in their progress, seems confident about eventual student success, and encourages all efforts at communication.

Student-Generated Vocabulary and the Vocabulary Notebook

Since Natural Approach classes may involve fairly free-ranging discussion that includes personal involvement of the students, it follows that a number of extra-textual vocabulary items will occur as students request words to tell about themselves. Student-generated vocabulary is written on the board, and students copy it into a vocabulary notebook that the instructor has asked them to bring to class each day.

Les enfants de Bernard et Christine s'appellent Camille (11 ans), Marie-Christine (8 ans) et Nathalie (6 ans).

Voilà la sœur de Bernard, Claudine Colin, avec sa famille. Son mari Victor travaille dans un bureau.

Toute la famille passe le mois d'août ensemble dans une maison au bord de la mer.

Christine parle beaucoup avec sa belle-sœur Claudine et sa belle-mère Marie Lasalle.

Les petites Lasalle adorent faire une promenade avec leur oncle Victor et leur tante Claudine.

Quelquefois, Victor Colin joue à la pétanque avec son beau-frère, son beau-père et ses neveux.

Definition Activities

These activities help students become accustomed to explaining what they mean in French and to using circumlocution when they cannot think of an exact term. These skills are essential to functional proficiency. In **Activité 12,** the instructor first asks the class to supply the name of the family member for each definition and then has students do the activity in pairs.

The Organization of the *Activités*

Oral activities are loosely arranged in order of productive difficulty within each section. This permits students to have more exposure to vocabulary and structures before they begin to produce them. **Activité 12** is typical of such activities. It is a **Définitions** activity. Students are asked to listen to definitions, then select answers from the list at the right. They do not have to produce any language themselves; they are obliged only to comprehend and to use the book when they speak. At the end of the activity, the instructor may elect to pair up the class for partner practice with the same activity for more input and speaking practice. **Activités 13** and **14** (page 57) contain richer input and end with supplementary activities that require some original speech. **Activité 15** (page 58), near the end of the section, is an interview that requires speech production.

Les francophones sur le vif

Les francophones sur le vif brings short direct replies from the Francophone world to author-written questions, drawing on answers from a variety of age groups and socioeconomic backgrounds. These direct answers bring fresh and different voices to the student text, giving different perspectives on everyday culture. We recommend that the instructor answer the questions that open this feature and also find out what students in class think of the different issues.

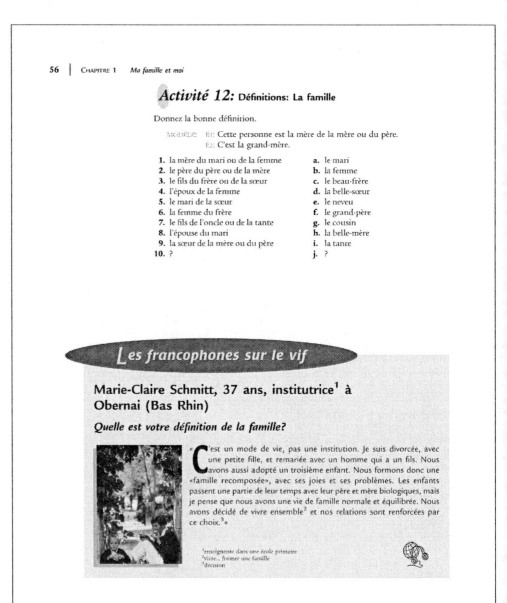

Activité 12: Définitions: La famille

Donnez la bonne définition.

MODÈLE: É1: Cette personne est la mère de la mère ou du père.
É2: C'est la grand-mère.

1. la mère du mari ou de la femme
2. le père du père ou de la mère
3. le fils du frère ou de la sœur
4. l'époux de la femme
5. le mari de la sœur
6. la femme du frère
7. le fils de l'oncle ou de la tante
8. l'épouse du mari
9. la sœur de la mère ou du père
10. ?

a. le mari
b. la femme
c. le beau-frère
d. la belle-sœur
e. le neveu
f. le grand-père
g. le cousin
h. la belle-mère
i. la tante
j. ?

Les francophones sur le vif

Marie-Claire Schmitt, 37 ans, institutrice[1] à Obernai (Bas Rhin)

Quelle est votre définition de la famille?

«C'est un mode de vie, pas une institution. Je suis divorcée, avec une petite fille, et remariée avec un homme qui a un fils. Nous avons aussi adopté un troisième enfant. Nous formons donc une «famille recomposée», avec ses joies et ses problèmes. Les enfants passent une partie de leur temps avec leur père et mère biologiques, mais je pense que nous avons une vie de famille normale et équilibrée. Nous avons décidé de vivre ensemble[2] et nos relations sont renforcées par ce choix.[3]»

[1]enseignante dans une école primaire
[2]vivre... former une famille
[3]décision

Enquête Activities

Enquêtes are personal opinion surveys that ask students to state their views on different topics or issues or to talk about their own habits. These are Stage 2 input activities. The instructor reads the items aloud (with added input), while everyone jots quick answers. The instructor may then elect to do a full-class survey of replies. However, **Enquêtes** can also be used to encourage spontaneous speech. After students have replied to the initial survey, rather than completing a full-class survey of answers, an instructor may choose to pair up students. They are then asked to compare their answers or to exchange other information. As a rule, students who share information become so interested in the topic that they begin to ask questions with **Pourquoi?**, **Quand?**, thus generating the need for explanations and free-ranging conversation.

À vous la parole! and *Allons plus loin!*

À vous la parole! appears after activities from time to time in every chapter, as here with **Activité 13.** This feature allows instructors to easily set up conversational situations or to encourage students to express themselves freely on the topic of the particular activity. We recommend that students be taught to do their best to express themselves within the limits of the language they know rather than using the dictionary or other resources, although the instructor can provide help as needed.

Allons plus loin!, seen after **Activité 14,** generally proposes projects for small groups or partners, such as preparing a travel brochure or creating a set of menus. Here, the example is a simple discussion appropriate for **Chapitre 1.**

Using the Web with *Cliquez là!*

Cliquez là! items appear from time to time in all chapters beginning with **Deuxième étape** and are related to the topical themes. Their purpose is to motivate students to begin using the French-language Web on their own. They are keyed to specific suggestions at the *Deux mondes* website, although they are also appropriate for students who prefer to browse on their own.

Activité 13: Enquête: Les activités de ma famille

Dans votre famille, qui fait les activités suivantes?

MODÈLE: _____ aime/aiment faire des achats sur Internet. →
Ma mère aime faire ses achats sur Internet. Elle déteste aller au centre commercial.

1. _____ travaille/travaillent dans un bureau.
2. _____ achète/achètent beaucoup de vêtements neufs.
3. _____ aime/aiment conduire vite.
4. _____ écoute/écoutent de la musique classique.
5. _____ reste/restent à la maison le samedi soir.
6. _____ rentre/rentrent tard très souvent.
7. _____ chante/chantent sous la douche.
8. _____ parle/parlent beaucoup au téléphone dans la voiture.

À vous la parole! Posez les mêmes questions à un(e) partenaire.

MODÈLE: É1: Est-ce que tu travailles dans un bureau?
É2: Non, mais je travaille dans un restaurant. Et toi?

Activité 14: Enquête: La famille et les amis

Dites **oui** ou **non.** Si vous dites **non,** corrigez la phrase.

Suggestions   mon copain/ma copine   Je ne... avec personne
mon/ma camarade de chambre   seul(e)
mon petit ami / ma petite amie

1. Je parle avec ma cousine quand j'ai des problèmes.
2. Je téléphone souvent à mes grands-parents.
3. Je passe le samedi soir avec mes copains.
4. Je regarde la télé avec mes camarades de chambre.
5. Je rigole avec mes frères.
6. J'étudie avec mes camarades de classe.
7. J'achète des vêtements avec ma mère.
8. J'écoute toujours les conseils de mon père.

Allons plus loin! Maintenant, comparez vos réponses avec les réponses de votre partenaire et expliquez quand vous dites **non.**

MODÈLE: Quand j'ai des problèmes, je parle avec ma tante. Elle est très discrète et elle écoute attentivement.

Cliquez là!

Visitez le site d'une famille française ou francophone. Qui sont les membres de la famille? Quel âge ont-ils? Comment sont-ils et qu'est-ce qu'ils aiment faire? Présentez «votre» famille à la classe.

www
www.mhhe.com/deuxmondes5

Entretiens

Entretiens are pair/partner interviews. They are Stage 3 activities that require full production of speech, although students can usually manage to incorporate words and phrases from the questions. In general, students become interested and add other questions while they are talking. This is to be encouraged, since explaining and describing are essential to true speaking proficiency. After assigning an **Entretien** to partners, the instructor may ask students to discuss each question together before moving on to the next or may choose to have two separate full-length interviews during the time the partners are talking. Both methods work well and engender talk that goes beyond the immediate requirements of the activity.

Errors in Speech

When students begin speaking spontaneously, they are likely to make grammatical errors because they are concentrating on expressing meaning and do not have time to monitor their speech. These early errors do not become permanent, and they do not affect students' future language development. Most forms and structures require a large number of communicative experiences before acquisition is complete, and direct error correction generally does not speed up this process. During communicative activities, the instructor should pay attention primarily to the student's message.

Any language correction should be done indirectly through rephrasing and expanding students' responses so that students' thought processes are not interrupted by overt correction. It is reasonable for the instructor to expect steady improvement throughout the course as students have an opportunity to acquire French, but students are not likely to end the school year with complete grammatical accuracy in all the language they have acquired. However, direct correction of errors is helpful in grammar exercises and can be applied profitably in writing tasks.

Activité 15: Entretien: Ma famille

Répondez aux questions. Ensuite, posez les questions à votre partenaire.

1. Est-ce que tu viens d'une famille nombreuse? Combien de personnes (approximativement) y a-t-il dans ta famille?
2. Est-ce que tes grands-parents sont vivants ou morts? Où habitent-ils? Quel âge ont-ils?
3. Qui est la personne que tu préfères dans ta famille? Comment est cette personne? Pourquoi est-ce que tu préfères cette personne?
4. Est-ce que tu discutes de tes problèmes importants avec tes parents? Pourquoi? Sinon, avec qui préfères-tu en parler?
5. À qui est-ce que tu ressembles physiquement? Et du point de vue personnalité?

> **AGENCE MATRIMONIALE**
> **«ESPOIR FAMILIAL»**
> 20, rue Paul Gourdon
>
> **RENCONTRES**
> 31 ans, célibataire, tendre, raisonnable, jolie et intelligente en plus! Milieu médical, elle désire faire des projets d'avenir avec jeune homme affectueux et protecteur.
>
> 58 ans, veuve, douce, un peu timide, elle aime la campagne, cuisiner; désire rencontrer compagnon simple mais gentil et affectueux.
>
> 36 ans, célibataire, dynamique, charmant, brun, 1,78m, sportif (squash, tennis, randonnée, planche à voile...); désire fonder un foyer, avoir des enfants.
>
> Grand-père, veuf, 75 ans, aisé, dynamique, aimant nature, voyages et sorties; désire rencontrer une dame 65/70 ans, mêmes intérêts.

Activité 16: Dans le monde francophone: L'agence matrimoniale «Espoir familial»

1. Est-ce que la personne de 31 ans est un homme ou une femme?
2. Est-ce que la personne qui aime faire de la planche à voile est veuve ou célibataire?
3. Quel âge a le «grand-père» dynamique?
4. Qui joue au tennis?
5. Qui vient d'un milieu médical?

À vous la parole! Vous désirez rencontrer une personne intéressante. Préparez une petite annonce pour l'agence matrimoniale «Espoir familial». Pour commencer, quel âge avez-vous? Et comment êtes-vous? Qu'est-ce que vous aimez faire?

Familles d'aujourd'hui

On dit que la famille est en crise, mais elle reste[1] importante pour les Français. Cependant, sa définition change selon la classe sociale, la région, les origines.

Jean-Claude Dutourd, 26 ans, chômeur,[2] habite avec ses parents. Évidemment,[3] c'est difficile, mais il n'a pas de travail, alors c'est une solution acceptable pour le moment. Ses parents sont patients: ils comprennent que ce n'est pas sa faute.

---

[1]remains [2]personne qui n'a pas de travail [3]< évident

Lectures

The Natural Approach views reading as an integral part of language acquisition. The **Lectures** are an essential part of the course and are strongly integrated thematically with the **Activités orales.** They consist of author-written and adapted pieces that provide an introduction to a variety of textual forms, including dialogue, narrative, and poetry. Although intended for beginning students, the language of the **Lectures** is authentic and natural. Most unfamiliar words

and expressions are glossed in simple French, since it is our belief that the best way to read French is to understand a text in French. Each **Lecture** is followed by a comprehension activity and by **À vous la parole!**, which provides a creative and integrative activity based on the reading.

Reading Strategies

Students must be aware that the ability to read French with facility cannot be developed through translation. The reader must make direct connections between language and meaning.

We suggest that students approach reading as they do listening. For all types of readings, encourage a global understanding rather than a word-by-word approach concerned with detailed accuracy. We suggest that the instructor introduce a text and have students skim it in class to get a general idea of what it is about before they take it home to read. They should be taught that reading a text several times without using a dictionary can enable them to comprehend the main ideas and more in a passage. When students come to realize that they can read a great deal of authentic French by making educated guesses based on the use of cognates, similar French words they know, visuals, and so on, they feel successful and are often able to learn to read quite rapidly and with a great deal of pleasure.

Un repas en famille, c'est parfois un pique-nique en pleine nature!

Naturellement, il y a parfois des frictions, mais, pour Jean-Claude maintenant, la famille est un refuge.

Pour **Élise Martinelli,** 55 ans, cadre[4] dans une grande entreprise, la famille est une valeur centrale. Elle a quatre enfants et sept petits-enfants; ils viennent la voir très souvent,[5] en général le dimanche. Ils discutent, ils chantent, ils jouent ensemble. Elle adore aller au zoo ou au parc avec ses petits-enfants. Son travail la passionne et elle est très occupée, mais la famille reste essentielle à son équilibre.

Amidou Traore, 17 ans, lycéen,[6] est originaire de Côte-d'Ivoire. Pour lui, la famille, ce n'est pas juste un père, une mère et des frères; c'est aussi des cousins, des oncles, des tantes... Chez lui, on a des relations très fortes, on forme un groupe uni. Dans sa cité,[7] il y a beaucoup d'Africains, alors c'est presque[8] comme un village. Si une personne a des problèmes, les autres sont solidaires.[9]

---
[4]Un cadre a un poste de responsabilité dans une entreprise. [5]fréquemment [6]étudiant dans un lycée, une école secondaire [7]une unité d'habitation dans une ville [8]approximativement (≠ exactement) [9]qui assistent les autres

Avez-vous compris? Déterminez qui parle.

MODÈLE: «Je n'ai pas de travail.»
C'est Jean-Claude Dutourd: il est chômeur.

1. «J'ai beaucoup d'intérêt pour mon travail.»
2. «Je ne suis pas d'origine française.»
3. «J'apprécie la patience de mes parents.»
4. «Où j'habite, il y a beaucoup d'Africains.»
5. «J'ai une famille nombreuse.»
6. «Je considère la famille comme une ressource nécessaire.»

Writing Activities

Each chapter ends with a writing task, **À vous d'écrire.** These tasks are usually based on real-life situations and are specific enough to provide a guide for content. Students should understand that they are not required to restrict themselves only to the information requested. They should have a clear idea of the instructor's expectations concerning how much to write and how the composition will be graded. For the early chapters, we suggest as a minimum a short paragraph of five to eight sentences. The compositions should be reflective of both the content and the level of the chapter. As students progress, they should be able to communicate past or future time as needed; their sentences should become more complex with parenthetical expressions or descriptive clauses. The instructor should decide in advance to what extent grades will reflect grammatical accuracy vis-à-vis content and what kinds of accuracy are the most important (missed accents vs. incorrect verb forms), and so on.

Espace vidéo

The **Espace vidéo** contains functional language clips filmed on location in France. These video segments correspond to each chapter's theme and provide students with authentic language situations. The segments are introduced with questions that serve as a comprehension aid while viewing. Additional activities for these functional language clips are available in the *Cahier d'exercices.*

The *Deux mondes* Online Learning Center (OLC)

The McGraw-Hill *Deux mondes* OLC houses activities that blend with the thematic **Activités** in the White Pages of the student text. They are task-based and keyed to specific Francophone sites on the Internet. Students and instructors will also find a number of other useful materials at the site, including supplementary self-checking exercises for all grammar points in the **Grammaire** section of the textbook.

60 | CHAPITRE 1 *Ma famille et moi*

✏ *À vous d'écrire*

Vous écrivez une lettre à l'agence Accueil France Famille parce que vous désirez passer deux mois dans une famille française. Dans votre lettre, décrivez comment vous êtes, les choses que vous aimez faire et le type de famille que vous préférez trouver.

MODÈLE:

Accueil France Famille
5, rue François Coppée
75015 Paris

Madame, Monsieur,

Je désire passer deux mois dans une famille française. Je m'appelle... , j'ai... ans et je suis étudiant(e) en... à l'université de... Je suis une personne plutôt... J'aime beaucoup... Si possible, je préfère loger dans une famille...
En attendant votre réponse, je vous prie d'agréer l'expression de mes sentiments distingués.

(signature)

Espace vidéo

Décrire quelqu'un. Dans le premier épisode, vous allez rencontrer les trois personnages principaux de cette vidéo. Ce sont des étudiants. Écoutez leur conversation. Comment s'appellent-ils? Qui est Marc? Est-il individualiste? Qui est M. Dépétri? Qu'est-ce qu'il porte aujourd'hui? Qui est Anne? Comment est-elle? Quelle personne aime méditer en plein air? Qui étudie la philosophie? Qui est B.C.B.G.? (bon chic bon genre = traditionaliste)

www

www.mhhe.com/deuxmondes5

Visitez le site Web de *Deux mondes* pour réviser la grammaire et les renseignements culturels qui se trouvent dans ce chapitre.

Vocabulaire

As students begin to talk, they should be encouraged to use the **Vocabulaire** sections at the end of the chapters as a reference tool. We suggest the instructor take a few minutes to explain that the vocabulary is arranged in alphabetical order by topic so that students learn to refer to a particular subject quickly when they forget a word during class. They should also refer to this section when doing writing activities. The list of obvious cognates at the end of each topical section helps remind students of the importance cognates can have in reading and enlarging one's functional vocabulary.

We recommend that students look over the **Vocabulaire** topical groupings and their vocabulary notebooks regularly during home study. Although students should be able to recognize these words, they should not be asked to memorize the vocabulary listings. It is impossible to develop the linguistic flexibility essential for true proficiency at any level without being exposed to a wide vocabulary, and it is detrimental to acquisition to be obliged to memorize large quantities of words.

The instructor should also point out the glossary at the end of the book, since words in the readings and all other vocabulary are listed there in alphabetical order.

Vocabulaire

La famille
Family

le beau-frère	brother-in-law
le beau-père	father-in-law; stepfather
la belle-mère	mother-in-law; stepmother
la belle-sœur	sister-in-law
le cousin / la cousine	cousin
le demi-frère	half brother
la demi-sœur	half sister
l'enfant (m., f.)	child
l'époux, l'épouse	spouse
la femme	wife
la fille	daughter
le fils	son
le frère	brother
la grand-mère	grandmother
le grand-père	grandfather
les grands-parents	grandparents
le mari	husband
la mère	mother
le neveu	nephew
la nièce	niece
l'oncle (m.)	uncle
le père	father
la petite-fille	granddaughter
le petit-fils	grandson
les petits-enfants	grandchildren
la sœur	sister
la tante	aunt

Mots descriptifs
Descriptive words

bon/bonne	good
célibataire	single, unmarried
compréhensif/ compréhensive	understanding
de taille moyenne	of medium height
mort(e)	deceased, dead
nombreux/nombreuse	numerous
poli(e)	polite
roux/rousse	red-haired
seul(e)	alone
tout(e)	all
trop	too
vite	quickly
vivant(e)	living, alive

Mots apparentés: **affectueux/affectueuse, ambitieux/ambitieuse, attentivement, calme, décisif/décisive, discret/discrète, égoïste, favori/favorite, flexible, généreux/généreuse, moderne, organisé(e), patient(e), physiquement, réaliste, réservé(e), sportif/sportive, strict(e)**

Activités favorites et distractions
Favorite activities and entertainment

Qu'est-ce que tu aimes faire?	What do you like to do?
J'adore...	I love . . .
J'ai horreur de...	I hate . . .
J'aime...	I like . . .
J'aime mieux...	I prefer . . .
aller au cinéma (au théâtre, à la plage, à la montagne)	to go to the movies (to the theater, the beach, the mountains)
chanter sous la douche	to sing in the shower
conduire une voiture	to drive a car
cuisiner	to cook
danser	to dance
dîner au restaurant	to eat at a restaurant
dormir tard	to sleep late
écouter la radio	to listen to the radio
faire des courses	to go shopping
du camping	to go camping
la fête	to party
une promenade	to take a walk
du ski	to go skiing
inviter des amis	invite friends over
jouer aux cartes (au billard, au football, au tennis)	to play cards (pool, soccer, tennis)
lire (le journal)	to read (the newspaper)
nager à la piscine	to swim in the pool
parler au téléphone	to talk on the phone
passer la soirée ensemble	to spend the evening together
regarder la télévision	to watch television
rester à la maison	to stay home
rigoler	to laugh, have fun
sortir avec des ami(e)s	to go out with friends
travailler dans le jardin	to work in the yard
voyager	to travel

61

Les endroits

Places

au bord de la mer	at the seashore
un bureau	office
une maison	house
à la montagne	in the mountains
une piscine	swimming pool

Mots apparentés: **un centre commercial, une discothèque, un hôpital**

Quand

Saying when

maintenant	now
quelquefois	sometimes
souvent	often

Substantifs

Nouns

un/une camarade de chambre	roommate
un chat / une chatte	cat
un chien / une chienne	dog
un copain / une copine	close friend, pal
un infirmier / une infirmière	nurse
une leçon particulière	private lesson
un numéro de téléphone	phone number
un petit ami / une petite amie	boyfriend, girlfriend
un poisson rouge	goldfish
un renseignement	piece of information
une réponse	answer
une ville	city

Mots apparentés: **une adresse, une aventure, un film, un match, la musique, la nationalité, un sport, les vacances** (*f.*)

Verbes

Verbs

acheter	to buy
déjeuner	to eat lunch
discuter (de)	to discuss
étudier	to study
faire des achats	to make purchases
habiter	to live (inhabit)
passer (un mois)	to spend (a month)

rentrer	to return home
ressembler (à)	to resemble, to look like
travailler	to work
venir	to come

Mots apparentés: **adorer, détester, préférer, téléphoner**

Mots et expressions utiles

Useful words and expressions

à	to, at
après	after
avec	with
beaucoup	a lot, many
C'est vrai?	Is that right (correct)?
chez moi (mes parents)	at my home (my parents' house)
D'où venez-vous? (**...viens-tu?**)	Where are you from?
Je suis né(e)...	I was born . . .
Moi aussi!	Me too!
Moi non!	Not me!
Moi non plus!	Me neither!
Moi si!	Yes (*I do*)!
mon/ma meilleur(e) ami(e)	my best friend
où	where
Pas possible!	Not possible!
pour	for
pourquoi	why
Quel âge avez-vous? (**...as-tu?**)	How old are you?
J'ai... ans.	I'm . . . (years old).
Tiens!	Well!
voilà	there is/are

Les pays et les nationalités

Countries and nationalities

l'Allemagne (*f.*)/**allemand(e)**	Germany/German
la Belgique/belge	Belgium/Belgian
la Chine/chinois(e)	China/Chinese
l'Espagne (*f.*)/**espagnol(e)**	Spain/Spanish
les États-Unis (*m.*)/ **américain(e)**	the United States/ American
la France/français(e)	France/French
le Québec/québécois(e)	Quebec/Quebecois

Mots apparentés: **l'Algérie** (*f.*), **algérien/algérienne; le Canada, canadien/canadienne; le Japon, japonais/japonaise; le Sénégal, sénégalais/sénégalaise**

Functional Grammar Titles

Grammar headings have functional labels wherever appropriate. We recommend that instructors call attention to these functional titles (here "Expressing relationships") and encourage students to use them as an introduction to the grammar points they are about to study. We believe that students should understand why they are asked to study grammar and that they should see it from the beginning as a tool to learning to use French.

English versus French

Note that the exercises in the **Première** and **Deuxième étapes** are introduced or contextualized in English. Beginning with **Chapitre 1**, however, all instructions and contexts for the grammar exercises are given in French. This makes it easier for those who are teaching entirely in French to do in class any grammar exercises they might wish.

Types of Exercises

Most grammar points are accompanied by two or more exercises, usually in either a completion or a communicative format. In general, the grammar exercises are contextualized to help engage thought in French, while one is also working on form. Completions like **Exercice 1** allow students to focus on accuracy while practicing grammatical forms in a natural discourse context. These exercises have the advantage of providing coverage of all or nearly all forms of a paradigm, though in the case of very complex paradigms like possessive adjectives, only a subset of the paradigm is covered in any one exercise.

Grammaire et exercices

1.1 Expressing relationships: Possessive adjectives

A. Here are the forms of the possessive adjectives in French.

ENGLISH	BEFORE SINGULAR NOUNS	BEFORE PLURAL NOUNS
my	mon, ma	mes
your (tu)	ton, ta	tes
his, her, its	son, sa	ses
our	notre	nos
your (vous)	votre	vos
their	leur	leurs

Definition: Possessive adjectives modify nouns by indicating ownership or relationship: my book, your sister.

Voici une photo de **mon** frère avec **sa** femme et **leurs** enfants.

Here's a photo of my brother with his wife and their children.

Pronunciation Hint

Final **-s** and **-n** are pronounced when the following word begins with a vowel: mes‿enfants but mes filles, mon‿ami but mon fils.

B. French possessive adjectives agree in gender and number with the nouns they modify. Exception: the possessive form ending in **-n** (**mon, ton, son**) is always used before a singular noun or adjective starting with a vowel or mute **h**, even if the noun is feminine.

   mon cousin Charles   **ma** cousine Clarisse   **mon** autre cousine Marise

C. Keep in mind that the number and gender of the possessive adjective are determined *by what is possessed*, not by the possessor. This is why **son, sa,** and **ses** all correspond to *his, her,* or *its,* depending on the context.

   Voilà Victor Lasalle avec **sa** femme Claudine et **son** fils Charles.
   Mme Martin regarde **son** livre.

There's Victor Lasalle with his wife Claudine and his son Charles. Madame Martin is looking at her book.

★ *Review **Grammaire A.3** and **A.5**.*

➤ "Number" refers to whether a word is singular or plural.

Exercice 1: En famille

Denise et Jacqueline parlent de leur famille. Remplacez les tirets par un des adjectifs possessifs: **mon, ma, mes; ton, ta, tes; son, sa, ses.**

   1. —Jacqueline, comment est _____ famille? Est-ce que _____ frères et sœurs sont jeunes?
   —Non, pas trop. _____ frère a 19 ans et _____ sœurs ont 12 et 14 ans.

63

Communicative Grammar Exercises

These exercises come in a variety of formats. Many of them lend themselves to optional in-class pair practice, although they are written to be done in writing by students working on their own. **Exercice 2,** for example, works well with either option. Students who study together outside class also find the communicative exercises useful for additional oral practice.

Coordination of Oral Activities and Grammar Exercises

The **Grammaire** is intended to be complementary to the White Page **Activités.** For example, in **Goûts personnels**

(**Chapitre 1**), the forms of **aimer** occur mainly as lexical items in the **Activités.** The focus in that section is on learning the meaning of a large number of infinitives so that students can talk about their favorite activities. In the corresponding **Grammaire 1.2** section, the conjugation of **aimer** is given primary importance. Here, students are asked to look closely at the forms and the pattern being described. This is the introduction to regular conjugations and is part of the spiraled presentation of verb conjugation and **-er** verbs.

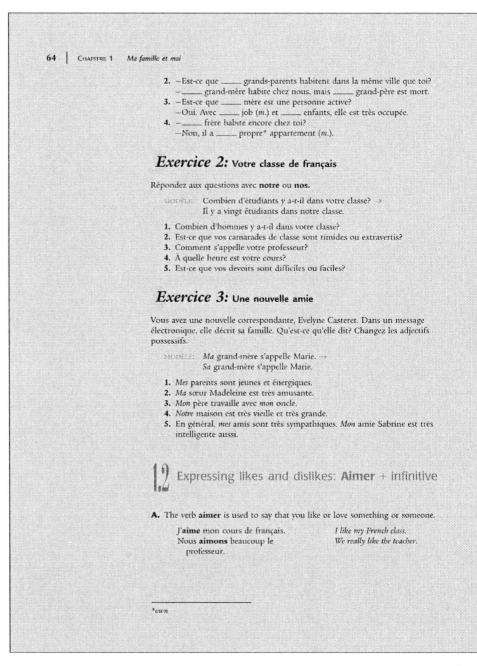

64 | CHAPITRE 1 *Ma famille et moi*

2. —Est-ce que _____ grands-parents habitent dans la même ville que toi?
   —_____ grand-mère habite chez nous, mais _____ grand-père est mort.
3. —Est-ce que _____ mère est une personne active?
   —Oui. Avec _____ job (*m.*) et _____ enfants, elle est très occupée.
4. —_____ frère habite encore chez toi?
   —Non, il a _____ propre* appartement (*m.*).

Exercice 2: Votre classe de français

Répondez aux questions avec **notre** ou **nos.**

MODÈLE   Combien d'étudiants y a-t-il dans votre classe? →
         Il y a vingt étudiants dans notre classe.

1. Combien d'hommes y a-t-il dans votre classe?
2. Est-ce que vos camarades de classe sont timides ou extravertis?
3. Comment s'appelle votre professeur?
4. À quelle heure est votre cours?
5. Est-ce que vos devoirs sont difficiles ou faciles?

Exercice 3: Une nouvelle amie

Vous avez une nouvelle correspondante, Evelyne Casteret. Dans un message électronique, elle décrit sa famille. Qu'est-ce qu'elle dit? Changez les adjectifs possessifs.

MODÈLE   *Ma* grand-mère s'appelle Marie. →
         Sa grand-mère s'appelle Marie.

1. *Mes* parents sont jeunes et énergiques.
2. *Ma* sœur Madeleine est très amusante.
3. *Mon* père travaille avec *mon* oncle.
4. *Notre* maison est très vieille et très grande.
5. En général, *mes* amis sont très sympathiques. *Mon* amie Sabrine est très intelligente aussi.

1.2 Expressing likes and dislikes: **Aimer** + infinitive

A. The verb **aimer** is used to say that you like or love something or someone.

J'**aime** mon cours de français.   *I like my French class.*
Nous **aimons** beaucoup le   *We really like the teacher.*
professeur.

*own

Grammar Display Boxes

The yellow boxes that accompany many **Grammaire** articles encapsulate important facts or details from the particular article. These are useful for both study and review, as well as for quick reference in class. The boxes often work in conjunction with the grammar margin notes in the Student Edition, making it even easier to use the **Grammaire** for reference.

Yellow and white shading are used consistently in the boxes throughout the text to highlight the "L-forms" of verb paradigms. The instructor should point out that L-forms for a particular verb are all pronounced the same though they may have different written forms. Students should be reminded of these differences between the written and the oral language whenever new verb conjugations are introduced.

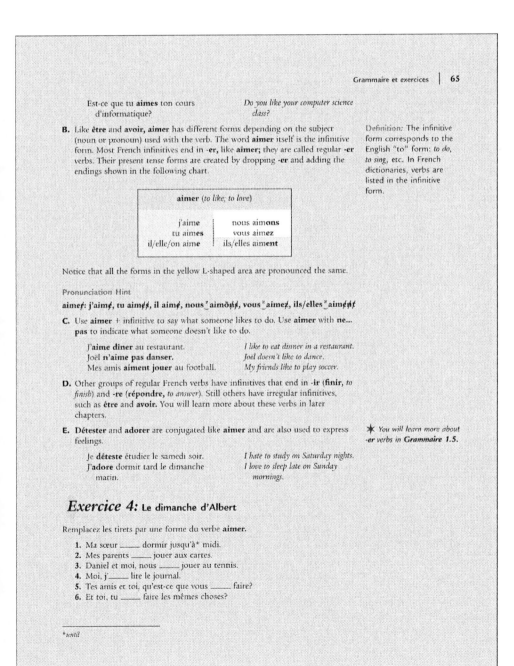

Est-ce que tu **aimes** ton cours d'informatique?

Do you like your computer science class?

B. Like **être** and **avoir**, **aimer** has different forms depending on the subject (noun or pronoun) used with the verb. The word **aimer** itself is the infinitive form. Most French infinitives end in **-er**, like **aimer**; they are called regular **-er** verbs. Their present tense forms are created by dropping **-er** and adding the endings shown in the following chart.

Definition: The infinitive form corresponds to the English "to" form: *to do, to sing,* etc. In French dictionaries, verbs are listed in the infinitive form.

aimer (*to like; to love*)	
j'aime	nous aim**ons**
tu aim**es**	vous aim**ez**
il/elle/on aime	ils/elles aim**ent**

Notice that all the forms in the yellow L-shaped area are pronounced the same.

Pronunciation Hint

aime̸: j'aim̸, tu aim̸s̸, il aim̸, nous ˇaim̃õn̸s̸, vous ˇaime̸z̸, ils/elles ˇaim̸e̸n̸t̸

C. Use **aimer** + infinitive to say what someone likes to do. Use **aimer** with ne... pas to indicate what someone doesn't like to do.

J'**aime** dîner au restaurant.
Joël **n'aime pas** danser.
Mes amis **aiment** jouer au football.

I like to eat dinner in a restaurant.
Joël doesn't like to dance.
My friends like to play soccer.

D. Other groups of regular French verbs have infinitives that end in **-ir** (**finir**, *to finish*) and **-re** (**répondre**, *to answer*). Still others have irregular infinitives, such as **être** and **avoir**. You will learn more about these verbs in later chapters.

E. **Détester** and **adorer** are conjugated like **aimer** and are also used to express feelings.

✳ *You will learn more about -er verbs in* **Grammaire 1.5.**

Je **déteste** étudier le samedi soir.
J'**adore** dormir tard le dimanche matin.

I hate to study on Saturday nights.
I love to sleep late on Sunday mornings.

Exercice 4: Le dimanche d'Albert

Remplacez les tirets par une forme du verbe **aimer.**

1. Ma sœur _____ dormir jusqu'à* midi.
2. Mes parents _____ jouer aux cartes.
3. Daniel et moi, nous _____ jouer au tennis.
4. Moi, j'_____ lire le journal.
5. Tes amis et toi, qu'est-ce que vous _____ faire?
6. Et toi, tu _____ faire les mêmes choses?

_____
*until

Grammar with Input

Most communicative grammar exercises are like **Exercice 5;** that is, students supply virtually all the language necessary to do the exercise. This lets students concentrate on the target forms without the distraction of having to produce other, more complex language. At the same time, however, students are getting good input from reading and thinking in French. If the exercises are done with a partner, the students also get good aural input.

Exercice 5: Passe-temps préférés

Répondez et puis indiquez un autre passe-temps préféré.

Suggestions

aller au cinéma	jouer aux cartes
danser	lire des livres / le journal
dormir tard	regarder la télé
écouter de la musique classique	surfer sur Internet

MODÈLE: Est-ce que vos amis aiment cuisiner? →
Mes amis aiment cuisiner, mais ils aiment aussi dîner au restaurant. (Mes amis n'aiment pas cuisiner, mais ils aiment dîner au restaurant.)

1. Est-ce que vos amis aiment surfer sur Internet?
2. Est-ce que votre mère aime jouer du piano?
3. Est-ce que votre père aime écouter du rock?
4. Est-ce que votre petit ami / petite amie aime faire une promenade?
5. Est-ce que votre professeur de français aime aller au cinéma?
6. Est-ce que vous aimez jouer au tennis le week-end?

Talking about dates and personal data: Numbers beyond 100

➤ The day always comes before the month: 25.12.04 = le 25 décembre 2004.

➤ Use **le premier** to express the first of the month.

➤ avoir

j'ai	nous avons
tu as	vous avez
il a	ils ont

A. To talk about the date, use one of these expressions.

Quelle est la date aujourd'hui?	*What's today's date?*
Aujourd'hui **c'est le** vingt (le huit, etc.) avril.	*Today is April 20th (8th, etc.).*
Aujourd'hui **nous sommes le** premier janvier.	*Today is January 1st (first).*

B. To express age, use **avoir** (*to have*) + number + **ans.**

—Joël, quel âge **as**-tu?	*Joël, how old are you?*
—**J'ai** huit **ans.**	*I'm eight.*
—Et ton frère Emmanuel?	*How about your brother Emmanuel?*
—Il **a** quatorze **ans.**	*He's fourteen.*

C. Here is how to tell your birthday and birthdate.

Mon anniversaire est le vingt et un septembre.	*My birthday is September 21st.*
Je suis né(e) en 1983.	*I was born in 1983.*

More on Grammar Display Boxes

Besides verb conjugations, key vocabulary such as numbers and other new language forms are always set off in vocabulary display boxes. This makes the material more salient and easily referenced by students during reviews. The Instructor's Edition margin notes give more suggestions on using these boxes and the other parts of the **Grammaire.**

The *Grammaire* as a Reference Tool

We attempt to provide the tools students need for the many types of activities they will do during their study of French. The grammar display box and margin notes on this page, for instance, are intended to help students with writing exercises and reading activities. Keep in mind, however, that the purpose of this **Grammaire** section is the functional use of numbers in communication situations. We do not encourage testing for small points of accuracy such as when to drop the **-s** of **cents** or to add **de** before a noun. Such details are best discussed and tested only after students have acquired a larger body of language material from which to work. At this point in their French career, it is much more important that they recognize the meaning of spoken and written numbers.

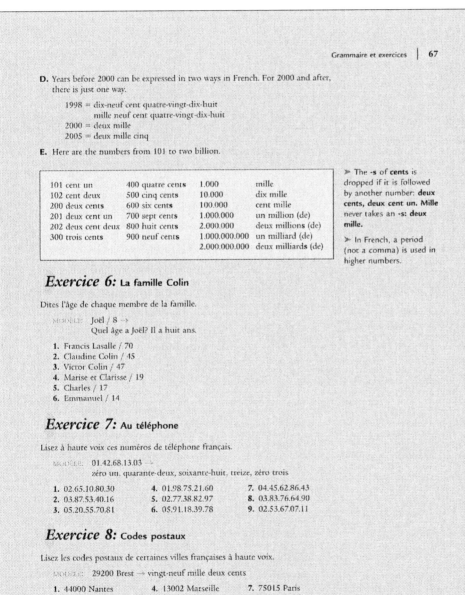

D. Years before 2000 can be expressed in two ways in French. For 2000 and after, there is just one way.

1998 = dix-neuf cent quatre-vingt-dix-huit
       mille neuf cent quatre-vingt-dix-huit
2000 = deux mille
2005 = deux mille cinq

E. Here are the numbers from 101 to two billion.

101 cent un	400 quatre cents	1.000	mille
102 cent deux	500 cinq cents	10.000	dix mille
200 deux cents	600 six cents	100.000	cent mille
201 deux cent un	700 sept cents	1.000.000	un million (de)
202 deux cent deux	800 huit cents	2.000.000	deux millions (de)
300 trois cents	900 neuf cents	1.000.000.000	un milliard (de)
		2.000.000.000	deux milliards (de)

➤ The **-s** of **cents** is dropped if it is followed by another number: **deux cents, deux cent un. Mille** never takes an **-s: deux mille.**

➤ In French, a period (not a comma) is used in higher numbers.

Exercice 6: La famille Colin

Dites l'âge de chaque membre de la famille.

MODÈLE: Joël / 8 →
        Quel âge a Joël? Il a huit ans.

1. Francis Lasalle / 70
2. Claudine Colin / 45
3. Victor Colin / 47
4. Marise et Clarisse / 19
5. Charles / 17
6. Emmanuel / 14

Exercice 7: Au téléphone

Lisez à haute voix ces numéros de téléphone français.

MODÈLE: 01.42.68.13.03 →
        zéro un, quarante-deux, soixante-huit, treize, zéro trois

1. 02.65.10.80.30	4. 01.98.75.21.60	7. 04.45.62.86.43
2. 03.87.53.40.16	5. 02.77.38.82.97	8. 03.83.76.64.90
3. 05.20.55.70.81	6. 05.91.18.39.78	9. 02.53.67.07.11

Exercice 8: Codes postaux

Lisez les codes postaux de certaines villes françaises à haute voix.

MODÈLE: 29200 Brest → vingt-neuf mille deux cents

1. 44000 Nantes	4. 13002 Marseille	7. 75015 Paris
2. 67000 Strasbourg	5. 59000 Lille	8. 33000 Bordeaux
3. 69009 Lyon	6. 64200 Biarritz	

Focused Practice or Comprehensible Input?

Instructors may choose to assign **Exercise 9** as homework. This exercise also has a communicative aspect that enables students to speak together with true meaning. Unlike the White Page activities, however, the input generated here is highly restricted: Students must use the same question throughout, and there is no choice when selecting an answer. Wrong answers can only be errors of usage. This is a focused practice of the target syntax and words. As such, it can make only a limited contribution to any student's stock of acquired language and will mainly be useful for learning the forms necessary for monitoring speech.

Exercice 9: Anniversaires

Posez la question et répondez avec les renseignements donnés entre parenthèses.

MODÈLE: Francis Cabrel (23.11.53) → Quelle est la date de naissance de Francis Cabrel?
C'est le 23 novembre 1953 (le vingt-trois novembre mille neuf cent cinquante-trois).

1. Elvis Presley (8.1.35)
2. Serena Williams (26.9.81)
3. Frédéric Chopin (1.3.1810)
4. Paul McCartney (18.6.42)
5. Sigmund Freud (6.5.1856)
6. Mickey Mouse (18.11.28)
7. Magic Johnson (14.8.59)
8. Yves Saint-Laurent (1.8.36)
9. Barry Bonds (24.7.64)
10. B.B. King (16.9.25)

1.4 Stating origin: The verb **venir**

A. Here are the forms of **venir**.

> Note that most French verbs have the same plural endings: **-ons, -ez, -ent**. With a few exceptions, verbs other than **-er** verbs have the same singular endings: **-s, -s, -t**.

venir *(to come)*	
je **viens**	nous **venons**
tu **viens**	vous **venez**
il/elle/on **vient**	ils/elles **viennent**

Use the verb **venir** and the preposition **de** to ask or say where someone is from.

—D'où **vient** Mme Martin?   *Where's Madame Martin from?*
—Elle **vient de** Montréal.   *She's from Montreal.*
—Et **d'où viens**-tu?   *And where are you from?*
—Moi, je **viens de** Kansas City.   *I'm from Kansas City.*

Pronunciation Hint

All singular forms of **venir** are pronounced alike: **viens**. The pronunciations of the plural forms are **venons**, **venez**, **viennent**.

Grammar for Recognition Only

Whereas we have approached grammar from the perspective of its functional use in corresponding **Activités** sections, we at times discuss points that are related to the main grammar explanation and that we believe may cause problems for students. As an example, **Grammaire 1.4** briefly discusses the forms **de, du,** and so on and the question **D'où vient... ?** because these items are used in the oral activities. However, they are not practiced in the exercises at this point because the primary focus of **1.4** is awareness of the forms of **venir.** Such early explanations are helpful for understanding the language used in the oral activities but are either too difficult or not particularly relevant to the students' current level of acquisition. In the grammar sections, the corresponding exercises will always reflect the main grammar point(s). In our example case, the use of the prepositions with names of countries and so on is explained in **Chapitre 8** after students have had much more experience with them.

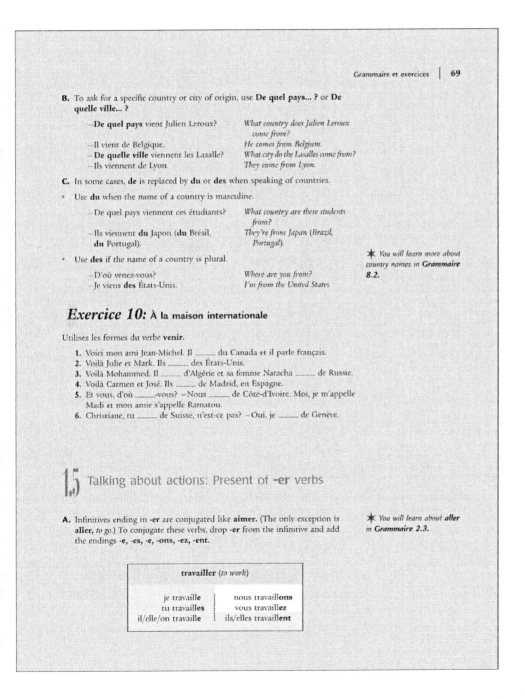

B. To ask for a specific country or city of origin, use **De quel pays... ?** or **De quelle ville... ?**

—**De quel pays** vient Julien Leroux? — *What country does Julien Leroux come from?*

—Il vient de Belgique. — *He comes from Belgium.*

—**De quelle ville** viennent les Lasalle? — *What city do the Lasalles come from?*
—Ils viennent de Lyon. — *They come from Lyon.*

C. In some cases, **de** is replaced by **du** or **des** when speaking of countries.

• Use **du** when the name of a country is masculine.

—De quel pays viennent ces étudiants? — *What country are these students from?*

—Ils viennent **du** Japon (**du** Brésil, **du** Portugal). — *They're from Japan (Brazil, Portugal).*

• Use **des** if the name of a country is plural.

✴ *You will learn more about country names in* **Grammaire 8.2.**

—D'où venez-vous? — *Where are you from?*
—Je viens **des** États-Unis. — *I'm from the United States.*

Exercice 10: À la maison internationale

Utilisez les formes du verbe **venir.**

1. Voici mon ami Jean-Michel. Il _____ du Canada et il parle français.
2. Voilà Julie et Mark. Ils _____ des États-Unis.
3. Voilà Mohammed. Il _____ d'Algérie et sa femme Natacha _____ de Russie.
4. Voilà Carmen et José. Ils _____ de Madrid, en Espagne.
5. Et vous, d'où _____-vous? —Nous _____ de Côte-d'Ivoire. Moi, je m'appelle Madi et mon amie s'appelle Ramatou.
6. Christiane, tu _____ de Suisse, n'est-ce pas? —Oui, je _____ de Genève.

1.5 Talking about actions: Present of -er verbs

A. Infinitives ending in **-er** are conjugated like **aimer.** (The only exception is **aller,** *to go.*) To conjugate these verbs, drop **-er** from the infinitive and add the endings **-e, -es, -e, -ons, -ez, -ent.**

✴ *You will learn about* **aller** *in* **Grammaire 2.3.**

travailler (*to work*)	
je travaille	nous travaill**ons**
tu travaill**es**	vous travaill**ez**
il/elle/on travaille	ils/elles travaill**ent**

The Role of Functional Usage

The exercises for **Grammaire 1.5** reflect the fact that functional usage is of primary importance in the *Deux mondes* approach to grammar. These exercises, intended as review of present tense forms of **-er** verbs, ask students to use verbs to express habitual action. In the explanations, other meanings of the present indicative are given in example sentences but are not practiced in the exercises (*I am studying, I do study*). These explanations are provided to help students with their overall comprehension and reading skills.

habiter (*to live*)	
j' habit**e**	nous habit**ons**
tu habit**es**	vous habit**ez**
il/elle/on habit**e**	ils/elles habit**ent**

Remember that the forms of **-er** verbs in the yellow L-shaped area are pronounced the same because their endings are silent.

Pronunciation Hint

In **travailler**, the letters **aill** sound like English "eye." Also note that because the initial **h** in **habiter** is silent, **je** contracts to **j'**, and you must make the liaison with all the plural forms: j'habite, nous ˅ habitons, vous ˅ habitez, ils ˅ habitent, elles ˅ habitent. This applies to all verbs beginning with vowels: **étudier** (*to study*): j'étudie, nous ˅ étudions, etc.

➤ **j'étudie** = I study, I am studying, *or* I do study

B. Notice that the French present tense is equivalent to three meanings in English.

Daniel travaille à la bibliothèque ce soir.	Daniel **is working** at the library tonight.
Denise travaille à la bibliothèque tous les samedis.	Denise **works** at the library every Saturday.
Oui, Denise travaille quelquefois le dimanche après-midi.	Yes, Denise **does work** on Sunday afternoons sometimes.

C. Here are some **-er** verbs you can use to talk about activities and actions.

chanter *to sing*	**dîner** *to eat dinner*	**parler** *to talk, speak*
chercher *to look for, go get*	**donner** *to give*	**regarder** *to look at*
	écouter *to listen to*	**rencontrer** *to meet*
cuisiner *to cook*	**inviter** *to invite*	**rentrer** *to return, come back (home)*
danser *to dance*	**jouer** *to play*	
déjeuner *to eat lunch*	**manger** *to eat*	**rester** *to stay*
dessiner *to draw*	**nager** *to swim*	**voyager** *to travel*

D. Some **-er** verbs like **préférer, acheter,** and **appeler** have a spelling change in their present tense forms before the silent endings (**-e, -es, -ent**). Verbs like **manger** and **commencer** have a spelling change in the **nous** form. See the charts in **Appendices A** and **C.3** for more information about spelling changes in **-er** verbs.

Exercice 11: La vie de Joël

Joël décrit les activités de sa famille et de ses amis. Complétez ses phrases avec la forme appropriée du verbe.

More on Communicative Grammar Exercises

Exercice 12 offers another kind of communicative grammar practice that combines verification of knowledge with a personal element. It is a two-part exercise in which students must first supply the missing verb forms to complete the sentence. In the second part, students react to the meaning of the sentence they have built to make personal responses, using the language in the exercise and little production. If done in class, we recommend that the instructor take sample answers for all the items as an input activity.

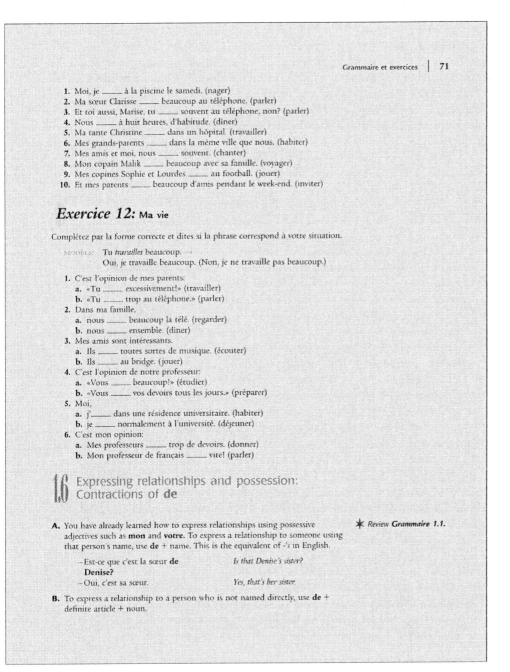

1. Moi, je _____ à la piscine le samedi. (nager)
2. Ma sœur Clarisse _____ beaucoup au téléphone. (parler)
3. Et toi aussi, Marise, tu _____ souvent au téléphone, non? (parler)
4. Nous _____ à huit heures, d'habitude. (dîner)
5. Ma tante Christine _____ dans un hôpital. (travailler)
6. Mes grands-parents _____ dans la même ville que nous. (habiter)
7. Mes amis et moi, nous _____ souvent. (chanter)
8. Mon copain Malik _____ beaucoup avec sa famille. (voyager)
9. Mes copines Sophie et Lourdes _____ au football. (jouer)
10. Et mes parents _____ beaucoup d'amis pendant le week-end. (inviter)

Exercice 12: Ma vie

Complétez par la forme correcte et dites si la phrase correspond à votre situation.

MODÈLE: Tu *travailles* beaucoup. →
Oui, je travaille beaucoup. (Non, je ne travaille pas beaucoup.)

1. C'est l'opinion de mes parents:
   a. «Tu _____ excessivement!» (travailler)
   b. «Tu _____ trop au téléphone.» (parler)
2. Dans ma famille,
   a. nous _____ beaucoup la télé. (regarder)
   b. nous _____ ensemble. (dîner)
3. Mes amis sont intéressants.
   a. Ils _____ toutes sortes de musique. (écouter)
   b. Ils _____ au bridge. (jouer)
4. C'est l'opinion de notre professeur:
   a. «Vous _____ beaucoup!» (étudier)
   b. «Vous _____ vos devoirs tous les jours.» (préparer)
5. Moi,
   a. j'_____ dans une résidence universitaire. (habiter)
   b. je _____ normalement à l'université. (déjeuner)
6. C'est mon opinion:
   a. Mes professeurs _____ trop de devoirs. (donner)
   b. Mon professeur de français _____ vite! (parler)

1.6 Expressing relationships and possession: Contractions of de

A. You have already learned how to express relationships using possessive adjectives such as **mon** and **votre**. To express a relationship to someone using that person's name, use **de** + name. This is the equivalent of -'s in English.

✱ *Review* **Grammaire 1.1.**

—Est-ce que c'est la sœur **de Denise?** *Is that Denise's sister?*
—Oui, c'est sa sœur. *Yes, that's her sister.*

B. To express a relationship to a person who is not named directly, use **de** + definite article + noun.

Chapter 2
Introduction to the *Deux mondes* Program

This Instructor's Manual and the marginal glosses in the Instructor's Edition were written to help you use *Deux mondes* effectively. Natural Approach (NA) materials are designed for a course in which students, interacting with you and with one another, develop the ability to communicate their thoughts and ideas in spoken and written French.

In this manual, we describe each component of *Deux mondes* and suggest how and when to use a specific type of activity or exercise. We firmly believe, however, that the ultimate success of the course and of the students depends on the instructor. Although these materials are provided to facilitate your efforts to create communicative experiences for your students, the materials alone will not suffice. Only the interaction between you and your students in natural, relatively spontaneous exchanges in French will result in a communicative experience. You will decide how to weave these activities and materials into a coherent experience that will ultimately result in proficiency in French. We do not include lesson plans per se but make suggestions and propose guidelines. In most cases, the oral and written activities are to be used as starting points for communication. We hope that these materials will not confine you but rather will free you to interact with your students in the sorts of communication activities that are the basis of the Natural Approach.

The Materials

There are two student texts: *Deux mondes: A Communicative Approach* (the main text) and *Deux mondes: Cahier d'exercices* (the workbook, which is both a laboratory manual and a writing manual). In both the main text and the workbook there are two preliminary chapters (**Première** and **Deuxième étapes**) and fourteen regular chapters (**Chapitres 1–14**). Each chapter of the main text contains three sections: the communication activities (**Activités**) with readings (**Lectures**), the chapter vocabulary (**Vocabulaire**), and the grammar and exercises (**Grammaire et exercices**). The **Activités et lectures** are the main focus of the course. They consist of suggestions for oral communication activities for the classroom and various kinds of readings that offer more possibilities for oral communication and for writing practice. The **Vocabulaire** is a reference list of most of the new vocabulary in the **Activités,** arranged in semantic or topical groupings. The **Grammaire et exercices** section includes explanations of grammar and word usage, followed by short verification exercises keyed to answers at the end of the book in Appendix D. There is also a French-English glossary of all new words in *Deux mondes* at the end of the book.

The chapters of *Deux mondes: Cahier d'exercices* correspond to the chapters in the textbook. They are divided into three sections, as are the textbook chapters. Each section of the *Cahier* has three main divisions: **Activités, Intégration,** and **Prononciation et le verbe français.** Each **Activités** section begins with **Activités de compréhension,** activities that are coordinated with the scripts of the audio program. These are followed by **Activités écrites,** which practice the new vocabulary and grammar for the particular section. The **Intégration** section at the end of the chapter includes a video-based activity (**À vos écrans!**), a reading that is recorded in the audio program for that particular chapter (**À l'écoute!**), and a writing task (**À vous d'écrire!**) that invites students to draw on what they have learned throughout this and past chapters. **La prononciation et le verbe français** contains pronunciation and spelling exercises, dictations, and verb study exercises. These materials are also included in the audio program for each chapter. The *Cahier d'exercices* is perforated for easy tear-out of homework exercises. The answers to all activities in the *Cahier d'exercices* are provided at the end of the student text for self-correction.

Complete transcripts of the *Deux mondes* video and audio program are available to instructors. The *Deux mondes* program also includes a Listening Comprehension audio CD packaged with the audio program with recordings of many **Lectures** from the student text, the Instructor's Resource Kit of supplementary activities, and a complete Testing Program. Additional activities and self-checking grammar exercises are also available at the McGraw-Hill *Deux mondes* Online Learning Center (mhhe.com/deuxmondes5).

The materials in *Deux mondes* provide the basis for a full academic year, or three semesters (30–45 weeks) at the college level. Approximately one week should be spent on each of the two preliminary chapters (**Première** and **Deuxième étapes**). Each regular chapter (1–14) can be covered in one and one-half to two weeks, depending on content and pace. For courses meeting four or five times per week, this will still allow time for supplementary activities and periodic testing. For programs in which classes meet three times a week, it may be advisable to use the book over a period of three semesters and to teach the last 4–6 chapters in second-year French.

Using *Deux mondes* in Quarter and Semester Systems

The *Deux mondes* package may be used in different academic environments and with different academic calendars. However, the amount of material presented should be adjusted. We provide schedules for two distinct course paces: standard and intensive. The intensive pace will be followed by French programs at large universities where many French students are false beginners or have had previous experience with another foreign language and, consequently, may acquire material more rapidly. The standard pace may be more appropriate if you have large numbers of true beginners and/or you plan to do many supplementary activities, either your own or those from the Instructor's Resource Kit.

Standard Pace	Intensive Pace
1. Semester system (150 hours of instruction, 5 hours per week, 30 weeks) Semester 1: **Première-Deuxième étapes, Chapitres 1–6** Semester 2: **Chapitres 7–14**	1. Semester system (150 hours of instruction, 5 hours per week, 30 weeks) Semester 1: **Première-Deuxième étapes, Chapitres 1–6** Semester 2: **Chapitres 7–14**
2. Quarter (trimester) system (150 hours of instruction, 5 hours per week, 30 weeks) Quarter 1: **Première-Deuxième étapes, Chapitres 1–4** Quarter 2: **Chapitres 5–9** Quarter 3: **Chapitres 10–14**	2. Quarter (trimester) system (150 hours of instruction, 5 hours per week, 30 weeks) Quarter 1: **Première-Deuxième étapes, Chapitres 1–4** Quarter 2: **Chapitres 5–9** Quarter 3: **Chapitres 10–14**
3. Semester system (120 hours of classroom contact, 4 hours per week, 30 weeks) Semester 1: **Première-Deuxième étapes, Chapitres 1–4** Semester 2: **Chapitres 5–11** **Chapitres 12–14** reserved for second year	3. Semester system (120 hours of classroom contact, 4 hours per week, 30 weeks) Semester 1: **Première-Deuxième étapes, Chapitres 1–6** Semester 2: **Chapitres 7–12** **Chapitres 13–14** reserved for second year
4. Quarter (trimester) system (120 hours of classroom contact, 4 hours per week, 30 weeks) Quarter 1: **Première-Deuxième étapes, Chapitres 1–3** Quarter 2: **Chapitres 4–7** Quarter 3: **Chapitres 8–12** **Chapitres 13–14** reserved for second year	4. Quarter (trimester) system (120 hours of classroom contact, 4 hours per week, 30 weeks) Quarter 1: **Première-Deuxième étapes, Chapitres 1–3** Quarter 2: **Chapitres 4–7** Quarter 3: **Chapitres 8–11** **Chapitres 12–14** reserved for second year
5. Semester system (90 hours of instruction, 3 hours per week, 30 weeks) Semester 1: **Première-Deuxième étapes, Chapitres 1–4** Semester 2: **Chapitres 5–9** **Chapitres 10–14** reserved for second year	5. Semester system (90 hours of instruction, 3 hours per week, 30 weeks) Semester 1: **Première-Deuxième étapes, Chapitres 1–5** Semester 2: **Chapitres 6–10** **Chapitres 11–14** reserved for second year
6. Quarter system (90 hours of instruction, 3 hours per week, 30 weeks) Quarter 1: **Première-Deuxième étapes, Chapitres 1–2** Quarter 2: **Chapitres 3–5** Quarter 3: **Chapitres 6–9** **Chapitres 10–14** reserved for second year	6. Quarter system (90 hours of instruction, 3 hours per week, 30 weeks) Quarter 1: **Première-Deuxième étapes, Chapitres 1–3** Quarter 2: **Chapitres 4–6** Quarter 3: **Chapitres 7–10** **Chapitres 11–14** reserved for second year

Goals of the Natural Approach

The context of foreign language instruction in the United States is quite different from that of most of the rest of the world. Beginning language students in the United States generally must choose from among Spanish, French, German, Japanese, Chinese, Italian, and Russian. Their decision is usually based on interest in the language or the culture of the people who speak that language. In some cases, students make their choice of language because it is widely spoken in the area where they live or where they will travel. By and large, however, it is impossible for students in the United States to determine what language will be of most use to them in the future. This is not true for language students in most other countries. English is the preferred language of study elsewhere because of its usefulness in work, study, and travel.

Taking these facts into consideration, we believe that students should learn how to acquire a language, since it is likely that they will want or need to repeat the process with a different language later in their lives. We want them to understand the acquisition process itself and, most of all, to enjoy it. At the end of a Natural Approach course, we want students to say, "Learning French was great! I really think I could learn another language if I needed to."

The rationale behind the NA and the specific techniques that we will recommend in this *Instructor's Manual* is based on our own particular view of the processes involved in classroom acquisition of a second language. Our views have been shaped by research in linguistics, psychology, psycholinguistics, and other disciplines and particularly by the work in first- and second-language acquisition. They are tempered by our years of experience in studying, learning, and teaching languages.

Language Proficiency

Foreign language instructors generally agree that beginning students should gain some functional ability to converse with native speakers. Since is difficult to determine what levels of proficiency are indicated and what constitutes those levels, however, it is useful to consider what it means to have acquired a second language when establishing proficiency goals for a class.

First-language acquisition for most people results in the ability to comprehend and speak their native language. Native speakers can understand input from a wide variety of sources and under a multitude of conditions, but they cannot understand everything. For instance, sometimes they are thrown off by a different accent, unfamiliar words, or unexpected topics. Often, they can understand more language than they are able to produce, since few native speakers can use all the vocabulary and structures that context permits them to understand. However, they can tell stories, argue, explain—in short, accomplish the many functions and tasks required for their personal needs.

Clearly, we cannot base our expectations for second-language learning on the level of proficiency of a native speaker. Very few people who begin their study of a second language after the age of sixteen ever reach that level. We can, however, expect students to be able to communicate their ideas and needs to a native speaker and to understand the native speaker's responses without experiencing undue stress caused by lack of language abilities. We can expect students' accents to be comprehensible and free of distortions that severely hamper a native speaker from understanding what they are saying. We can expect that their range of vocabulary will be wide enough so that they will not feel restricted in their conversational topics. Although we cannot expect their grammar to be perfect, it should be functional at the level of their communicative needs.

The primary goal of a second-language acquisition course using *Deux mondes* is basic functional proficiency in speaking and understanding spoken and written French in authentic, everyday communicative contexts. This includes the ability to deal effectively with nonlinguistic aspects of communication and, especially, to conform to essential cultural patterns.

In addition, we believe that proficiency includes the ability to continue to grow linguistically. Many students do not expect to pursue their formal study of French after completing their required courses. However, through travel, population shifts, the media, and even multilingual materials produced for users of commercial products, students will continue to encounter French and to use it. In our classes, we must lay a good foundation for continued acquisition.

Scope and Sequence

Première étape   Premières rencontres

La communication en classe	A.1 Giving instructions: Commands with **vous**
Qui est-ce? Les camarades de classe	A.2 Identifying people: **C'est... , je m'appelle**
Comment sont-ils? La description des personnes	A.3 Gender and articles
Les vêtements et les couleurs	A.4 Describing people: **Être**, subject pronouns, and **ne... pas**
Les nombres (0–34)	A.5 Plural nouns and articles
Rencontres	A.6 Addressing others: **Tu** and **vous**

Deuxième étape   Le monde étudiant

Qu'est-ce qu'il y a dans la salle de classe?	B.1 Expressing existence: **Il y a**
La date et l'alphabet	B.2 Asking questions
Les nombres de 40 à 100 et l'heure	B.3 Spelling in French: The French alphabet
Les cours	B.4 Telling time: **Quelle heure est-il?**
La description des autres	B.5 Expressing possession: The verb **avoir**
	B.6 Describing with adjectives: More on gender
	B.7 Irregular plurals

Chapitre 1   Ma famille et moi

La famille	1.1 Expressing relationships: Possessive adjectives
Goûts personnels	1.2 Expressing likes and dislikes: **Aimer** + infinitives
Origines et renseignements personnels	1.3 Talking about dates and personal data: Numbers beyond 100
La vie de famille	1.4 Stating origin: The verb **venir**
	1.5 Talking about actions: Present of **-er** verbs
	1.6 Expressing relationships and possession: Contractions of **de**

Chapitre 2   Le vie quotidienne et les loisirs

Le temps, les saisons et les loisirs	2.1 Talking about activities and weather: The verb **faire**
Les activités quotidiennes	2.2 Talking about everyday activities: Reflexive verbs
Les habitudes et les projets	2.3 Going places and future actions: The verb **aller**, contractions of **à**
Aptitudes et rêves	2.4 Making general statements: The subject pronoun **on**
	2.5 Abilities and desires; The verbs **pouvoir, vouloir,** and **savoir**

Chapitre 3   En ville

S'orienter en ville	3.1 Saying where things are: Prepositions of location
La ville et les transports	3.2 Asking questions: Interrogative words
Les achats	3.3. Verbs like **prendre**
Les distractions	3.4 Expressing necessity: **Il faut** and the verb **devoir**
	3.5 Pointing things out: Demonstrative adjectives
	3.6 Expressing quantities: Partitive articles
	3.7 The verbs **sortir** and **dormir**
	3.8 The verb **courir**

Chapitre 10   Les voyages

Voyages à l'étranger	10.1 Expressing obligation: **Il faut que** + subjunctive
En voiture!	10.2 More about the subjunctive: Irregular-stem verbs
Comment se débrouiller	10.3 Verbs for traveling: The verbs **conduire** and **suivre**
Les achats, les produits et les matières	10.4 Double object pronouns
	10.5 The superlative: Expressing extremes
	10.6 Making distinctions: **Lequel** and **celui**

Chapitre 11   Les moyens de communication

L'univers de l'électronique	11.1 Saying what you would do: The conditional
On se distrait, on s'informe	11.2 The relative pronoun **dont**
Les pièges de l'inforoute	11.3 More on relative pronouns: **Ce qui, ce que, ce dont**
	11.4 Commands with pronouns: Giving orders
	11.5 Talking about hypothetical situations: More on the **imparfait**

Chapitre 12   La santé et les urgences

La santé	12.1 Saying what you want others to do: More on the subjunctive
Les maladies et les traitements	12.2 Changes of state: **Passé composé** vs. imperfect
Les accidents et les urgences	12.3 The present participle
	12.4 Expressing events in the recent past: **Venir de** + infinitive
	12.5 Narrating in the past tense: **Passé composé** vs. imperfect

Chapitre 13   La famille et les valeurs en société

L'amour, l'amitié et la famille	13.1 Reciprocal actions: More on reflexive pronouns
La vie de famille	13.2 Describing actions: Adverbs
Valeurs et décisions	13.3 Expressing feelings: More on the subjunctive
	13.4 A past in the past: The **plus-que-parfait**
	13.5 More on expressing possession: Possessive pronouns

Chapitre 14   Les enjeux du présent et de l'avenir

L'intégration sociale	14.1 *Should have:* The past conditional of **devoir**
L'héritage du passé	14.2 Saying what you would have done: The past conditional
Les enjeux du XXIᵉ siècle	14.3 More on the subjunctive: Conjugations
	14.4 More on the subjunctive: Expressing doubt and uncertainty

Chapter 3
The Natural Approach and *Deux mondes*

The Natural Approach is a philosophy and an approach to the teaching of second languages that is widely used in North America to teach foreign languages such as Spanish, French, and German. It is also used to teach English as a second language (ESL) to non-native speakers of English, both in North America and abroad. Although the NA had its origins in classroom practice, Professor Stephen D. Krashen's theoretical model of second-language acquisition and his extensive experimental research have substantiated much of what began as teacher intuitions. Since *Deux mondes* is written from a Natural Approach perspective, it is helpful if those who use it have some understanding of the theories and practices that have informed its development. For that purpose, we include the following articles on the Krashen theory of acquisition and the Natural Approach principles as they relate to it.

Second-Language Acquisition Theory: The Krashen Hypotheses

The second-language acquisition theory developed by Professor Stephen D. Krashen of the University of Southern California evolved from a considerable amount of experimental research, classroom-oriented as well as theoretical. The theory consists of five interrelated hypotheses. We will describe our own version of each briefly, then draw conclusions for classroom practices based on them.[1] Keep in mind throughout the discussion that these hypotheses do not represent some ultimate truth about second-language acquisition but rather our best guesses about how the process takes place, based on both formal and informal research evidence.

1. The Acquisition-Learning Hypothesis

The acquisition-learning hypothesis claims that we have two independent ways of developing language ability:

- Language acquisition is a subconscious process; while it is happening, we are not aware that it is happening. In addition, once we have acquired something, we are not usually aware that we possess any new knowledge; the knowledge is stored subconsciously in our brains. The research strongly supports the view that both children and adults can subconsciously acquire language.
- Language learning is what we did in school. It is a conscious process. When we are learning, we know we are learning, and learned knowledge is represented consciously in the brain. When we talk about "rules" and "grammar," we are usually talking about learning.

The process of error correction does not affect acquisition. However, it can affect language learning. When we make a mistake and someone corrects us, we can change our conscious version of the rule we were using.

Acquisition appears to be a much more powerful process for developing language ability than is language learning, and our main, although not exclusive, focus in the Natural Approach will be on language acquisition.

Classroom Applications

The sort of knowledge obtained through the study of grammar and grammatical exercises (learning) is different from the knowledge obtained through communicative experiences (acquisition). For this reason, the central focus of *Deux mondes* is on the oral communication activities and readings of each chapter. But the study of grammar is also important for many students. Knowing how French words and sentences

---

[1]For more detailed information, consult S. D. Krashen and T. D. Terrell, *The Natural Approach: Language Acquisition in the Classroom*, Alemany / Janus Press (2051 Industrial Parkway West, Dept. F, Hayward, California 95545).

are put together may facilitate the processing of input, and that is why we include grammar explanations and verification exercises as an adjunct to the oral communication activities and readings.

2. The Input Hypothesis

The Input Hypothesis attempts to explain how language acquisition occurs. The evidence strongly supports a simple hypothesis: We acquire language when we understand messages or obtain input that is comprehensible.

Comprehensible input can be aural or written. In fact, there is growing evidence that reading is a very good source of comprehensible input. According to the Input Hypothesis, production (spontaneous talking and writing) is a result of language acquisition, not a cause.

The evidence for the Input Hypothesis comes from both second-language acquisition research and from research in literacy. Evidence from second-language classroom studies has shown that language classes that contain more comprehensible input produce consistently better results than traditional classes. Results for literacy development are similar; listening to stories and reading also improve language performance.

Applications

What students will produce depends on what they are able to understand from input. During oral acquisition activities and readings in *Deux mondes,* students' attention should be on the exchange of ideas and information. Acquisition depends on comprehensible input: First on the comprehension of new words and grammatical structures used in communicative contexts, and then on the production of those words and structures during meaningful interactions. This means that teacher-talk input is indispensable and, furthermore, that no amount of explanation and practice can substitute for real communicative experiences.

3. The Monitor Hypothesis

The Monitor Hypothesis attempts to explain how acquisition and learning are used. Language is normally produced using our acquired linguistic competence. Conscious learning has one main function: as a "monitor," or editor. After we produce some language using the acquired system, we sometimes inspect it and use our learned system to correct errors. This can happen internally before we actually speak or write, or as self-correction after we produce the sentence.

To use the conscious monitor, three conditions must be met: (1) The speaker (writer) must know the rule; (2) he or she must have enough time to apply the rule; and (3) he or she must be thinking about correctness, or be "focused on form." Keep in mind that these conditions are hard to meet.

- *Knowing the rule.* Language texts do not contain all the rules for a given language; teachers do not always teach all the rules in the text, and even the best students do not learn all the rules or remember all the rules they have learned.
- *Having enough time.* In real conversations people rarely have enough time to think about rules unless the topic is familiar and the rules are well known and simple.
- *Focusing on form.* While focusing on form may improve accuracy a little, it can also disrupt communication. Thinking about rules while the other person is talking makes it difficult to pay attention to meaning.

Applications

If language is normally produced using our acquired linguistic competence, it follows that acquisition activities are of first importance to beginners. Grammar rules will become useful only after learners have acquired enough language to need them. For this reason, acquisition-oriented activities and readings play a central role in *Deux mondes.* Grammar exercises that ask students to pay close attention to correct application of grammar rules are mainly to be done as written homework. This system allows adequate time for reflection on and use of those rules. We suggest that students be evaluated primarily on their comprehension and communicative ability, rather than on the grammatical correctness of their speech. The latter will improve as their acquired linguistic competence increases, but beginners should not be held responsible for errors in new or partially acquired material. The Monitor Hypothesis reminds us that the ability to produce forms on a written exam, or even in a free writing activity, should never be equated with the ability to use those forms in natural, spontaneous speech.

4. The Natural Order Hypothesis

The Natural Order Hypothesis claims that we acquire the parts of language in a predictable order. Some grammatical forms are acquired early, and others come later. The order of acquisition for first and second languages is similar but not identical. In English, for example, the progressive form -*ing* is acquired well before the third-person singular -*s*. In English as a first language, there might be six months to a year between the emergence of -*ing* and -*s*. In English as a second language, -*s* may lag many years. A number of people speak English very well but have not yet acquired the third-person singular -*s*.

Research has revealed two interesting points about the natural order.

- The natural order appears to be immune to deliberate teaching; we cannot change the natural order by explanations, drills, and exercises. You can drill a given structure over and over, but it will not be acquired (that is to say, occur spontaneously in speech) until its time has come.
- The order of acquisition has nothing to do with ordinary notions of "simplicity" or "complexity." Some structures that appear to be simple are acquired late, and some that appear to be complex are acquired early.

Unfortunately, research has not yet told us exactly what is the overall natural order for the acquisition of all rules of grammar of any language. Moreover, the order of acquisition and the order of learning may be different. For example, all students of languages such as French, Spanish, and German study the rule of gender agreement for nouns and their modifiers quite early in their course of study. However, the ability to produce correct forms without conscious editing takes much longer—for most adults, several years. Most students are only beginning to acquire the ability to produce gender agreement automatically in their speech by the end of their first year of study, although they learn the rule and the concept quite early in the course. Thus, it appears that although some grammar rules are learned early, and relatively quickly, the ability to use those forms occurs only after long periods of communicative contact.

Applications

The basic syllabus for *Deux mondes* is topical and thematic. We choose the situations students are most likely to encounter and the topics they most likely want to address. Given a particular situation and topic, we try to specify linguistic tools necessary for communication; that is, we choose the important vocabulary, grammatical forms, and structures that students will need to understand others and express themselves on a particular topic in a given situation. We use a grammatical syllabus as the basis for the **Grammaire et exercices** section. However, we do not expect acquisition and the study of grammar to coincide perfectly. For example, students may study grammar and do exercises with the past tense forms in a particular chapter of the **Grammaire,** but the **Activités** that encourage the acquisition of past tense must be spread over a longer period of time. In many cases acquisition seems to occur without any grammar study at all. This appears to be especially true of syntax. Given good input and enough communicative experience, most students acquire the ability to produce correct word order without any explicit study of the rules or exercises that practice them.

5. The Affective Filter Hypothesis

The Affective Filter Hypothesis claims that attitudes and feelings do not have a direct impact on language learning but can hinder language acquisition. Acquisition takes place best in affectively positive situations where students attend to the input. If a student is anxious, uninterested, does not perceive the culture in a positive way, or is experiencing other reasons for inattention, the Affective Filter will impede or prevent that individual from acquiring language through input.

Applications

Students need to be interested in the activities in which they participate and feel comfortable with their classmates. Classroom interactions should be carried out in a supportive, rather than a competitive, environment. Opportunities for group work in *Deux mondes* help create a sense of classroom community that is very conducive to communication. *Deux mondes* creates a positive classroom atmosphere by encouraging student interest and involvement in activities that relate directly to their lives and the world around them. We encourage the instructor to help students understand and appreciate Francophone cultures through diverse activities in the book, the Instructor's Edition margin notes, and other supplementary materials available with the program.

Natural Approach Principles in *Deux Mondes*

Here are the guiding principles of the Natural Approach that we have incorporated into *Deux mondes.* They derive both from a set of beliefs about how one acquires another language and an approach to teaching that attempts to accommodate those views.

Comprehensible Input Is Essential in the Classroom

The primary goal of the classroom is to provide comprehensible input, the essential component necessary for language acquisition. In *Deux mondes,* the Pre-Text Oral Activities in the **Mise en train** section, the supplemental activities from the Instructor's Edition marginal notes, and the **Activités, Lectures,** and other White Page features in the student text are intended to provide students with interesting and relevant comprehensible input. This input occurs in the classroom through the use of these and other materials that center on topics of interest to the students. The techniques are varied and include TPR, input association activities, and use of visuals, polls, games, and many types of partner and small group activities.

Comprehension Precedes Production

According to the Input Hypothesis, the ability to produce language spontaneously is the result of acquisition. It follows, then, that the students' ability to use new vocabulary and grammar is directly related to the opportunities they have had to listen to and read that vocabulary and grammar in meaningful and relevant contexts. Opportunities to express their own meaning should follow comprehension. We have included introductory comprehension activities for all major semantic word groups, grammatical forms, and structures introduced in *Deux mondes.* These can help students begin the acquisition process before they use them in activities requiring the use of those words, forms, and structures. See in particular the **Mise en train** activities in the Instructor's Edition notes that end each chapter, as well as the notes that accompany the illustrated displays that begin each section of the **Activités.** We believe that this material greatly facilitates the task of the instructor and makes it easier to ensure that new language is introduced for comprehension before students are expected to use it.

Speech Emerges in Stages

Speech is allowed to emerge in the Natural Approach. There is no pressure on students to use language in production beyond their capacity. They are encouraged to speak whenever they wish, however, and the marginal notes in the Instructor's Edition suggest techniques for helping them when they begin to do so. According to our experience, students feel more at ease and are more receptive to aural input when they are not required to speak French immediately. Their comprehension of spoken French develops faster, they speak more fluently, and they pronounce the language better when they do begin to speak.

The Natural Approach expects that beginners will pass naturally through three developmental stages, not simply at the beginning of the course but throughout the course as new material is presented, and provides for the following stages in the language acquisition process:

- Stage 1: Comprehension
- Stage 2: Early Speech
- Stage 3: Speech Emergence

In the Comprehension phase (Stage 1), students need not respond in the target language. During this pre-speech phase, instructors use techniques that ask students to demonstrate their comprehension with **oui** or **non,** a classmate's name, or a gesture. Most of the **Activités** in the **Première étape** are Stage 1 activities.

As they reach Stage 2 (Early Speech), students begin to respond spontaneously with simple language (usually with single words or short phrases). New topics and structures in the **Deuxième étape** are introduced through Stage 1 activities, but the **Mise en train** and **Activités** for the **Deuxième étape** also include Stage 2 activities. These range from asking students to make a simple choice (**Est-ce une robe ou une jupe?**) to printed activities that give strong linguistic support while permitting students to talk about interesting topics at a level beyond their capacity for spontaneous speech at that point. These printed activities are an excellent source of both aural and reading input.

In Stage 3 (Speech Emergence), students can actually converse together, ask questions, request clarification, and explain. To do so, they spontaneously draw on the range of language that they have acquired from earlier oral and written input during Stage 1 and Stage 2 activities. Their French will not necessarily be grammatically correct, but it will be functional. To foster and develop this growing ability, **Chapitre 1** begins to include activities that motivate students to talk about their own lives and interests, encouraging them to express themselves with more complexity and at greater length.

From **Chapitre 1** and in each subsequent chapter of the book, the needs of all three stages are accommodated. When new topical vocabulary occurs in a chapter (Stage 1), there are pre-text input activities from **Mise en train** and other sources. As acquisition of that material begins and students are starting to use the new material spontaneously (Stage 2), there are opinion surveys, options, and other Early Speech input activities that allow students to converse truthfully without having to produce much language. The content and form of Stage 3 activities, placed near the end of topical sections, inspire spontaneous exchanges of greater length and complexity. These activities include interviews, simple logic problems, role-plays, explanation of choices, and group projects.

Speech Emergence Is Characterized by Grammatical Errors

When students start putting words together into sentences, they make many errors. These errors will gradually disappear as acquisition progresses. Because conscious learning only supplements language acquisition, direct error correction appears to play a limited role. Therefore, we do not expect students to wait until they have French completely under control before they are allowed to use it. Consider what must happen for error correction to work: The learner must notice the correction, understand the correction, and apply the conscious rule to arrive at a better version of what he or she is trying to say. This process is difficult to effect when one is attempting to communicate meaning. In fact, it often causes communication to break down because the speaker is distracted from the expression of an idea and is forced instead to think about a grammatical rule.

Research shows that early speech errors that occur during communication activities do not necessarily become permanent, nor do they affect the students' future language development. In fact, there is ample evidence that errors are a natural part of the language acquisition process. Some forms and structures require a large number of communicative experiences before acquisition is complete, and no amount of direct correction of speech can hasten the process. Most students like to speak French and are eager to communicate with others, if they feel that they are not being scrutinized for linguistic accuracy while they are talking. They need to realize that one of the best ways to expedite the acquisition process is to think and communicate ideas in French. In communication activities, it is quite acceptable, perhaps even necessary, to allow students to make errors.

Although we do not expect students to speak French without errors, we do expect steady improvement in their speech throughout the course. This improvement occurs as they are exposed to more input, develop a better understanding of how the language works, and do home study. During communication activities, we recommend that the instructor respond naturally to what students say, not to how it is said. For occasions when a correction seems necessary, we suggest the use of indirect correction (expansion). This way, the instructor replies to the student's idea while including the correct form(s) in that reply. The answer does not interrupt the flow of ideas, and it provides good input, particularly for those students who are at a point in the acquisition process where such input is meaningful. Here is an example: STUDENT: **J'avez trois frères.** INSTRUCTOR: **Ah bon, vous avez trois frères! Moi, je n'ai pas de frères, mais j'ai une sœur.**

Some teachers are concerned that uncorrected errors will become permanent. We believe that there is little danger of "fossilization" occurring in Natural Approach classrooms, where the goal is to expose students to intensive, good quality aural and written input of all types on a regular basis.

Group Work Encourages Speech

As soon as students begin to say words spontaneously in French, let them work in pairs and small groups. We suggest doing some group work very early on, starting at the end of the **Première étape** and using it extensively thereafter. Group work allows many more students to speak the target language during the class period. Most students enjoy interacting with others on a personal basis and feel freer to express themselves in groups. Group work also gives the instructor the opportunity to move from group to group, making sure that the activity is going well, answering questions, and helping individuals with vocabulary as needed. The time students spend working in small groups should increase throughout the course, so that toward the end of the course, they themselves become the source of much of the communicative interaction.

Classroom Environment Affects Acquisition

According to Krashen's Affective Filter Hypothesis, a low-anxiety environment is essential for acquisition. If students are nervous or inattentive for other reasons, acquisition cannot take place. In a good acquisition environment, students realize from the outset that they can understand the French spoken in class. They are at ease because they know they can concentrate on expressing their ideas without fear of interruptive language correction. The goal during communicative activities is for students to express themselves as best they can and to develop confidence that they can communicate in French. The more they feel successful in speaking, the more they enjoy their learning and develop a positive attitude toward their experience with the language. Later, we suggest a wide variety of techniques for creating a positive and productive classroom environment.

Grammar Study Plays a Supplemental Role

Knowledge of grammar can be useful for self-monitoring in both speaking and writing. Grammar study can help to make input more comprehensible to students and can lead to a greater appreciation of the structure of a language. In addition, many students derive satisfaction from learning about what they are acquiring, particularly as their body of acquired material increases.

Keep in mind, however, that "learned" knowledge does not necessarily turn into "acquired" knowledge; acquisition occurs through comprehensible input. The oral activities and readings in *Deux mondes* should be done in a purely communicative way, with both teacher and student focusing entirely on meaning. In class, grammar explanations should be brief and occur only when they relate to an immediate communicative need that has arisen.

The **Grammaire** is intended primarily for home study. It is written in simple, direct language that is easy for students to understand, and answers are provided against which they can check their work at home. Having students assume primary responsibility for learning the rules at home means that class time can be devoted to developing the communications skills. In class, many instructors prefer to use French as part of teaching grammar in context.

The Goal of the Natural Approach Is Proficiency in Communication Abilities

Proficiency, or communicative competence, is the ability to convey information and feelings in a particular situation for a given purpose. In Natural Approach classes we determine, for example, if the student is able to ask a native speaker how to get from one location to another and understand directions given by the native speaker. Accuracy plays a part in proficiency but is in no sense the only goal of the course or even a prerequisite for communicative proficiency.

Any foreign language course may have additional goals: reading and writing, for example. For this reason, we include extensive marginal notes on the use of the various reading materials in *Deux mondes* and on developing writing ability, in addition to suggestions in this Instructor's Manual. All the materials include more oral and written activities than needed for a single, year-long college-level course. How much of these materials the instructor chooses to use depends on the goals for the particular course. The most important point, however, is that proficiency develops from comprehension and communication experiences, not from covering a certain amount of material in this or any other book.

Chapter 4
Teaching with the Natural Approach

The Natural Approach offers a distinctive way of teaching that is intended to help students acquire language rather than to simply study about it. It is based on the assumption that meaningful, comprehensible input is the essential ingredient that sets in motion and fuels the acquisition process. For this reason, the content of the traditional syllabus is approached from a perspective that puts natural listening experiences and comprehension in a position of primordial importance. The other "skills" are by no means neglected. Instead, they are treated in conjunction with further opportunities for generating comprehensible input and are viewed as an important part of developing full linguistic proficiency.

In the following articles, we describe the Natural Approach to standard classroom teaching concerns, including teaching techniques for each area of development that we have used successfully with our students over the years. We believe that it is helpful to instructors who are currently teaching with *Deux mondes* and to those who are about to begin using the book to understand what lies behind the teaching suggestions in the marginal notes and elsewhere in the Instructor's Edition. We hope that the following discussions provide this background information.

Teaching Comprehension and Speaking

Class activities should provide both comprehensible input and interactional activities that allow students to progress through the natural stages of acquisition: comprehension, early speech, and speech emergence. The purpose of this section is to clarify the relationships shared by the acquisition process, comprehension and speaking, while placing emphasis on the use of particular teaching techniques that aid in the development of communicative proficiency.

Comprehension

The student who begins a Natural Approach course concentrates first on the development of listening ability. It is important, then, to understand how beginning students interpret the utterances they hear in their instructor's speech. The immediate goal in the first few classes is to develop the students' ability to use comprehension strategies. Beginning students are able to comprehend an utterance if they recognize the meaning of key words in the utterance and are able to use context to derive the meaning of the utterance itself: Comprehension = key words + context.

Looking at comprehension in this way implies that students need several kinds of experiences in the classroom. First, input must consist of utterances in a meaningful and interesting context. Second, students must understand the key words in each utterance. Finally, the instructor must use body language, gestures, intonation, and other aspects of paralanguage, as well as visuals, objects, and anything else available to make the meaning of the utterance clear.

Students pay attention to words emphasized by the instructor. Several techniques can draw attention to the most important parts of an utterance.

- Say a key word louder than the words that surround it: **La femme sur cette photo porte une jupe rouge.** Emphasize the word **jupe**, pronouncing it louder, perhaps drawing it out longer while pointing to a skirt or to a picture of a skirt.
- Pause slightly before saying the key word, pointing to a picture: **Regardez l'homme sur cette photo. Qu'est-qu'il porte? Il porte un... slip de bain.**
- Use repetition and reentry of the key word to draw students' attention to the word. Point to what someone is wearing: **Susan porte un chemisier blanc. Son chemisier est blanc. C'est un chemisier blanc. Il n'est pas bleu. Il n'est pas rouge. Susan porte un chemisier blanc.**

The task of the instructor is to use the key word meaningfully, so that through input, students come to associate the meaning with the key word. The task of the students is to attend to the input in such a way that the meaning is linked to its form in French. How does the linking of form and meaning take place? What does not seem very helpful is memorization of vocabulary and grammar presented without context.

The key element in acquisition appears to be communicative experiences. We link words to meaning by hearing or reading them when they are used in context. Context can include but is not restricted to:

- the use of visuals (such as pictures, drawings, and posters);
- the use of concrete objects or items (a ticket, a pair of gloves);
- the use of movements (acting out words, as in TPR activities).

In addition, affective factors such as the following can help students acquire new words:

- association of words with particular classmates (the fact that a particular classmate has long blond hair, has blue eyes, and wears glasses helps to associate meaning with the words for *blond, hair,* and *glasses*);
- association of new words with the interests of classmates (for example, acquisition of the word **cuisiner** is easier if someone in the class particularly likes cooking);
- something unusual in a picture or other visual;
- use of humor to draw attention to certain words.

Linguistic factors can also help. Words can be more salient:

- when spoken louder or by the speaker pausing slightly before saying the word;
- when they have particular sounds, length, or rhythm;
- when they have similarities with other languages a student knows (cognates, borrowings, or invented similarities).

Cultural factors are also important, since words may be acquired during discussions or experiences involving the use of slides, movies, videotapes, games, parties, skits, readings, and so on.

Instructors should not expect a word to be completely acquired after one use or even after several uses. Research suggests that acquisition of vocabulary does not occur all at once but in small increments. It typically takes many meaningful occurrences of a word for complete acquisition to take place. The responsibility of the Natural Approach instructor is to create vivid experiences that will help students form strong associations.

Teacher-Talk

Since second-language acquisition theory posits that input plays a major role in acquisition, an extremely important part of Natural Approach instruction is the input the instructor supplies in the form of "teacher-talk." This input has certain characteristics.

1. It focuses on meaning. Everything in the input is aimed at getting across information about some topic or situation being addressed.
2. It is comprehensible. Students are able to follow the main ideas of the input.
3. It is slightly above the students' current level of competence. This means that students understand enough of the key words and structures to be able to comprehend new vocabulary and structures by using what they do understand and the context of the input (that is, knowing about the topic under discussion, looking at visual aids, attending to gestures, and so on). Not every utterance coming from the instructor must be at the students' current level of competence. If teachers simply try to make input comprehensible and interesting, a great deal of what they say will be at the appropriate level.
4. It is interesting and relates to students' experiences. The instructor must use knowledge about the students to personalize the discussion arising from the stimuli of the oral activities and then orient it toward topics of personal interest.
5. It allows for spontaneous and innovative student responses without being threatening. The attitude of the instructor during the give-and-take of the input must be one of attention to meaning. Any attempt students make to communicate is accepted in a positive fashion.

6. It is simplified input. All language acquirers, including children acquiring a first language, must have access to simplified input. In this context, simplified means many things. The rate of input is somewhat slower than regular adult-to-adult, native speaker input. It is more clearly enunciated. The focus is usually maintained on a single topic longer than normal, and the information may be given in several forms and repeated several times. The range of vocabulary and structures used in the input is limited without being artificial. (Note that many of these accommodations will happen naturally as you communicate with your students.)
7. It is varied and natural. Since the focus is always on the message, the instructor reacts naturally to students' responses, thereby creating new situations and additional information in the input. In this way, the instructor re-enters frequently used vocabulary and structures many, many times without having to plan a specific review.

Speaking

Although the emphasis in NA is on acquisition through comprehensible input, most students want to practice speaking the language they are learning. In addition to the affective and motivational value of speaking, when students begin to respond in the target language, class interactions and activities become much more interesting, and there is a greater potential for variety than when students simply listen to and indicate comprehension of input. It is also possible that the use of words and forms to express an idea in speech (output) will strengthen the connections between meaning and form established through the input. For all these reasons, in the Natural Approach one must allow ample opportunities for students to express themselves in the target language.

As we have mentioned, in the Natural Approach, proficiency in speaking emerges in stages. Stage 1 is the comprehension stage in which students are obliged only to indicate that they have understood. In Stage 2, students are encouraged to respond with single words or short phrases. The instructor should formulate questions so that students are asked to produce only the words that they have had a chance to acquire. The idea is to avoid "translation searches" in which the students go through a thought process like "dog—how do you say dog in French?" for each word and grammatical form they wish to produce. For this reason, we begin speech production in Stage 2 with "either/or" questions: **Est-ce que la femme sur cette photo porte une jupe rouge ou bleue? Est-ce que Tom a une barbe ou une moustache?** Even simple interrogatives such as **Qu'est-ce que c'est?** or **Où sont les fleurs?** are attempted only when we are relatively sure that students will be able to produce the correct word without conscious translation from English. The following is a sequence of question types, increasingly complex, that provides opportunities for encouraging speaking in Stage 2.

1. Yes/no questions
2. Either/or questions
3. Simple interrogatives: **Qu'est-ce que? Où? Quand? Qui?**
4. Open sentences: **Ce monsieur porte un...**
5. Lists of words: **Que voyez-vous sur cette photo?**

The transition from the production of single words to longer phrases and more complete sentences in Stage 3 is facilitated by dialogues and interviews. In any model dialogues we use key words in short, complete sentences. Open dialogues are particularly effective in the early stages because they provide the grammatical context, and students have only to provide words they have already acquired.

The transition from controlled contexts to more open activities is somewhat difficult because it is impossible to know what students will want to say. Invariably, in some situations, students will be unable to retrieve a word in French, either because it has not been encountered enough or because they have not yet heard the word in your input. In either case, it is natural that they give the English word first and ask **Comment dit-on ___ en français?** When used occasionally, such spot translations are not damaging per se, but we want to avoid putting students into situations in which an entire utterance is new and must be translated word by word. The instructor must keep the focus on communication and make clear that the class can be and is being conducted in French.

We recommend that you do not push students into Stage 3 too quickly; allow them to answer with short replies until they are ready to attempt more complex responses. When students are pushed to respond using words and grammar they have not yet acquired, they invariably fall back on their native language to formulate a reply and then translate word for word. This probably does no great damage to the acquisition process should it occur occasionally, but it is unnecessary and requires a great deal of mental energy and does nothing to foster acquisition.

In Stage 3, when students do begin to produce French, they will make a number of errors: Errors of pronunciation, word usage, grammar, and, as the discourse becomes more complex, syntax. As we noted earlier, errors are a normal part of the acquisition process, and we do not recommend direct correction of speech errors during class interactions. Error correction is interruptive to the exchange of ideas and creates affective barriers to acquisition even when it is done in a positive manner. However, because learners will not acquire what they do not hear in the input, you must use student responses as a basis for a more complete and correct version of what they wish to express. We call this "expansion of student responses" and will discuss it in more detail later.

Encourage students to express themselves using what they have acquired, even when this means going slightly beyond their present level of proficiency. They will soon discover that the language they know can be used to explain and to express ideas that may seem relatively complex. Bear in mind, however, that danger exists in pushing students to express ideas that they have neither the vocabulary nor the structure to express. For example, asking a student in the early speech stage (Stage 2) a **pourquoi?** question will almost always lead to difficulties. When students are pushed to respond using words they have not begun to acquire, they will fall back on their native language to formulate the reply. In class, provide students with daily proof that they can understand French and, in turn, make themselves understood.

Teaching Reading and Writing

In general, people read for information and for pleasure, but in the context of language teaching, there are additional reasons to learn to read. Written texts can be good sources of comprehensible input that contribute directly to the acquisition process, and they are an important source of cultural information that can stimulate exciting class discussions. Too often in a foreign language course, students have been taught only to read intensively, to focus on word-by-word accuracy rather than learning the techniques that can enable them to be flexible in their approach to the reading. This results in their learning to translate without gaining the useful skills that go with really learning to read.

In our experience, those who are learning to read in French must be taught right from the start how to focus on the meaning, to get absorbed in "the story." When a student applies techniques useful for reading in French and the material is truly interesting to that individual, strong personal involvement with a text is more likely to occur. For pleasure reading in French, students enjoy texts that have a plot; newspaper articles, biographies, and straightforward stories make excellent choices for most beginning readers. The Internet is an amazing resource, even for early readers. No matter how difficult the French, those with particular interests almost inevitably get drawn into sites they find irresistible, complete with context, visuals, and lots of cognates. An avid hiker, for example, might find full details about trails and campsites in the Alps, complete with maps and suggestions on how to prepare. On the Internet, students read for pleasure because it's interesting and important to them. They quickly learn that they do not need to know every word to understand a text.

Deux mondes contains many types of reading texts. In **Chapitre 1,** the reading **Les Francophones sur le vif** is based on questions from an opinion survey that gives the respondents' replies in personal, informal French. The **Infos** give factual information in a standard narrative form. The **Lectures** are a sampler for trying a wide variety of content, language, and culture. They include narratives, poetry, adaptations of short stories, extracts from Francophone literature, and author-written selections, all recorded on the CD-ROM so that students can listen to them as well. In the Audio Program that coordinates with the *Cahier d'exercices,* **À l'écoute!** provides songs, poetry, adaptations of short stories, fairy tales, and myths from around the Francophone world. Both *Deux mondes* and the *Cahier* contain many pieces of authentic material (realia) ranging from simple ads to longer passages. We have also tapped into the rich vein of authentic materials on the Internet, as well. At the *Deux mondes* website, task-based **Activités** require information learned by reading native French at specified websites. The **Cliquez là!** boxes in the textbook suggest exciting ideas and topics that encourage students to use the Web on their own.

The instructor may or may not choose to assign all the readings in the *Deux mondes* program. In fact, many programs use additional readings of their own. Our main goal is to give the instructor plenty of varied reading materials and to help show students that they can read a surprising amount of French from the outset. We want students to become aware of the huge variety of reading matter that is available in French. We also hope to help students acquire reading techniques that will enable them to successfully approach and comprehend texts in French by themselves. The ultimate goal is to help students enjoy their reading so much that they will choose to continue it on their own long after they have ceased their formal studies.

Introducing Reading

In Natural Approach activities, students begin to read almost immediately. During the first oral input of Stage 1 (the **Mise en train** activities), most Natural Approach instructors write some of the key words of the input on the chalkboard. This practice allows students to begin the process of connecting French sounds to familiar letters—if not consciously, then intuitively. The "reading" involved in these activities is minimal and silent. Some students report "rehearsing" words the instructor writes on the board as they copy them in their vocabulary notebooks. We recommend that you do not ask students to read these words aloud because they will not have had enough input to correctly produce French sounds for what looks like "English" letters. In addition, they will be concentrating on pronunciation rather than the meaning of the words, thus impeding the acquisition process.

As students engage in the interactions in the **Première** and **Deuxième étapes** (Stages 1 and 2), they will have more opportunities to hear words and match them with the printed versions. In addition, they can work through the exercises on pronunciation and spelling in the *Cahier d'exercices*. Those exercises explicitly point out the sound-letter correspondences of French. The emphasis during this stage, before formal reading begins, is on extracting meaning from the printed word without translating into English.

The first **Info** in **Chapitre 1** is **Portrait de famille**, on page 48. Read the title aloud, then ask students to look at the photo and describe the family members they see. Next, read the text aloud, slower than normal but with normal phraseology. Repeat the reading, going sentence by sentence and calling attention to cognate words. Ask students to help identify them. Since the notion of cognate words may be new to some students, list them on the board and ask for the English words they resemble. Next, ask students to skim the text to find answers to simple questions: **Est-ce que 30 % des Français restent célibataires? Il y a combien d'enfants dans la famille typique?** Finally, read the entire text aloud once more, with students joining in if they wish.

The first sustained narrative reading is the **Lecture, «Familles d'aujourd'hui»,** on page 58. We recommend that the instructor work with this reading in class to ensure that students understand what is expected of them when a reading is assigned. After introductory input, ask students to look at the picture, the title, and to skim the introduction.

1. *Introduce the story.* Read the title and introduction aloud, then ask: **Est-ce que la famille est importante pour les Français? Est-ce que le mot *famille* a la même définition pour toutes les classes sociales? Pour toutes les régions?**

2. *Students skim to look for a factual frame of reference.* Emphasize that they are not to translate into English but rather to attempt to extract meaning directly from the French. In this first cursory reading, they should try to find the names of the three interviewees and something about them. When students have finished, say the names while asking questions that identify the interviewees: **Qui est (chômeur), Élise ou Jean-Claude? Quel âge a... ? Est-ce qu'Élise est grand-mère?**

3. *Students scan the text for further information.* In this second reading, they should be asked to read the first paragraph, trying not to translate. When they finish, ask about Jean-Claude's comments: **Est-ce que Jean-Claude habite avec ses parents ou avec des amis? Est-ce qu'il aime habiter avec ses parents? Dans sa famille, est-ce qu'il y a parfois des frictions? Et dans votre famille aussi? C'est normal d'avoir des frictions dans la famille?**

   Work on cognate awareness during the discussion. For example, point out that **friction** is a cognate word of the English word *friction,* and write it on the board in a column headed **Mots apparentés.** Next, ask the class to locate other cognates in the reading that should be added to the list.

4. *Do a final reading.* To show students that their understanding of the text increases through multiple readings, ask them to reread the full text silently, trying to get the gist entirely in French. Afterward, review the larger ideas of the text with the class: **Pour ces trois personnes, est-ce que la famille est importante? Comment est la famille pour Jean-Claude? (un refuge) Et pour Élise, est-ce que la famille est nécessaire? Pour Amidou, la famille est comme un village. Qui sont les membres?**
5. *Do the questions in Avez-vous compris?* Ask the questions quickly while students answer as a group. The questions are deliberately broad to help hold students' attention and interest. Asking too many comprehension questions also causes students to become less absorbed by the content.

It is impossible to predict how many times you will need to go through the readings in subsequent chapters with students before they establish good reading habits. However, helping them to grow comfortable with the notion of reading in French will ensure that they move away from the push to translate and increase their likelihood of becoming effective, independent readers.

Reading Strategies

The readings in *Deux mondes* are intended to provide new ideas and additional, comprehensible input. We hope that they help students become confident readers who enjoy reading in French. We do want to stress, however, that our main interest is not in teaching students how to read per se. Just as we believe that language acquisition follows naturally from exposure to good input and being attentive to ideas instead of forms, we also believe that the use of good reading strategies is best acquired indirectly. We suggest that the instructor incorporate the strategies given below whenever possible, while reading in class with the whole group. After the instructor has used them successfully on several occasions without calling attention to them, many students begin to apply them effortlessly to their independent reading.

1. *Begin with contextual clues.* Before beginning to read, use illustrations, the title and the introduction, and any other initial cues that help indicate the topic of the reading.
2. *Cognates.* Use cognates to make predictions about content and to guide students' imagination.
3. *Global reading.* Read in stages.
   - First reading: Read rapidly to get the main idea.
   - Second reading: Read to clarify the main idea and notice important details.
   - Third reading: Read to answer questions and to relate content to your own experiences.
4. *Main idea (second reading).*
   - Pay attention to the first paragraph. It will give you the main idea of the reading.
   - Remaining paragraphs develop the main idea with more details.
5. *Context.* Use context to determine the meaning of unknown words; make guesses relying on context.
6. *Morphological analysis.*
   - Look for prefixes or suffixes.
   - Analyze the word's root.
   - Could the word be a derivative?
   - What is its function in the sentence: subject, predicate, object?
7. *Be an active reader.* Anticipate, predict. An active reader asks himself or herself questions: Why is this said? Is this a contradiction? An active reader predicts the outcome and is alert for clues that modify those predictions as the reading continues.
8. *Use literary images to attain a better understanding.*
   - Metaphors are an implicit comparison between two different objects.
   - Similes are an explicit comparison between two different objects.

Teaching Writing

The first steps in learning to write French begin during the **Mise en train** activities of Stage 1 (**Première étape**) when students copy key words from the board into their vocabulary notebooks. Many Natural Approach instructors assign students to write out the answers to grammar exercises and, at times, to questions on readings. (Only rarely will students be expected to write anything for an oral activity.) Such writing practice is necessary and helpful but is in no sense "creative" writing in which students express themselves in French without copying directly from models. Writing exercises involving free composition are found mainly in the *Cahier d'exercices.*

Starting with **Chapitre 1,** one writing activity is included in each chapter in the main text in **À vous d'écrire.** In the early chapters, students are asked primarily to complete sentences with words and phrases or to follow a model very closely. In later chapters, they are asked to write letters, descriptions, and short essays. Models, pieces of realia, or sets of questions provide guidance for these activities so that students can develop the ability to express their personal views in writing without feeling overwhelmed. In the *Cahier d'exercices,* writing activities for the **Première** and **Deuxième étapes** require one-word answers and short phrases. Beginning with **Chapitre 1,** students are asked to write complete sentences and to start to write some simple narratives. As they progress through the *Cahier,* writing activities become more creative and varied.

Introducing Writing

You can start "creative" writing (free composition) at the end of Stage 2 (**Deuxième étape**), even though students are not yet speaking in complete sentences. Since the input topics have been about the students themselves, choose this topic for the first essay. Ask for a volunteer to serve as the person the other students will describe. Write the title of the essay on the board and have students copy it: **Un(e) camarade de classe.** Then ask students to brainstorm what they want to write about their classmate by giving you words and phrases. Write their output on the board as they give it to you (it will occur in a random and unconnected order), making corrections for gender, number, and so on, as necessary using the technique of indirect correction. (STUDENT: **Il est grande.** INSTRUCTOR, WRITING ON BOARD: **Oui, il est grand.**) After you have five to ten descriptive phrases such as **cheveux blonds, il est étudiant, T-shirt,** or **intelligent** on the board, have students pick the word or phrase with which they would like to begin their composition. Suppose they say **étudiant.** You respond orally: **Oui, Maurice est un étudiant dans la classe de français.** Write that sentence on the board. Suppose the next phrase is **cheveux blonds.** Write **Il a les cheveux blonds.** The following is an example of a first essay generated in class.

Un camarade de classe

Maurice est un étudiant dans la classe de français. Il a les cheveux blonds et les yeux bleus. Il n'est pas grand, il n'est pas petit. Il est de taille moyenne. Il porte un jean et un T-shirt rouge aujourd'hui. Il est intelligent et sportif. Il préfère le tennis. Il déteste le lundi matin.

After you have helped the class create this essay, ask students to write a second one about another classmate or friend. Circulate around the room, helping students individually. They will particularly need help with constructions that have occurred in your input but that they have not yet seen and used in the text (**il préfère, déteste**). We suggest that you do two or three group essays before assigning the first composition from the text or *Cahier d'exercices.*

We recommend that students do a communicative writing task once a week. In some cases, it may be impossible to collect, correct, and grade all writing assignments. When you do collect essays to which you intend to assign a grade, ask students to hand in a first draft. On that draft, circle errors that they should be able to correct on their own. For errors that they will not recognize, either correct them yourself or leave them (items such as subjunctive forms have no meaning to first-semester students, for example). Some instructors find it useful to color-code the errors they mark as an extra help for students. For example, you might use blue for spelling and vocabulary, red for morphology (agreements, conjugations, and so on), and green for syntax (word order, punctuation, linking of clauses, and so forth). Ask students to rewrite the essay, making the corrections you have indicated; then collect and grade the second draft.

Teaching Culture

In common usage, the term "culture" is often mistakenly used in reference to the manifestations of culture such as behaviors, attitudes, traditions, and objects. Strictly speaking, culture is a virtual framework that we can understand only through these manifestations and only in reference to itself. The problem is that our approach to an alien culture is inevitably framed by our own cultural norm and habits. This leads to a comparative approach. When we think and say, for instance, that the French are "more stylish" or "less organized" than Americans, we are in effect judging one culture by the standards of another rather than trying to grasp that culture's internal coherence.

Teaching culture in a "language" class is better achieved through constant exposure to culturally determined aspects of life in a foreign society such as language, behavioral patterns, modes of consumption, housing, work habits, and attitudes toward relationships and leisure. In fact, culture is better acquired in this way than in formal presentations, which tend to be comparative at that level and, therefore, judgmental.

In *Deux mondes*, we have tried to present language in culturally rich and authentic contexts. We hope to facilitate the acquisition of language and culture simultaneously, in the most natural fashion. Whenever a discussion about culture arises, we hope the instructor will steer students toward a descriptive approach of what people say, think, and do and away from a comparison between the target culture and their own. Throughout the Instructor's Edition, there are regular suggestions for expanding the content of the **Activités** and **Lectures** to enrich their cultural dimensions and to stimulate classroom discussions.

Teaching Pronunciation

We would like students using *Deux mondes* to develop good pronunciation habits. By "good" we mean that their pronunciation of French will be close enough to a native speaker's so as not to call undue attention to the mispronunciations. We suggest that students be urged to concentrate first on listening carefully rather than on imitating and repeating. One of the major benefits of Stage 1 input activities is that they allow students to hear French sounds in context so that they can develop a "feel" for French pronunciation before they attempt to produce. We believe that this listening period is especially important to developing good rhythm and intonation.

Even when a solid listening stage is provided, many students still experience problems in recognizing and producing certain sounds. For example, many students have difficulty pronouncing the French uvular **r** or the vowel sound of **tu** without explicit practice. In addition, French presents special difficulties with respect to the relation between spelling and pronunciation, given such phenomena as silent final consonants, liaison, and nasal vowels. For this reason, pronunciation and spelling are treated in specific sections of the *Cahier d'exercices*.

When the class is engaged in meaning-focused activities, we recommend that pronunciation errors be treated similarly to grammar errors; that is, not by direct correction but rather by modeling of the correct pronunciation. However, when a pronunciation error genuinely interferes with communication (for instance, when **deux heures** is pronounced as **douze heures**), it is appropriate to consider this a failure to communicate and request clarification (**deux heures ou douze heures?,** emphasizing the vowel distinction). You may also wish to emphasize certain sounds or sound distinctions that cause frequent errors by taking a few minutes in class to point out the problem and do some quick practice as a whole class. Above all, avoid singling out students with pronunciation difficulties. You can give special attention to students who need help while they work in small groups or pairs. In a few cases, students may need individual help during your office hours.

The complex relation between French spellings and pronunciation leads most students to make more errors in pronunciation when reading from a text than when speaking spontaneously. For this reason, avoid asking students to read aloud from texts such as reading passages that contain unfamiliar vocabulary and whose complexity goes beyond what students are able to produce in speaking. During the presentation of a reading activity, we recommend that you draw students' attention to basic rules such as the fact that final unaccented **-e** (and **-es** and **-ent**) is not pronounced, that a final consonant is usually not pronounced unless followed by **-e,** and that final **-er** and **-ez** are usually pronounced [e].

The Tools of Proficiency: Vocabulary and Grammar

The four skills—listening, speaking, reading, and writing—are the primary focus of *Deux mondes.* Two tools are essential for students to become proficient in any of these skills, however: vocabulary and grammar. Here we describe how each functions in *Deux mondes.* Since acquiring vocabulary is far more important than grammar rules for understanding comprehensible input in the early stages of the students' career, we will treat it first.

Teaching Vocabulary

Our approach to teaching vocabulary is derived from the Natural Approach principle that speech emerges in stages. Thus, *Deux mondes* has been written with the expectation that students will hear new vocabulary before they see and use it. In the student text, the primary vocabulary of each chapter is introduced in meaningful contexts via the vocabulary displays and **Activités.** In the Instructor's Edition, however, the **Mise en train** activities and the marginal notes provide suggestions on how to teach the chapter vocabulary orally before students do the activities in the text. The Instructor's Edition notes for the vocabulary displays and for each oral activity in that chapter list key new vocabulary for those particular activities. This arrangement allows the instructor to identify at a glance any new material in an exercise that is essential to success in doing that activity. Here are the steps we suggest you follow for each chapter in the book.

1. Students listen and begin comprehending new language (Stage 1). At this introductory point, the instructor uses **Mise en train** activities to give students ample opportunity to acquire language before having to produce it. Students show they understand by supplying names of people, by answering **oui** or **non,** or by following TPR (Total Physical Response) commands. We suggest that you aim to introduce, for recognition only, the words that are suggested in the **Mise en train** activities and any other words you wish to add, including words from upcoming chapters. We recommend that students hear new words and structures in a variety of contexts, and that you recycle the same language over several days while also adding new items during each input session. Remember that students progress rapidly in the early stages of the Natural Approach because they have only to recognize words not to produce them. Of course, most of these extra words will be reintroduced many times in subsequent activities and will finally appear formally in one of the later chapters. This "review" of vocabulary speeds up progress in later chapters, since students will always encounter words with which they are familiar, even when dealing with new topics.
2. Students begin to use the new language during the Pre-Text Oral Activities (Stage 2). The instructor begins to modify his or her techniques so that students can "copy" speech by using the words and simple phrases they hear. This means that the instructor begins including questions that offer a choice of simple answers. The following are some examples based on magazine pictures. **Première et deuxième étapes:** (photo of a man) **Il est jeune ou vieux, ce monsieur? Est-ce qu'il a une barbe ou une moustache? Chapitre 6:** (photo of tennis champion) **Qu'est-ce que John McEnroe faisait souvent quand il était petit? Est-ce qu'il chantait dans une chorale ou est-ce qu'il jouait au tennis? Chapitre 11:** (photo of person with a cold) **Qu'est-ce qu'il faut qu'on fasse pour éviter les rhumes, à votre avis? Faut-il qu'on prenne des vitamines tous les jours ou est-ce qu'il vaut mieux qu'on mange une nourriture riche en vitamines?**
3. Students begin using the textbook. This usually occurs almost simultaneously with Stage 2 above. The activities in each chapter of the main text are arranged in order of difficulty. Each new section provides most of the language needed to do the activities. This means that students both see and hear the new language as they engage in communicative exchanges with partners or in groups. Because they have the requisite vocabulary at their fingertips, students are free to focus on ideas and are relieved of the burden of having to "think up" vocabulary on their own.

Keep in mind that the process described above will probably occur daily in your classroom throughout the year. New words and structures will enter through listening input during every class, while students will be able to use other language in a restricted fashion. Often, students begin to use words in real speech long after they are introduced in a particular chapter, and in fact, words that are recognized only in a particular chapter will be produced spontaneously during an activity in a subsequent chapter.

Student-Generated Vocabulary and the Vocabulary Notebook

To discuss the themes and topics you introduce in class, students will need to express their own ideas. Since each class is composed of a different set of individuals, the ideas they express will be different from those of another class and will require their own particular vocabulary. We recommend that you regularly provide students opportunities to suggest vocabulary they want to learn and that you have students keep a vocabulary notebook in which they record all new items you put on the chalkboard.

The need for personal expressions may arise in several different ways. For example, during a **Mise en train** activity the instructor may show students a photo of someone sailing and say to the class, **Il aime faire de la voile. Et moi aussi, j'aime faire de la voile. Est-ce qu'il y a quelqu'un d'entre vous qui aime aussi faire de la voile?** Several students indicate interest, so you pursue the topic: **Ah, il y a beaucoup de personnes qui aiment faire de la voile.** Then you talk with someone who did not indicate interest: **Et vous, Richard, vous n'aimez pas faire de la voile? (non) Alors, quel sport préférez-vous?** At this point, the student may need to respond in English. Imagine that he says he likes rock climbing. The instructor gives the French and writes the term **faire de l'escalade** on the board for students to see and to copy into their vocabulary notebooks. This term becomes a part of the vocabulary of that particular class and may be included in tests. Some suggestions on how to develop and use a vocabulary notebook follow.

1. Write all new key vocabulary items on the chalkboard during input and oral activities and have students copy those words into their vocabulary notebooks.
2. Have students review their vocabulary notebooks regularly, and, in particular, have them spend five minutes or so looking over the most recent entries before they come to class each day.
3. Keep track of the words by asking a different student each day to make a copy of that day's vocabulary.

In our experience, the vocabulary notebook will add about one-third more words to those you select as the primary vocabulary for a chapter. In the early stages, we recommend that students be held responsible for recognition only and not be required to produce or spell the words correctly. However, after students have had ample exposure and have begun to acquire particular words, they should be able to use them in creative activities and writing, and students should be held responsible for them for testing purposes.

The Role of Grammar Instruction in the Natural Approach

Although grammar is clearly secondary to vocabulary in expressing meaning, we do not want students to acquire pidgin French. When they focus on communication and meaning during spontaneous speech, students will use simplified and sometimes erroneous structures. Gradually, however, their speech improves throughout the course and becomes more "grammatical." We believe that most of this improvement takes place because of their increased ability to understand and attend more carefully to input. However, most Natural Approach students report that the study of grammar is helpful in improving their speech. We think that grammar study can be useful in three ways: (1) It improves listening comprehension; (2) it focuses attention on a specific grammatical marker; (3) it provides forms and rules to use in monitoring.

The study of grammar can help the learner make sense of the input. For example, some related forms are so different that even in a clear context learners may not recognize them (for example, the irregular forms of **être**). The study of grammar can emphasize certain characteristics that otherwise might take a great deal of time to figure out. For example, it is probably helpful to point out that plural nouns are indicated in spoken French by a change in the article (**le/la/les**) rather than by the ending of the noun itself. Finally, we cannot produce "optimal" monitors if the students have no information to help them monitor. The study of grammar helps to make minor improvements in speech and is very useful in reading and writing tasks.[1]

The **Grammaire et exercices** section of the student text presents grammar rules that students will use to monitor their written work and, in some cases, their speech. There are short explanations of the rules of morphology (word formation), syntax (sentence formation), and word usage (lexical sets). (Spelling and pronunciation rules and practice are found in the *Cahier d'exercices*.) We have tried to reduce the length and detail of explanations since we believe that excessive study and memorization of grammar rules and exercises are not very helpful to the beginning students. Above all, the student should not be expected to learn and use the material in this section without errors in writing and speaking. This material serves

---

[1]For further discussion, see Tracy D. Terrell, "The Role of Grammar Instruction in a Communicative Approach," *Modern Language Journal* 75 (1991): 52–62.

primarily as an introduction, a guideline, and a reference, nothing more. The exercises are meant primarily to verify comprehension of the material and to provide concentrated input with the new structure. It must be remembered that real communicative experiences result in acquisition of grammatical forms and structures. The acquisition of grammar takes a long time. Students should not think that a conscious mastery of French grammar is a prerequisite to communication with native speakers of French.

Grammar in *Deux mondes*

Instructor's Edition notes in the margins of the **Grammaire et exercices** sections often include specific suggestions for what we believe to be appropriate expectations for a given grammatical structure. For instance, some structures are presented for comprehension only (for example, compound tenses other than **passé composé**); some are intended to be practiced in monitored, form-focused activities but not yet expected to be used correctly in spontaneous speech (for instance, relative pronouns **qui** and **que**). Still others are expected to begin to occur in spontaneous speech, although always with inconsistent accuracy (for example, present tense of **aimer** + infinitive). This diversity of expectations is the logical consequence of a cyclical, progressive view of language acquisition and has important consequences for the grammatical syllabus of the course. Certain topics traditionally included in first-year French textbooks are not included here (for instance, causative **faire** construction and passive voice). Others that are frequently omitted from certain first-year texts are included (compound tenses other than **passé composé**). However, one should keep in mind that mastery or productive use of these structures is not expected. We believe this is an advantage in several respects. Not only does it better prepare students to deal with these structures during subsequent study, but, more importantly, it allows us to expose students to a wider sample of the French language in natural uses. In other words, it increases the possibilities for meaningful input and thus facilitates the acquisition process.

In addition to specifying varying expectations for diverse grammatical topics, the syllabus acknowledges the cyclical nature of language learning and acquisition through the "spiraling" of certain complex grammatical topics; that is, certain topics are covered only partially in the initial presentation and then are re-entered and expanded in one or several subsequent units that are usually spaced throughout the remainder of the text. For example, reflexive (pronominal) verbs and the imperfect tense are each treated in four different grammar sections: Between **Chapitres 2** and **13** for reflexives and between **Chapitres 6** and **12** for the imperfect.

Using the *Grammaire et exercices*

The material in the **Grammaire et exercices** should be integrated with the rest of the materials from other sections. The specific way you use the **Grammaire et exercices** will depend on your own teaching style and your students' learning preferences and background. Some instructors prefer to assign the grammar and exercises before they begin the corresponding section in the **Activités et lectures;** others assign parts of the grammar and exercises as they are working on a particular section; still others use the grammar and exercises as a follow-up after they have completed the corresponding section of the **Activités et lectures** in class.

Students should be aware that the sections in the grammar do usually relate to the activities they are doing in class. However, we emphasize that the **Grammaire et exercices** section is not responsible for developing the ability to use grammar in spontaneous speech. Still, for many adults, a clear grammar explanation, even if it does not really help the acquisition process, is very satisfying. Only in a specific class situation can you judge the appropriate time and emphasis to give to grammar assignments. We suggest that you avoid detailed grammar explanations in the classroom whenever possible. They rarely help more than a few students and inevitably take away valuable time from acquisition activities.

When we do wish explicitly to draw students' attention to a grammar feature, our own preference is to wait until students have been exposed to considerable input including the feature. To clarify the meaning or use of a grammatical feature, we recommend giving input in the same ways that are used for new vocabulary but where occurrences of the grammatical feature in question are concentrated. The marginal notes in grammar sections of the Instructor's Edition include numerous suggestions on how to do such input presentations for grammar. The goal is always to use the feature in a natural way to talk about something of interest to your students, but also to make the new forms more apparent through their concentration in the input. An extended example of an input presentation for **aimer** + infinitive and the different types of infinitives is given in this manual (see Infinitives [**Chapitre 1** Pre-Text Oral Activities]). Most input presentations do not need to be this lengthy, but the principles are the same. When doing input presentations, you will probably want to write an example with each different form on the board as it occurs in your input. This procedure will help to establish the correlation between spoken and written forms, and it can then be used following the input to draw students' attention to the complete paradigm, or to elicit the students' own expression of their understanding of the use of these forms.

Most of the grammar exercises are short and "moderately" communicative. We usually recommend that grammar exercises be done in writing because we believe that it is more conducive to a focus on grammar. However, in many cases, the exercises can be done orally between instructor and students or even in student pairs. We recommend that you distinguish carefully between an exercise in which the focus is on grammar and an acquisition activity in which the focus is on the message. Otherwise, students will get the idea that they should focus on grammar in all oral activities. Many instructors assign the grammar exercises as homework and check them quickly during the following class period. Note that although grammar errors are not corrected directly in activities (but rather by natural expansions), grammatical errors are corrected during learning exercises since the focus is indeed on grammar and correctness. Since the answers to all grammar exercises are found in Appendix D of the student text, students can check their own work at home, and you may simply have them ask questions about items they found problematic.

OUTLINE OF GRAMMAR SPIRALING

The following chart is a general outline of the spiraling of grammar points in *Deux mondes*. For specific grammar references, see the index in the main text.

Overview

ADJECTIVES
A.3   Gender, agreement, and articles
A.5   Plural nouns and articles
B.6   Describing with adjectives: More on gender
B.7   Irregular plurals
1.1   Expressing relationships: Possessive adjectives
3.5   Pointing things out: Demonstrative adjectives and **-ci/-là**
4.1   Describing: Placement of adjectives
4.2   Making comparisons
8.1   Expressing *all* and *everything*: Using **tout**

ADVERBS
4.2   Making comparisons
10.5   Expressing extremes: The superlative
13.2   Describing actions: Adverbs

ARTICLES
A.3   Gender and articles
A.5   Plural nouns and articles
B.1   Expressing existence: **Il y a**
B.5   Expressing possession: The verb **avoir**
1.6   Expressing relationships and possession: Contractions of **de**
2.3   Going places and future actions: The verb **aller;** contractions of **à**
3.6   Expressing quantities: Partitive articles

AVOIR (EXPRESSIONS WITH)
4.7   Describing states of being: Idioms with **avoir**
6.3   Describing past states: More on the imperfect
12.2   Changes of state: **Passé composé** versus **imparfait**

Chapter 5
Classroom Management

Modes of Address

We recommend that you address individual students as **vous** and that students also use **vous** with you. The use of **tu** would be culturally inauthentic between student and instructor in most French-speaking university settings. In addition, if the instructor used **tu** with students, they would have few opportunities to hear **vous** in the input. However, students should use the pronoun **tu** in all cases where they talk with one another. The textbook uses **vous** when addressing students, but **tu** occurs in interviews and other activities where students are expected to talk to one another.

Classroom Environment

We believe that language acquisition in the classroom happens most effectively when certain conditions are met. Students must be exposed to natural and comprehensible input; they must have ample opportunities to interact in French; and the atmosphere of the classroom must be both encouraging and stimulating. When students are interested in what is happening in class, they pay attention to the input. When they feel free of constraints that make them feel awkward, they use their French for communication with others without reserve.

None of the above is meant to imply a lax atmosphere in which entertainment takes precedence over language learning. In fact, students seem to acquire fastest when they know the rules of the class and are expected to live up to them. It is important that they know how to judge where they stand in terms of classroom behavior, homework requirements, and evaluation procedures. Within this context, however, it is possible to for the instructor to create an environment that makes it interesting to come to class and exciting to learn French. Although no strategy will work for all classes and for all teachers, the following are some suggestions that we have found to be very helpful.

1. Personalize the instructor-student relationship. Each student should feel that the instructor takes a personal interest in his or her progress. Learn your students' names immediately and begin to accumulate personal information about each one. Use this information to make comments during oral activities, linking the activities to the students' interests and experiences.
2. Encourage all attempts to communicate. Limit direct error correction to grammar exercises; such correction should not occur during oral activities or during any conversation in which the focus is on meaning rather than structure. Praise attempts at guessing and risk-taking in both comprehension and speech production. Promote creativity and risk-taking as more important than any errors students might make.
3. Encourage a positive attitude about eventual success. The goal of a first-year course is to communicate with native speakers, not to understand and speak the target language as fluently as native speakers.
4. Set realistic, useful, and attainable goals. Most students will not be able to develop perfect accents, nor will they be able to monitor extensively enough to correct all errors in their speech. However, all students can be proficient and successful communicators in French.
5. Make the class enjoyable. Smile, laugh, react, reveal, explain, and play games but, most of all, enjoy yourself. Language acquisition and instruction does not need to be a chore.
6. Appeal to the students' desire to learn. Make the course a cultural as well as a linguistic experience. Bring in topics and information that will pique students' natural interest and curiosity. Show slides, movies, and videotapes. Bring newspapers, magazines, and other authentic documents to class. Show students how to make use of the resources offered by the Internet. Recount your own experiences, your travels, and your encounters.

7. Make it obvious how your course relates to the students' general educational experience. *Deux mondes* makes it easy for you to introduce discussions of real interest in French, even at fairly early levels. As opportunities arise, initiate discussions of historical and current events. Point out the historical relationships among the Romance languages and between French and English by discussing cognates and other linguistic items. A good language course is a "content" course. Instead of speaking French just to speak French, students learn best when they are provided with a stimulating context that enlivens their studies.

Selecting Class Activities and Making Lesson Plans

Lesson plans are not provided for *Deux mondes* since we believe that the instructor should feel free to use the materials made available in this program to supply exciting input and to allow the development of interesting interactions with and among students. The activities in *Deux mondes* are not meant to be "covered" as in a traditional textbook; rather, they are intended as springboards for meaningful interactions using the target language.

A normal Natural Approach instructional hour consists of three to seven interactions. These interactions are selected from the Pre-Text Oral Activities, the topical displays, the **Activités orales,** the **Mise en train** activities and **Activités supplémentaires (AS)** found in the margins of the Instructor's Edition, the White Pages topical displays and **Activités,** readings, comprehension texts, and writing activities. In addition, you will want to include games, skits, presentations, videos, slides, movies, and your other favorite input and interactional activities. In general, the grammar explanations and exercises, as well as many activities in the *Cahier d'exercices,* are meant to be used as homework assignments. However, students like to have a follow-up of some sort on homework in class. In most classes, you will want to save a small amount of time for grammar discussions and perhaps for checking one or more of the exercises that students have studied. In some cases, students are not able to do much homework, and you will have to spend more class time on grammar and exercises.

The sequence of class interactions is not fixed, but here is one possibility that you may want to try.

5 minutes	warm-up/review with picture file (PF)
10 minutes	comprehensible input based on new topical display
20–25 minutes	**Activités orales** and **Activités supplémentaires (AS)**
5–10 minutes	video, songs, reading
5 minutes	preview of new grammar assignment

The length of the interactions is not fixed either. Some may be as short as one minute, whereas others may last much longer. Generally, students' attention starts to wander after about ten minutes. For this reason, you must determine both the length and the order of the interactions you select for a particular class period. The topical divisions of each **Activités orales et lectures** section are ordered as logically as possible, as are the activities within a topic. However, in most cases, there is enough flexibility for modification; indeed, it is somewhat boring to proceed simply from one activity to another with no variation.

We have tried to provide more than enough materials for a variety of interactions on each topic. For some topics, you may wish to add other activities; for other topics, you may wish to omit several activities. There may even be entire topics (and vocabulary and grammar items) that you decide to omit as irrelevant to your students.

We believe that variety, pace, and recycling are three important factors you should keep in mind when you are designing lesson plans. Beginning with **Chapitre 1,** there should be a balance between instructor-centered input and pair- or group-centered activities. Students need to speak if they are to learn how to speak, and pair or small-group activities ensure that all students have as much opportunity to practice as possible. Switch back and forth from instructor-centered to group-centered activities to change pace and maintain student attention, and have students change partners several times during a series of activities so that they are exposed to a variety of input and ideas.

A lively pace in class keeps students on their toes. You do not need to wait until everyone finishes before you end an activity. As a rule of thumb, you may stop any activity when approximately two-thirds of the class have finished. However, students should not feel pressured or rushed if they are to formulate and express their thoughts in French.

Recycling is important because students need considerable exposure to language for acquisition to take place. For example, just because they have learned vocabulary to describe environmental problems or have learned to use infinitives with **venir de** in a particular chapter does not mean that they have acquired these items. *Deux mondes* provides a large amount of recycling and spiraling, but some classes may require even more practice. If such is the case, we recommend that you make up additional activities or reuse activities from previous chapters. Interviews and other open-ended activities lead to interesting new exchanges with each new partner.

Homework

The class hour is the only opportunity most students have for hearing and speaking French. For this reason, class time should be reserved almost entirely for communicative activities. Students can do much of the work that has been traditionally a part of active class time during their study time outside class. Reading long assignments, listening to recorded materials, doing written exercises, and reading grammar explanations should be done outside class whenever possible.

We believe that homework and study are very important, and we recommend that students be made aware of their importance from the beginning. Make sure that students leave the class with a clear idea of what they are to do after each session. We also suggest that they study in small time increments throughout the day instead of in a large block, such as they might allot for a history or an English assignment. For example, it is easy to listen to the Audio Program in the car, and the shower is an excellent place to work on verb forms. Another study technique that pays good dividends is to go over the new words copied into vocabulary notebooks and the day's **Activités** as soon as possible outside class and just before coming to class the next day. Lengthier study sessions are best reserved for grammar explanations and exercises, longer readings, and for assignments in the *Cahier d'exercices*. It is also a good idea to listen repeatedly to the audio recordings over more than one day and to invent spontaneous dialogues and monologues with oneself in French, spoken aloud if possible.

Homework assignments and coverage in class vary according to the particular teaching situation and students. Many instructors find that students are more faithful in preparing for class if they are asked to hand in assignments on a regular basis and are graded accordingly. In some cases, instructors find that they are obliged to include homework activities in the class hour because the students are working adults who do not have time to read and study outside class; other students may lack the background for such activity and need extra help. One must remain flexible and work with the conditions one has. Whatever the teaching situation, however, it is equally important not to lose sight of the basic principle of the Natural Approach: Communication skills are acquired through comprehensible input and communication of meaning to others. Most students are interested in developing the ability to speak French, and this should be the primary focus in class.

Evaluation

Deux mondes provides a testing program from which to select materials for creating tests in listening, speaking, reading, writing, and grammar. These materials alone, however, may not provide you with the range of evaluation you need for your course. Evaluation is a complex issue that we will not attempt to discuss in detail here. However, since we advocate comprehension and communicative ability as primary goals, we provide the following comments and suggestions on these issues that may be useful to you when preparing tests or evaluations outside the Testing Program. They are based on the assumption that material to be tested should be offered in meaningful context and that students should understand the basis on which grades are determined.

1. Comprehension. The listening tests in the Testing Program check noncollaborative listening ability—that is, situations in which the listener is a bystander. However, collaborative listening ability is an important objective in communicative teaching. In collaborative listening, speakers participate in constructing the discourse and are able to negotiate, to a certain extent, what they hear. One way to evaluate collaborative listening ability is to judge how well students understand conversations with the instructor or others. A recorded conversation that is used to grade speaking ability can also be used for this purpose. In such a case, the instructor can judge the extent to which messages are understood, as well as how many are misunderstood completely.

Instructors may also wish to give short listening quizzes. This can be done via instructor input that occurs daily in class. In these, you might check for items such as recognition of vocabulary that you expect students to recognize at the end of the week's work, recognition of tense as a time indicator, the ability to guess meaning from context, and so on. Following are some suggestions for listening quizzes.

- Tape pictures to the board and have students give the letter (or number) of the picture you are describing. Teacher-talk would depend on the level and could range from simple descriptions to stories based on the pictures.
- Make statements or spontaneous narratives based on information learned during class time and have students write the name of the classmate.
- Tell brief stories and ask students to indicate whether they occur at the present time or will happen in the future (or occurred in the past).

2. Speaking. The Testing Program provides materials and suggestions for testing students' general speaking proficiency and includes chapter-specific questions designed to elicit vocabulary for particular topics and particular structures. For the latter, you might wish to let students know which particular speech functions and topics to prepare. The amount of time required for testing can be reduced by having two or more students engage in conversation rather than using one-on-one interview.

Here is a simple procedure that students enjoy and that allows the instructor to test the entire class at once. Prepare two sets of questions (A and B) and set up recorders in the classroom. Before students begin, everyone receives a copy of the questions and the instructor reads them aloud to be sure everyone understands. Students are told they will ask their partner a set of questions and are instructed to react naturally to the partner's responses. They are also instructed to speak softly (to cut down background noise) and are put in charge of the machine they will use.

The class numbers off to assign the question sets, and those holding Set A choose a speaking partner who holds Set B. The test should last from five to seven minutes. Afterward, collect the tapes and grade them. This procedure generates a surprising amount of natural language, since it resembles familiar everyday partner activities, and students almost inevitably go beyond simply asking questions and lead their partners into explaining or giving opinions.

3. Vocabulary. We do not expect students to produce all the words in the **Vocabulaire** in their speech. For testing purposes, some instructors prefer to assign all the words in the **Vocabulaire;** others choose to assign the words they consider the most important. These might include the words in the art displays and selected **Activités,** along with vocabulary generated in class (vocabulary notebook). Whichever method best suits your program, vocabulary should be tested in context and that comprehension of meaning be the primary emphasis. Production of words, and spelling, are best checked within the context of writing.

4. Writing. Evaluation of writing is a complex matter, since the instructor needs to consider multiple factors, such as accuracy in spelling, vocabulary, morphology (agreements, conjugations, and so on), and syntax (word order, punctuation, linking of clauses, and so forth), as well as clarity of statement and organization in the presentation of the message. Additionally, some instructors wish to see evidence that students can use the material they have been studying during the testing period.

Besides determining how much to count for such errors, a qualitative analysis needs to be made: Is the student writing at the level the instructor can reasonably expect at a particular time in the course? Certainly, in the middle of the second semester, a composition that uses basic French from the first semester, although completely free of errors, cannot be entirely acceptable and should not be graded higher than one that contains errors but shows a strong command of the language acquired at that point. It is important to resolve such issues and to let students know your grading standards. Making a judgment in this area can be helpful when you are dealing with both true and false beginners.

Picture File

A good picture file (PF), essential for use with *Deux mondes,* is created with real pictures from magazines and newspapers and is much more attractive than the pictures that are available from commercial publishers. Cut pictures from magazines and newspapers and trim them to eliminate English and other distracting elements. Paste or tape them to heavy construction paper and, if possible, laminate them to protect them while they are handled. Some Natural Approach instructors request that their students bring in one picture per week as part of a "show-and-tell" session. In this way, a large PF is built up quickly and without too much work or expense. The pictures in your PF will be more useful if they fulfill certain requirements.

- Each picture should focus on a particular thing or event but should also contain enough other items or events to lend interest. Pictures of a single item (for example, a banana) are less useful, since they do not lend themselves to much more than a flash-card drill.
- Each picture should be interesting or eye-catching. It should contain something that draws students' attention as you talk about it.
- Each picture should be large enough to be seen easily.

We recommend that in making a PF you save all pictures that students bring in and categorize them for use later. Searching for a particular item at random is too time-consuming.

The PF is useful in various ways at different levels. In Stages 1 and 2, the pictures have two main functions. First, they make the input comprehensible. In some cases, there are new words that we do not wish to associate with students in the class (for example, adjectives such as *fat, thin,* and *ugly*). In other cases, it is difficult in class to dramatize a new item adequately (for instance, activities such as cooking, sailing, and cleaning). Second, particular characteristics of a picture (the background, the people, or the action) will often aid students in associating the meaning of a new word or structure with its target language form. In Stage 3, pictures are used to stimulate responses or to initiate a discussion. They may also be used to stimulate creative writing. Finally, pictures are used extensively in the Natural Approach in quizzes, especially in the initial stages of language acquisition.

Here are some examples of how the same picture can be used at different levels throughout the school year. *Picture:* advertisement for cigars showing a man and a young boy standing beside a lake, each holding up a fish he has just caught. There is a forest in the background, and the man (father) is smoking a big cigar. Both are smiling, proud, and happy. The boy's fish is very large, and the man's fish is quite small. In the earliest stages, this picture can be used to teach vocabulary such as **petit garçon, homme, enfant;** physical characteristics; names of clothing; colors; adjectives such as **grand, petit, content;** and the names of the objects in the picture. It can be used in conjunction with other pictures for items such as **Est-ce qu'ils sont debout ou assis?** A little later it is useful for teaching family relationships (**père/fils**); possession; comparison (**Est-ce que le fils est plus petit que son père? Est-ce que le poisson du fils est plus grand que le poisson du père? Est-ce que le père est plus content que le fils?**); preferences; expressions with **faire** (**Ils aiment la pêche. Ils font de la pêche? Est-ce qu'ils font aussi du camping, probablement?**); and verbs like **fumer** and **sourire.**

As students learn past tenses, the photo can be used again. (**Ils ont fait de la pêche. Le père n'a pas eu beaucoup de chance. Quand Jack était petit, il aimait pêcher avec son père. Jack avait perdu une dent à cette époque-là. Ils viennent de faire de la pêche. Il vient de perdre une dent.**) Still later, the picture can be used as part of a series illustrating good and bad health habits. (**Il ne faut pas qu'on fume.**) As students' language becomes more complex, the photo can be used for items such as **Est-ce que ce petit garçon va imiter son père à l'avenir? Fumera-t-il un jour?** or **Si vous aviez des enfants, quel sport feriez-vous avec eux? Est-ce que vous fumeriez devant eux?** These are only some of the many uses for this particular photo. It could be used for many different purposes and for most chapters of *Deux mondes,* depending on theme, topic, and linguistic need.

Following is a basic list you might use for selecting magazine pictures and other realia, arranged thematically to coordinate with the chapters of *Deux mondes.* Keep in mind that the pictures recommended for any one chapter may work well in another. For more on creating a picture file, consult *The Magazine Picture Library* by Janet McAlpin.[1]

---

[1]McAlpin, Janet. *The Magazine Picture Library.* London/Boston: G. Allen and Unwin, 1980.

Suggested Pictures by Chapter

PREMIÈRE ÉTAPE

Clothing / physical description: photos of people (hair color/style, height, glasses . . .) wearing a variety of clothing

Colors: pictures or objects to illustrate color words

Counting in class: number cards up to 30

Naming people: pictures of celebrities

DEUXIÈME ÉTAPE

Classroom objects: pens, pencils, eraser, paper, and so on

Adjectives: photos of moods like **content, triste** and of people types like **sportif, intellectuel**

Days/months: large calendar

Numbers 40–100: number cards

Telling time / numbers: clock with moveable hands, bingo grids

CHAPITRE 1

Age: photos of celebrities/others

Family: nuclear/extended (family tree, family scenes)

Aimer + infinitives / places: photos of leisure activities (reading, watching TV, and so on), common sports, and places such as beach, movies, pool, park, mountains

Nationalities/languages: flags, products

Higher numbers: pictures of items for guessing price (cars, clothing . . .)

Plans: photos to suggest what someone is going to do/is going to occur

Ownership: photos (**le chat du petit garçon...**)

CHAPITRE 2

Weather, seasons: photos

Leisure activities / common and less common sports: photos (include rock climbing, surfing . . .)

Daily routine: photos of people, objects for shaving, shampooing, and so on

Pouvoir/vouloir/savoir: photos of what people can / know how to do, what people want / want to do

CHAPITRE 3

City: street maps, photos of public buildings/places

Transportation: photos of train/bus, and so on

Location: photos/drawings for **à côté de, derrière...** ; campus map

Stores/products: photos, real items

City activities: photos of nightclubs, theaters, festivals, and so forth

CHAPITRE 4

Housing: photos of different types of housing

Comparison: photos or items for larger, smaller, faster, and so on (adjectives and adverbs)

Home, furnishings/appliances: photos

Housework: photos of people/items like lawn mower; real items like broom

Neighborhood: photos of shops/people like florist, mail carrier, pharmacy

Connaître: photos of world monuments/celebrities

CHAPITRE 5

Passé composé: photos of actions / photos that show finished action like dropped an object, tore a garment, won the game

Historic events and myths: photos of paintings / drawings / famous people; realia such as books, medals

Negation: photos about which one can say not yet, nobody, nothing, and so on

CHAPITRE 6

Childhood/teen activities: objects (jacks, Monopoly, doll, video game)

Holiday/special events: photos of birthday parties, and so on; holiday ads

Indirect object pronouns: photos of phoning, speaking, giving, and so forth

Emotions: photos to illustrate emotional scenes: **se battre, se disputer, s'énerver,** and so on

CHAPITRE 7

Foods/beverages: photos of basic foods; real items; nutrition/diet chart

Food stores: photos

French cuisine: photos/slides of French foods (**coq au vin, profiteroles,** and so on; people eating meals)

Cooking/table: photos or objects for place setting, table cloth, and so forth; frying pan, measuring spoons, and so on; recipes

Restaurants: photos/slides of different types of restaurants, personnel; restaurant guides

Time sequence: photos to illustrate before/after

CHAPITRE 8

Countries: slides/photos of people and places

Topography: photos of mountains, hills, desert, and so on

Judgments with **devoir***:* photos of problems (*they should / ought to . . .*)

Environment: photos of city (crowded, vandalism, noise) and environmental issues and concerns (stagnant pond, city dump, smokestacks belching smoke)

Materials: objects in silver, gold, iron, cotton, and so forth (ring, watch, toy frying pan, handkerchief . . .)

Shopping: photos/slides of markets, stores, specialty shops, products

Francophonie: photos/slides of people/places; maps; small flags; products; pictures of art; books and poems; websites

CHAPITRE 9

French university: magazines like *l'Étudiant;* websites and **Minitel;** advertisements for different types of **formation**

Professions: photos (chef, policeman, and so on)

*Action in progress (**depuis**):* photos to suggest actions still in progress (president since . . . , married since . . . , travel in space since . . . , and so forth)

Future: photos of events about to happen; photos that allow you to say what will probably happen (when she finishes breakfast, she will . . .)

CHAPITRE 10

Travel: items like passport, shots, itinerary, tickets

Francophone world: slides/photos of places and what travelers might see/do

Money: real coins, bills; photos of money

Car: photos of interior and exterior of cars

Driving: photos of repairs, towing, filling gas tank, road signs, and so on

Se débrouiller: photos of changing money, hotel, post office, phone, and so forth; realia like **télécarte, Carte Orange,** hotel receipts

CHAPITRE 11

Computer/Internet/Web/Minitel: photos, advertisements

Cinema: posters/slides/photos for French and Francophone films, actors

Media: French TV/radio schedules, newspapers, magazines; websites

Advertising: French/Francophone ads that reflect cultural values; ads that are deceptive, humorous, and so on

Conditional: photos of events that allow you to ask students what they would do (if you broke your leg, if you had a flat tire at night . . .)

CHAPITRE 12

Physical fitness: photos of joggers, exercisers, visiting dentist, and so forth; nutrition charts, posters about fitness / no smoking, and so on

Illness: photos to suggest symptoms, medical care, and remedies/treatments

Causes / changes of state: photos to illustrate situations (smoke makes him sick, exercise makes him feel good, presents make her happy, and so forth)

Accidents: photos (car accident, broken limbs, falls, cuts, and so on)

Recent past: photos of events that have just occurred; newspaper headlines

Background events: photos of events (describe what was going on when the event occurred)

CHAPITRE 13

Family: photos of ceremonies like weddings, funerals, christenings

Family life: photos of family activities; raising children; teen/parent dispute, grandparent/grandchild taste differences, and so on

Reciprocal actions: photos of speaking together, loving each other, giving each other, and so forth

Feelings: photos of people's emotions about events (he's happy/sad/angry that she . . .)

CHAPITRE 14

Francophonie: photos/slides of people/places; maps; small flags; products; pictures of art; books and poems; websites

Immigration/acculturation: photos of ethnic activities; magazine and newspaper headlines/articles; poems and stories

Historical events: photos of paintings / drawings / famous people

Should have / would have: photos of problems (they should have / I would have . . .)

Future: photos of inventions/dreams such as found in *Popular Science*

Chapter 6
Mise en train and Input Techniques

This chapter explains in some detail how to use the **Mise en train** activities that occur in each chapter in the Instructor's Edition of *Deux mondes*. Because it is a closely related topic, we also explain in some detail how to do the techniques we recommend for making these activities interesting and exciting. Where appropriate, the techniques are described for more than one level of linguistic development.

The *Mise en train* Activities

These are input activities that are printed in the margins of the Instructor's Edition, on the last page of each chapter. They are oral activities for introducing new vocabulary, grammar forms, and structures before the class does the oral activities in the text itself. The purpose of the **Mise en train** activities is to help the instructor to use new words in a communicative context, inviting interaction with students. All chapters have **Mise en train** activities, but those in the **Première étape** are especially important since they represent the first comprehensible input that students will hear; they also set the tone and pace of the class. Most of the **Mise en train** activities call for extensive use of a Picture File.

Input Techniques in Stage 1 (Comprehension)

In the following sections we provide a detailed description of the major suggested Pre-Text Oral Activities for Stage 1. These examples are based mainly on the **Première étape,** but the same techniques will apply to Stage 1 presentations for all chapters.

Total Physical Response (TPR)

TPR, as used in the Natural Approach, is adapted from the methodology developed by Dr. James Asher, professor of psychology at San Jose State University, San Jose, California.[1] During Stage 1, TPR in its simplest form consists of commands given by the instructor that students act out. In Stage 2 and, particularly, in Stage 3, students may also give commands to one another and/or to the instructor. You will find that students quickly acquire a great deal of vocabulary using this technique.

The first time TPR is introduced, you may wish to briefly explain in English what you are going to do and what you expect of the students. The point is to show students that they can understand French without any English translation and to help them begin acquiring basic verbs and other vocabulary that they will use throughout the course. Include the same commands daily until you feel that students understand them easily, adding a few new ones each day.

Introduce the new commands one at a time, reviewing them frequently. At first, students may listen and watch you do the action. Or you may bring them into the action immediately by doing the commands with the class and indicating that they are to do the same action. For the former, begin with **Levez-vous (s'il vous plaît).** Say the command clearly and stand up while saying it. Then say **Asseyez-vous,** executing the command yourself. Do the sequence several times; then have students do it with you. Finally, give the commands and have students execute the action alone. All TPR activities should follow this same pattern. Introduce the command, practice it with the class, and test comprehension by giving the command and having the class perform it alone.

An average TPR activity lasts from three to seven minutes and introduces five to fifteen new commands. The following is a simple TPR sequence that you might wish to use at the beginning of the **Première étape: Levez-vous, marchez, courez, asseyez-vous. Levez-vous, marchez, courez, marchez,**

---

[1]For details see J. Asher, *Learning Another Language Through Actions: The Complete Teacher's Guide*, Sky Oaks Publications, Los Gatos, California, 1977.

sautez, asseyez-vous, and so on. TPR is an excellent way to teach the many instructions necessary for daily class routine during the early days of the course. For example: **Prenez votre livre. Ouvrez-le à la page 10. Maintenant, tournez à la page 21. Passez-moi votre copie. Fermez la porte,** and so on.

At more advanced levels, TPR activities provide excellent input for teaching a wide variety of vocabulary and structures such as verbs, adverbs, and prepositions of location. If possible, use logical sequences of commands in a variety of contexts such as taking the bus (**Montez dans l'autobus, donnez votre billet au contrôleur, cherchez une place libre**). Gradually incorporate more complex ones such as a typical day's routine for a university student. By repeating a sequence over a period of several days, you can gradually add interesting and imaginative vocabulary. Example: **Vous êtes en retard! Courez à votre voiture! Ouvrez la portière, sautez dans la voiture, introduisez la clé dans le contact. Ah, voilà enfin l'université! Mais zut! Il n'y a pas de place libre dans le parking. Conduisez, cherchez, garez. Vous êtes en retard pour votre cours! Courez! Montez vite dans l'ascenseur. Appuyez sur le bouton du 7ème étage! Mais comment! L'ascenseur ne bouge pas! Quelle panique! Criez «au secours»! Vous êtes très inquiète parce qu'il y a un examen important aujourd'hui. Alors, pleurez, tordez les mains...**

Student-Centered Input with Names as Responses

This technique is used to introduce new words or grammatical forms and structures during Stage 1. Students indicate their understanding by answering with their classmates' names or, in some cases, with **oui/non.** Several vocabulary topics appear for comprehension in the **Première étape.** We will describe each separately; however, they should be mixed in your speech.

- *Color and length of hair.* Draw students' attention to their classmates' physical characteristics (use only positive ones). For example, Lisa Clark might be **la fille aux cheveux bruns,** and Jim Armstrong **le garçon aux cheveux blonds.** Review often: **Comment s'appelle l'étudiante aux cheveux bruns? (Lisa) Et quelles autres personnes ont les cheveux bruns? Oui, Mike a les cheveux bruns, et Karen a...**
- *Physical characteristics.* Often the fact that male students have **une barbe** or **une moustache** will provide identification cues. Eye color and glasses are also distinguishing features.
- *Clothes.* Articles of clothing with color words are easy identification tools. For example, Judy Lindstrom might be **la fille qui porte le chemisier rose.** Use key words like **chemisier, chemise, pantalon, jupe** with a few colors such as **rouge, noir, blanc, vert,** and **jaune.** Changes for gender agreement do not normally interfere with comprehension.

Here are some techniques for introducing these topics.

- *Ask someone's name.* **Je m'appelle ___.** (Write your name on the board.) **Mademoiselle, comment vous appelez-vous?** Then make some comment about an identifying feature—hair color, clothing, and so on. Suppose the student's name is Linda Smith: **Regardez Linda. Linda porte une jupe rouge.** (Point to the skirt.) **C'est une jupe rouge? Oui, c'est une jupe rouge.** (Point out other red things.) **Cela est rouge, et ça aussi. Alors, comment s'appelle la fille qui porte une jupe rouge?** Students answer with the student's name. Expand each response: **Oui, Linda est l'étudiante qui porte une jupe rouge.**
- *Ask the class to point out a student with the characteristics you announce.* **Montrez-moi une fille (étudiante) aux cheveux blonds.** (Use mime techniques to illustrate the meaning of **montrez.**) All students need to do is to point to a woman with blond hair (there may be several). The instructor picks one of them and asks the student's name. Then the procedure continues as in the preceding paragraph.

Use both procedures, switching back and forth from one to the other. Suppose, for example, that we already know Linda Smith as **la fille qui porte une jupe rouge;** you can then ask if there is another student in the class with a red skirt. If there is, then that student's name is learned together with some other detail. Laurie, who is wearing a red skirt, may also be wearing a white pullover sweater (**un pull blanc**).

With this technique, you can usually introduce at least twenty new words in a fifteen-minute activity. Make sure the class understands by using frequent review questions that require only the student's name as answer: **Qui porte une jupe rouge dans la classe?** and so on. Remember that the goal of Stage 1 activities is to give students the opportunity to interpret meaning by using key words and context.

After a day or two, begin to write the words on the board. Adjectives can be in either masculine or feminine form, as they occur in conversation; nouns might be written with **un** or **une.** If students are particularly knowledgeable about grammar, write the adjectives on the board in double form: **vert/verte** or **vert(e).** Students should copy these words in their vocabulary notebooks.

Picture File Input

The use of a Picture File (PF) makes the introduction of new vocabulary and structures an exciting experience and facilitates acquisition of the words. The PF should be used for full, rich input instead of the presentation of single words or structures. Most instructors make extensive use of their PF both for presentations and for later review while introducing a new **Activité.**

In Stage 1, the techniques are essentially the same as those outlined earlier. Instead of describing the students themselves, use pictures from your PF. Show people of different ages and physical characteristics. Describe a picture: **Voici la photo d'une très jolie fille. Elle a les cheveux noirs.** Then give the picture to a student and say **Maintenant Mike a la photo d'une jolie fille aux cheveux noirs.** Introduce a new picture, using the same technique, then review: **Et qui a la photo d'une jeune fille aux cheveux noirs?** Continue introducing new key words with each picture and reviewing old ones until about half the students are holding a picture. The activity begins to resemble a low-pressure memory game, since students have only to reply with names, but students find it interesting, and they also get intensive input and learn the names of their classmates.

Mix questions about the pictures with questions about the students themselves. Example: **Qui a la photo d'un homme qui porte un pantalon blanc? (Gene) Oui, c'est vrai. Gene a la photo d'un homme qui porte un pantalon blanc. Qui dans la classe porte aussi un pantalon blanc? (Laura).**

The use of a PF allows you to introduce words for items not readily available in class. They also can provide concrete images and are interesting to students, both of which hasten the acquisition process.

Expansion Techniques in Stage 1

Many Natural Approach instructors expand what students say. For example, if the instructor asks **Qui porte une jupe rouge?** and students answer **Marge,** the logical expansion is **Oui, c'est vrai. Marge porte une jupe rouge.** The expansion is easily understood because of its discourse position, and it adds considerable input. This expansion may then be followed by another question related to the first. **Est-ce que la jupe de Marge est courte?** Students answer **oui.** The expansion is **Oui, sa jupe est courte. Elle n'est pas longue,** and so forth.

Here are some other examples of expansion to be used in Stage 1.

- **Qui porte un pull blanc? (Jan) Oui, aujourd'hui Jan porte un pull blanc. Qui d'autre porte un pull aujourd'hui? (John) Oui, John porte aussi un pull. Mais le pull de Jan est blanc. Est-ce que le pull de John est aussi blanc? (non) Non, il n'est pas blanc. Il est rouge.**
- **Il y a trois garçons qui ont une barbe. D'accord?** (Hold up three fingers as you say **trois.**) **(oui) Qui a une barbe? (Paul, Al, Mike) Oui, Paul a une barbe, Al a une barbe** (pause and emphasize the word for and) **et Mike a une barbe. Il y a trois étudiants qui ont une barbe. Est-ce qu'il y a des filles qui ont une barbe?** (now students usually laugh, indicating comprehension). **Non, les femmes n'ont pas de barbe. Une femme n'a pas de barbe, n'est-ce pas?**

Note that **aussi, mais, il y a, a/ont, est/sont, aujourd'hui, il/elle, qui,** and **autre** have all been introduced and understood in context.

An expansion can also be a grammatically correct rephrasing, by the instructor, of a student's grammatically incorrect utterance. This technique permits the instructor to avoid the interruption of direct error correction during communicative activities. Usually, it comes into play as soon as the class moves beyond the beginning of the course and students are able to comprehend enough for it to be effective. For example, if a student says **Ma mère est quarante-cinq ans,** the instructor might say: **Ah, votre mère a quarante-cinq ans. Ma mère est bien plus âgée. Ma mère a soixante-deux ans.** Note that the discourse remains natural; the expansion is not an artificial correction and does not disturb the flow of the conversation. After a few weeks, you will notice students picking up on indirect corrections and muttering the correct phrase under their breath. This is a sign that they are paying attention and are acquiring French.

Input Techniques in Stage 2 (Early Speech)

After initial Stage 1 presentations of new material, Stage 2 activities encourage students to begin to use what they have heard. At this point, they are not capable of producing much of the new material in their speech spontaneously. The techniques we are about to describe are intended to provide more input and to help students speak without having to produce the words by themselves. These explanations are mostly keyed to the introductory **étapes.** Remember that these are examples. The activities we describe here can be used, with appropriate modification, in the Stage 2 phase for all new material in all chapters of *Deux mondes*.

Either/Or

The most important question technique in Stage 2 (comprehension) activities is the "choice" question. Beginning with the **Deuxième étape,** this technique figures in Pre-Text Oral Activities throughout the book. Here are some examples.

- *Numbers.* Begin by including the numbers from one to ten in your input. Count students, walking around the room pointing to each one and counting aloud slowly. Students should mostly listen, but some will want to count along, and some will say the numbers aloud. Repeat the procedure several times—go forward, and backward, always giving the same student the same number. Hold up fingers and count to ten slowly. Continue until most of the students have voluntarily joined in. Hold up fingers and ask either/or questions such as **C'est un ou trois? C'est cinq ou six?** Always expand answers: **Oui, c'est ça, c'est trois.** Continue until numbers through ten are easily recognized by most students. Ask either/or questions so that each time students respond, the response is simply a repetition of what you have just said: **C'est huit ou dix? (huit).** For some classes, you may wish to put the figures on the board as you hold up fingers and use the either/or technique to begin associating the visual with the sounds. Some instructors like to do simple arithmetic on the board, only asking that students choose answers. **Deux et deux, c'est quatre ou c'est cinq? Six moins quatre, c'est deux ou c'est trois?**
- *Colors and clothes.* Use Stage 1 questions (yes/no, names as responses) to review vocabulary, and then begin to include choice questions. **Qui porte une veste bleue? (Lucie) Est-ce que Marie porte un chemisier rouge? Et la jupe d'Anne, est-ce qu'elle est bleue ou rouge?** Students respond with a single word that you expand: **(rouge) Oui, la jupe d'Anne est rouge. Est-ce que le pantalon de Paul est rouge aussi? (non) C'est vrai. Son pantalon n'est pas rouge. Il est de quelle couleur, alors? Est-ce qu'il est noir ou bleu?** Many students will begin to speak spontaneously. Attend to the semantic correctness of the students' responses and simply expand the responses that have grammatical errors: **Est-ce que la jupe de Laura est jaune? (Non, blanc). Bravo, Marc! La jupe de Laura est blanche.**

Open Sentences

This technique encourages simple production and should be used for material with which students are familiar, since they will be asked to think of the words themselves in order to complete sentences. For example, after students can understand a number of adjectives, you might say: **Sur cette photo il y a une femme. Elle est très...** Students might say **jeune/vieille, jolie/laide, mince/grosse, grande/petite,** according to the picture and the vocabulary they have learned. Expand the responses: **Cette femme est... (jeune). Oui, c'est une femme jeune et mince, n'est-ce pas?**

Lists

Ask for a volunteer to stand up. Direct attention to the clothes the student is wearing and have the class help you compile a list of statements: **Qu'est-ce que Mike porte? (pantalon) Oui, il porte un pantalon. De quelle couleur est le pantalon de Mike? (vert) Oui, il est vert. Il porte un pantalon vert. Qu'est-ce qu'il porte d'autre? (chemise) Oui, il porte une chemise. Est-ce que la chemise de Mike est bleue? (non, jaune) Bien sûr, elle n'est pas bleue, elle est jaune.**

Interrogatives (*Qu'est-ce que? Qui? Combien?*)

Use your PF to talk about people and their appearance. Include photos of famous people. **Qui est cette personne? (Tom Cruise) Est-ce que c'est un homme ou une femme? (homme) Oui, c'est un homme. C'est un acteur, n'est-ce pas? Qu'est-ce que Tom Cruise porte sur cette photo? (pantalon) Décrivez le pantalon qu'il porte. (bleu) Oui, il est bleu. Est-ce qu'il est neuf? (vieux) Non, il n'est pas neuf, il est vieux. Est-ce qu'il porte des chaussures? (oui) Combien? Deux ou trois? (deux) Bien sûr! Oui, il porte deux chaussures. De quelle couleur sont ses chaussures? (noires) Oui, elles sont noires. Les chaussures de Tom Cruise sont noires.**

All these question techniques should be mixed naturally in the input. Whenever students give a response that is factually correct but that contains a grammatical error, attend to the semantic correctness of the response; during your reaction to the information, you can give the appropriate grammatical form as an expansion.

Association Activities

Association activities are primarily Pre-Text Oral Activities but they can be used in conjunction with various other activities in the student text. They are used to introduce new vocabulary and grammar and help to create a pleasant, relaxed atmosphere in which you and your students learn more about one another. In these activities, students can contribute vocabulary that is not in the text but that is of high interest to themselves.

The goal is to associate certain information with each student, and the instructor and students try to remember with whom each piece of information is associated. Initially, the information will be relatively simple (birthplace, place of residence, classes). As students become more advanced, however, they will need to ask for terms they do not know. In such cases, they may respond in English. The instructor then provides the French and puts the term on the board to be copied in the vocabulary notebooks. These words become a part of the active vocabulary of the class.

In the following sections, we will describe in detail how to do the association techniques we recommend as Pre-Text Oral Activities for **Chapitre 1** (aimer + infinitives) and **Chapitre 5** (passé composé). Remember that the same model can be used to introduce many areas of vocabulary, other tenses, and other grammatical structures.

1. Infinitives (*Chapitre 1*)

For this Pre-Text Oral Activity, you will ask each student to think of an activity he or she likes to do. The purpose is to learn the meaning of a large number of verbs (infinitives). To begin, write **J'aime (_____)** on the board, with your infinitive in parentheses. Let students know they each must think of something different (related activities such as to play basketball and to play football are acceptable). If someone names an activity already mentioned, indicate that it is "taken." **Ah, Jason aime faire de l'escalade, Mark. Alors, quelle est une autre activité que vous aimez faire?**

As students name activites, write the infinitive forms on the board and pronounce each word or phrase several times. (Since the activity will repeat on other days, you may prefer to use a transparency.) For example, suppose a student has said *I like to ski;* you repeat by saying **Beth aime faire du ski. Faire du ski. Elle aime faire du ski.** Write the infinitive on the board as you add questions like **Où? Où est-ce que vous aimez faire du ski? À Aspen? À Vail?** The answer should be a name (not a sentence) such as **Snow Summit.** Expand with questions like **Est-ce que Snow Summit est une bonne station de ski?** Before moving to another student, review: **Alors, qui aime faire du ski? (Beth) Oui, c'est Beth qui aime faire**

du ski. As you continue, return to Beth's answer while reviewing replies: **Qui aime faire du ski? (Beth) Oui, Beth aime faire du ski. Et qui aime faire la cuisine? (Sal) Oui, Sal aime faire la cuisine et Beth aime faire du ski.**

When you do these activities, we recommend that you use more or less complete predicates (of course, students need not). This way, students will have a chance to acquire nouns that normally accompany the verbs. In addition, it is usually easier to remember the meaning of a verb if there is a common noun associated with it. For example, students will remember **manger une glace au chocolat** more easily than just **manger** or just **glace.**

Review this activity during subsequent class periods and continue to add associations until there is a different infinitive for each student in the class. Each day, start with simple questions: **Qui aime faire du ski? (Beth) Oui, c'est Beth qui aime faire du ski. Qui aime faire la cuisine? (Sal) Oui, il aime préparer des plats italiens. Est-ce que Mike aime dormir?** Rewrite the previously reviewed predicates on the board (or show previous transparency). As you review, ask for information from students who did not give you an activity in the previous class and add their verbs to the written list. Students should copy the new infinitive phrases in their vocabulary notebooks.

During all association activities, maintain the focus on comprehension and meaning. Weave into your input questions such as **Qui aime _____? Qui n'aime pas _____? Combien de personnes aiment _____? Combien de filles aiment _____?** together with your comments. This is still a comprehension activity, but students can respond using single words, especially nouns and adjectives they have heard often enough to have acquired. You may also include simple choice questions. The point is a natural exchange in which students are not required to produce sentences or long phrases on their own. Example: **Qui aime conduire? (Jim) Jim, est-ce que vous avez une voiture? (oui) Quelle marque de voiture? (Toyota) Est-ce que Toyota est une marque française? (non) C'est une marque japonaise, n'est-ce pas? (oui) Alors, est-ce que Jim aime conduire ou est-ce qu'il aime dormir? (conduire) Est-ce qu'il a une voiture? (oui) Et sa voiture, elle est française ou japonaise?**

Gradually, give students the opportunity to produce the new verb forms in whole-class discussions. Ask questions exactly as in the preceding activities, but this time integrate the question **Qu'est-ce que ___ aime faire?** For example: **Qui aime faire la cuisine? (Sal) Oui, Sal aime faire la cuisine. Et Monique, est-ce qu'elle aime faire la cuisine? (non) Non? Alors, qu'est-ce qu'elle aime faire? (courir) C'est vrai, Monique? Vous aimez courir? Vous courez pour faire de l'exercice? (oui) Oui, elle aime courir pour faire de l'exercice. Quand est-ce qu'elle aime courir? (matin) Ah, le matin. Elle aime courir le matin.**

2. *Passé composé* Forms (*Chapitre 5*)

This activity introduces past tense forms and adverbs for past time. Because the idea is to help students develop awareness of past tense markers, the activity is intended to elicit mainly familiar verbs, to keep the focus on the past tense meaning. However, some new verbs will probably be introduced. Most forms in the input will be in first and third person, because these are the most common forms and the forms students will find the most useful. However, you need not artificially restrict your speech; if the context is clear enough, the use of plural forms will not impede comprehension. Students will quickly grasp the notion that the past tense requires compound forms, but past participle forms and the use of **être** or **avoir** will be acquired only over time, after students have had multiple opportunities to hear and use them in communicative contexts.

Follow the same procedure as described above for introducing infinitives. Write **La semaine dernière, j'ai ___** on the board and list one thing you did. Use a calendar page (or dates) to indicate that you are talking about the past and to explain the meaning of **la semaine dernière.** Then have students name one (different) activity they did last week. Answers will probably include present tense forms and incorrect forms such as **j'ai allé.** Some may need to reply in English. Focus on the communication and write all activities correctly on the board or transparency, with subjects: **Louis a étudié, Patricia est allée au cinéma, Lawrence s'est couché à trois heures du matin.**

When you have accumulated several activities from your students, review with simple questions. **Qui est allé au cinéma? (Patricia) Est-ce que Louis s'est couché à trois heures du matin? (non) Non? Il ne s'est pas couché à trois heures du matin? Je me suis trompé? Alors, qui s'est couché à trois heures du matin?** Gradually increase the list, reviewing from time to time. After you complete the list and do a final review, erase the subjects (or cover, if using a transparency) and have students try to recall who did each activity.

After the intensive input already described, point out that most of the verbs are used with **avoir,** and only a few with **être.** Clearly indicate which verbs are conjugated with **être** and demonstrate how to form their past participles. Here are ways to provide input with other forms: Use the list to ask how many people in class did the various activities last week (**vous** questions) and ask for a show of hands; have volunteers ask you if you did the activities (**Est-ce que vous avez étudié? Est-ce que vous êtes allé[e] au cinéma?**) and answer truthfully (**Oui, j'ai... , non, je n'ai pas,** and so on); describe what both you and the class did or didn't do. (**Nous avons fait des courses. Nous n'avons pas vu** *Mighty Aphrodite.*)

Chapter 7
Using the White Pages

In this chapter we discuss in some detail the contents of the communicative activities in *Deux mondes*, including the vocabulary and art displays, the **Activités,** and the variety of other features that appear regularly in the main section of the book. We include a description of each feature, along with teaching suggestions. Since pre-text and extra-text oral input activities figure heavily in the background of *Deux mondes* and are often mentioned in this Instructor's Manual and elsewhere, we believe that it is important to begin the chapter with a brief discussion of the Instructor's Edition of *Deux mondes*.

The Instructor's Edition of *Deux mondes*

The Instructor's Edition (IE) contains the student text pages of *Deux mondes*, along with detailed marginal notes to use when teaching the content of each page. There is a margin note for every vocabulary art display and **Activité,** every grammar explanation, and for many of the grammar exercises. The margin notes also include suggestions for extra oral input and games, indicated by **AS** (**Activités supplémentaires**), as well as extenders to grammar exercises and oral input with structures, indicated by **ES** (**Exercices supplémentaires**).

One could say that the Instructor's Edition is really a manual on how to teach with *Deux mondes*. This does not mean that all those who use *Deux mondes* choose to follow the "manual," because *Deux mondes* is easily used with many styles and approaches to teaching. However, most instructors find the IE margin notes very helpful in making lesson plans because they indicate what new vocabulary is present in each **Activité,** contain a system of cross-referencing for using the **Grammaire,** and can be of real help when preparing to teach an **Activité** or a reading or to introduce a grammar explanation.

For those wishing to establish a Natural Approach classroom, the Instructor's Manual is invaluable. The **Mise en train** activities that appear at the end of each chapter allow the instructor to make sure that all important new vocabulary topics are covered in input activities before students use that material in the book. The margin notes are filled with suggestions for providing rich and meaningful oral input, for integrating language teaching with culture, and for finding teaching resources.

The Instructor's Edition is available at no cost to all instructors in programs that have adopted *Deux mondes*. To obtain a copy, contact the McGraw-Hill sales representative in your area or see the McGraw-Hill Website at **http://www.mhhe.com.**

The Vocabulary Displays

Each thematic or topical section in every chapter of *Deux mondes* begins with a visual display depicting new vocabulary and grammatical structures that will be prominent in the **Activités** for that section. Many displays are also planned to facilitate or stimulate cultural discussion. The Instructor's Edition notes accompanying the displays include suggestions for their use. Note that you may obtain from McGraw-Hill a set of overhead transparency masters that reproduce the displays. Many instructors use these in addition to the text to provide a change of pace.

If the instructor has done the **Mise en train** activities from the Instructor's Edition, most of the vocabulary in a display will have already been covered during the Pre-Text Oral Activities, thus allowing the displays to serve as a springboard for review and further input. If the instructor has chosen not to do the **Mise en train** activities, the display allows the instructor to make the initial vocabulary presentation for the section in a communicative context. Whichever way the instructor has chosen to use the book, the vocabulary displays make it easier to provide good listening input and to develop cultural insights and knowledge.

When teaching the display, first describe one or two of the drawings and intersperse questions and comments to retain students' attention and keep them involved: **Ce jeune homme aime faire une** promenade à la campagne. Moi, j'aime faire une promenade au parc. Et vous? Qui dans la classe aime faire une promenade?

As you progress to more drawings, include frequent review of what you have already said. For example, give a description and ask the class to identify which drawing you are talking about. For new material, first restrict yourself to questions that require only simple answers (**oui, non,** a name, or a known word): **Est-ce que cette jeune fille fait de l'escalade? Quel étudiant dans cette classe aime faire de l'escalade?** When students seem to comprehend the new material, ask questions in a way that makes it easy for them to begin to use the material themselves (choice questions): **Est-ce que Charles aime lire des magazines ou un bon livre? Qu'est-ce que Raoul aime faire le samedi soir? Est-ce qu'il aime aller au cinéma ou est-ce qu'il préfère conduire sa voiture?**

Remember that in the Natural Approach, the purpose of the display is to provide input. Students will pick up pronunciation and meaning of the new words indirectly from oral input activities where they are used in interesting contexts. Having students pronounce a list of new words removes those words from meaningful context and actually slows acquisition by causing students to focus on isolated form and sounds. The feeling of constraint this can cause is also detrimental to acquisition, since it interferes with the close attention students need to pay to input. For students and instructors who would like such practice, the laboratory audio program includes an audio reading of the **Vocabulaire** for each chapter, and the tape program and *Cahier d'exercices* offer a phonetics program that is both thorough and easy to use.

The Oral Activities

All the White Page activities are labeled by type at the start of each activity (**Récit, Ça fait penser,** and so on). In this section, you will find a description of each type, with examples keyed to specific activities in the fith edition. Where appropriate, we make suggestions for teaching the activity. Remember that these are only suggestions, techniques that have worked well for us. We hope that they help you better understand the intentions behind the activities, supply ideas as needed, and that they are useful in triggering your own teaching ingenuity.

Activity Types

Associations

Some **Associations** are partner activities; others may be input activities that are intended to be led by the instructor. Unlike **Définition** activities, they ask students to make different types of associations, using popular stereotypical "knowledge" or solid factual knowledge. Whether for partner-talk or whole-class discussion, they can be used to generate a great deal of input. Here are examples of the most common types of **Associations:**

1. *Sorting information:* In **Activité 12, Chapitre 3,** and **Activité 4, Chapitre 14,** students are asked to arrange a set of statements into "portraits" of individuals based on stereotypical assumptions. Students usually enjoy activities of this type and end up disagreeing in a friendly way about how to phrase at least one or two of the statements. We suggest that the instructor do the activity with the class before assigning it, so that students hear all the sounds and can understand the words. Partners should be given about 10 minutes for the activity, and the instructor should plan another 5–10 minutes for a follow-up discussion, which may uncover even more differences of opinion in the class.
2. *Matching based on factual knowledge:* These activities ask students to make associations in cases such as matching names for workers with the place in which their work is done, determining the dietary needs for people in different states and situations, or identifying members of groups. **Activité 4, Chapitre 2,** for instance, lists activities such as **faire de la gym** and names of places. If students know the vocabulary, the activity can immediately be assigned for partner discussion, and the instructor can lead a general discussion and input session to follow up the activity. However, **Activité 4, Chapitre 8,** should be approached as an input activity because it contains many new cognate words. Although students can understand the new vocabulary in context, they have

not yet had sufficient exposure to produce or pronounce the terminology on their own. That activity can be very short but can also provide an excellent opportunity to use the maps in the book as well as giving comprehensible input.

3. *Matching based on stereotypes:* **Activité 5, Chapitre 5,** asks students to identify the probable activities of several celebrities. The instructor should first introduce the celebrities and explain the activity. Next, we suggest that the instructor read the predicates and let the class name the appropriate celebrity. When everyone understands the activity and the words, it is assigned to partners. The decisions students make will be based on their stereotyical views about what is required for success in the fields represented by the celebrities. This means that students may need to give reasons for their views, and differences of opinion may engender further conversation. During follow-up, the instructor should do the activity again with the class, ostensibly to see if all the answers are still the same as the first time and, if not, discover what prompted the change in opinion.

Casse-tête

Activities in this category include riddles and puzzles that can be solved through reasoning logically and making use of clues that are provided. The riddles are Stage 2 input activities, since they use topical vocabulary and structures intensively and are led by the instructor, who guides the discussion. A good example is **Activité 11, Chapitre 4,** where students listen to riddles and identify the household tasks they describe. Besides the topical vocabulary, object pronouns are used naturally in the input. The instructor might also put students in pairs to ask each other the riddles in the book and others that they may make up. Another option is to form groups of three, in which two people listen and answer with books closed while the third person reads riddles from the book.

Most puzzles are similar in form to **Activité 4, Chapitre 5, Le cadeau d'Adrienne Petit.** They are Stage 3 activities because students will need to engage in free discussion that goes beyond the language in the activity. Here the instructor presents the problem and gives the clues, making sure they are understood by everyone. Students then work in pairs to figure out the answer. There is no right answer; the only criterion is that any answer must be logically defensible. During the follow-up discussion, differences of opinion will probably arise, as they will during the partner work, engendering much discussion of the topic by the students.

Dans le monde francophone

These activities are built around authentic, unedited materials that contain unfamiliar words and structures, which should not be taught as active vocabulary. Instead, the instructor is asked to encourage students to apply the reading skills they already know and to learn new ones. The level and function of the activities vary according to the text, so no one instructional method can apply. However, the format of these activities remains the same throughout the text. **Activité 5, Chapitre 5,** is an example of a typical **Dans le monde francophone** activity from the early chapters. Students are asked to use the content of the realia to answer questions or solve a problem.

When introducing the activity, the instructor should ask questions to draw the class into the authentic material in a nondemanding way. **Ces trois villas sont près de Marseille, dans le sud de France. Ils sont dans trois villages, Gémenos... Une villa a une piscine. Est-ce la villa à Gémenos ou celle à Cassis? Où est la villa qui est la plus chère?** After students have had a chance to review the content of the realia and have answered the preview questions, the instructor reads the statements, and the students reply. They do not have to produce language to do this activity, but the instructor may invite the class to think of other statements to ask about the houses, or may have partners do the activity after class discussion.

Many **Dans le monde francophone** activities require that students use the information to perform a task. For example, to do **Activité 11, Chapitre 11,** students must understand the messages in the realia in order to name the misdeeds of those who fail to follow good etiquette. Even at advanced levels, it is always important to focus on message rather than details. The authentic materials provide a good opportunity for students to practice the reading skills they already know and to learn new ones. The use of each authentic text should be a reminder that by starting with the larger aspects of the text, one can often reason one's way to a much fuller understanding than was immediately apparent at the outset.

Définitions

Définitions are Stage 2 input activities in which students match definitions or descriptions to vocabulary items. They occur throughout the book and are intended to develop the ability to explain and to use circumlocution. The instructor introduces the activity and acquaints the class with the choices they may use to answer. In most cases, there is one right answer, but occasionally this may not be true. The instructor reads the definitions; then everyone responds with the answer. When the instructor verifies that answer, students self-check what they have said. After the activity, the instructor may add other definitions. Many instructors assign the **Définitions** to partners after the whole-class input activity. (See **Act. 12, Ch. 1,** and **Act. 1, Ch. 11,** for examples.)

Dialogue

These Stage 2 input activities occur in the early chapters in *Deux mondes.* They provide useful contextualized input and practice of conventional polite exchanges. They come in two forms.

- *Open Dialogues:* These are written in familiar language so that students can talk about themselves with others in class. Each open dialogue is written so that students need only supply personal facts as they read the statements from the book aloud. They do not have to produce the language themselves. Instead, they receive initial aural input from hearing the instructor model the activity and then both written and oral input as they do the dialogue with their partners. We suggest that the instructor model the dialogue two or three times with volunteers from the class. (See **Act. 2, Ch. 1,** for an example.)

- *Model Dialogues:* These are third-person dialogues among the *Deux mondes* characters. They contain models of language that students might want to use in typical exchanges with others. The instructor should model the dialogue alone, clarifying any unfamiliar language as it arises. Next, the instructor should model the dialogue by reading it with the help of a volunteer, then exchanging roles with the volunteer and repeating it at least once more. Thereafter, it is assigned to partners, who are instructed to play the roles, then exchange roles and repeat the dialogue. Students should be encouraged to use the "read, look up and say" method so that they look their partners in the eye and say each statement with as natural an inflection as possible. Suggestions are made for variations of student practice in the Instructor's Edition margin notes. (See **Act. 10, Ch. 2,** for an example.)

Discussion

Discussions are oral input activities that can also be used for student interactions if the instructor so chooses. In Stage 2 **Discussions,** students listen and read as the instructor works with the activity in an input session. Afterward, partners may be assigned to do the activity together. These Stage 2 partner exchanges center on the students themelves. They will feel "real," but they involve no real production of language; instead, students use the words provided in the activity. (See **Acts. 4** and **5, Ch. 1,** for examples.)

In Stage 3 **Discussions,** input is also the primary goal; however, the activity is also planned to elicit free-ranging student-talk, and the topics are not always personal as they are in the Stage 2 **Discussions.** (See **Act. 12, Ch. 1,** as an example.)

- *Stage 2 activities* (see **Acts. 4** and **5, Ch. 1**): The instructor reads a statement and reacts to the options that go with that statement: «En été, je préfère sortir avec mes amis.» Oui, c'est vrai. Je préfère sortir en été et j'adore sortir avec mes amis. «En été, je préfère rester à la maison et lire.» Ah non! Pas moi! En été, je préfère la nature et le sport. J'aime rester à la maison et lire en hiver. Students are involved in the teacher-talk as usual during input sessions, but the students mainly look at the items and listen to the instructor. The input contains many words from the topical vocabulary of the section in which the activity occurs. Afterward, most instructors prefer to assign the activity to partners. Students are invited to add to the options but should react to all those in the book. Note that for many **Discussions,** the conversational **Modèle** follows the input activity, as in **Activité 5, Chapitre 1,** and is accompanied by **Exprime-toi!** to provide vocabulary options so that students can express themselves more fully.

- *Stage 3 activities* (see **Act. 12, Ch. 10**): The instructor introduces the activity, including the **Modèle,** to illustrate what students are to do. Thereafter, the instructor discusses each **Situation** so that unfamiliar language can be explained. The instructor leads a class discussion of possible solutions to the situations and may need to write useful new vocabulary on the board. Afterward, the activity is assigned to partners or small groups for discussion. Students can consult the board for vocabulary if needed. As a follow-up, the instructor reviews the **Situations** and surveys what solutions have been proposed.

Échanges

These Stage 2 partner activities ask students to exchange brief pieces of information about their preferences, habits, activities, and so forth. In general, they provide good input and require little production but allow some real expression of ideas and often stimulate discussion beyond that required by the activity. *Échanges* may take the form of questions and answers or may ask students to make a statement and then ask for their partner's reactions.

- **Activité 3, Chapitre 1:** This activity is based on choices that give intensive input with the target vocabulary of the section. The instructor may do the items before assigning the activity to partners to remind students of the vocabulary and its pronunciation. The instructor should certainly do a few items to demonstrate what students are to do. Students need produce language only if they wish.
- As students become more advanced, the input becomes more complex. In **Activité 6, Chapitre 5,** for example, the input is with expression of past time using the **passé composé.** Students will need to produce only a small amount of original language since they can pick up the new structures from the questions. In **Activité 4, Chapitre 6,** however, the exchanges remain short, but students are asked to add explanations to their answers, hence to create new language. For both these activities, the instructor's introductory and follow-up input will intensively use the target structures or vocabulary.

Enquête

Enquêtes are Stage 2 input activities that can be used for partner discussion after the initial exercise has been completed. They are information surveys about the students themselves. Usually they ask for factual information, although occasionally they ask for personal opinions. The instructor reads the survey items aloud, explaining and clarifying as needed, while students write or check off answers; usually answers are restricted to **oui/non** or **vrai/faux.** The instructor then does a class survey, counting answers and putting them on the board. For variation, a volunteer may be allowed to lead the survey after the class has become familiar with the procedure. After the answer survey, the activity may then be assigned to partners or small groups in which students compare and discuss their replies. (See **Act. 13, Ch. 1; Act. 7, Ch. 2;** and **Act. 15, Ch. 4;** for examples.)

Entretien

In general, the **Entretiens** are Stage 3 partner interviews that require production. Their content grows progressively more complex as students advance linguistically. However, they are always written so that student answers can be fairly simple unless students choose to add more. The instructor goes over the items with the class in the beginning to make sure that students understand the questions and any new vocabulary needed to do the activity. Next, students work in pairs. We suggest that the two partners answer and discuss each question before moving on to the next one. However, some instructors prefer to arrange a more formal interview session, in which Partner A actually interviews Partner B, asking all the questions and including other questions that expand answers or clarify information. At the end of this interview, Partner B then repeats the process and interviews Partner A. Later, each student reports on the interview by writing a composition or telling another person what the interviewee said. At times, you may find it useful to select only one or two questions from an interview, rather than assigning the entire activity. In whole-class follow-up discussion, survey what students or their partners said earlier, expanding their answers, making comments, and so forth. (See **Act. 12, Ch. 2; Act. 7, Ch. 10;** and **Act. 6, Ch. 13;** for examples.)

Interro

Interros are Stage 2 input activities that are based on a chart or drawings. Students hear considerable input as the instructor presents the activity, and then they have an opportunity to practice asking and answering questions based on those facts. Some **Interros** are designed to allow students to include personalized questions. Before the instructor assigns an activity to partners, it is important to ask a large number of questions about the information in the visual. For example, **Activité 6, Chapitre 1,** includes detailed but simple questions such as the following: **Qui a 32 ans? Est-ce que Charles est lycéen ou journaliste? Qui est étudiante à Paris? Quelle personne aime nager dans la mer? Est-ce qu'Adrienne aime nager le samedi ou le dimanche?** This familiarizes students with all the details, reminds them of question forms, and allows the instructor to explain new words. The instructor should write on the board an example of each new type of question during the input session for use as reference during the activity.

After introductory input, the activity is assigned to partners. Students should be encouraged to go beyond the **Modèle** and ask other types of questions. Afterward, ask more questions or invite the class to ask you questions about the information. (See **Act. 10, Ch. 8,** for another example.)

Ordre logique

All activities classified as **Ordre logique** are designed to produce Stage 2 input. They focus on new topical vocabulary and structures while also fitting logically into the thematic context of the particular chapter or section. In general, there is a correct order for the items, although some may be debatable. The **Ordre logique** activities are especially useful for intensive input with predicates, as in **Activité 5, Chapitre 2,** where students put verbs for personal hygiene and daily routine into a typical chronological order. **(Je me réveille. Je me lève. Puis, je m'habille.)** Often, they generate input with topical idiomatic vocabulary such as the steps one takes when renting a lodging. (See **Act. 7, Ch. 4.**)

To do an **Ordre logique** activity, the instructor leads the discussion, first reading the items in the list aloud to make sure that students understand them. Next, the instructor guides the discussion: **Quelle est la deuxième démarche? Est-ce qu'on cherche des appartements dans le journal, ou est-ce qu'on signe le contrat?** From time to time, the instructor reviews: **Alors, la première démarche, c'est... , la deuxième... et... Maintenant, quelle est la sixième démarche?** Finally, the instructor may ask the class to help list the steps: **Alors, la première démarche... (On décide dans quel quartier on voudrait vivre.)** By this time, students should be so familiar with all the steps that production should be no problem, especially since the class should do this as a group, and no one individual is put on the spot. As a follow-up, the instructor might ask the class to look at the activity from another angle and to give the order in which a very disorganized person might perform some of the steps. **(Il signe le contrat, puis il visite l'appartement.)**

Récit

Récits are "story boards" of 8–12 drawings that appear in almost every chapter. They are Stage 3 activities, since ultimately they ask students to develop and tell a story. Each **Récit** has a functional speech focus such as narration in present tense or the expression of future time. The focus is indicated in a printed context or by a **Modèle** like the one in **Activité 11, Chapitre 2: «Qu'est-ce que Clarisse va faire vendredi prochain?»**

How you elect to use the **Récits** depends on your particular class and its needs. Some instructors describe a few frames in detail on one day, repeat that and add a few more on the next day, and so on until the story is gradually complete. Another method is for the instructor to use the frames to narrate a more or less skeletal story on the first day, then retell it with added details the next day, and other days thereafter. With either method, time should be allowed so that students get to work in pairs with the frames each day they are discussed by the instructor. The final goal is for each student to be able to narrate the entire story to a partner. This usually occurs only after everyone has practiced the various parts with one (or different partners). It is best to do the final narration with yet another new partner so that both partners hear a fresh version.

Here is an example of introductory input for **Activité 11** in **Chapitre 2.** As students look at the book: **Cette jeune fille s'appelle Clarisse. Elle est étudiante à l'université. Voilà toutes les activités que Clarisse va faire vendredi. Regardez le premier dessin. Sur la première image, c'est le matin. Quelle** heure est-il? (7 h 15) Alors, vendredi prochain, Clarisse va se lever à sept heures et quart. Qu'est-ce que vous pensez? Est-ce qu'elle va avoir beaucoup d'énergie? (non) Est-ce qu'elle va être un peu fatiguée? (oui) Intersperse personal questions such as: **Dans notre classe, combien de personnes se lèvent à 7 h 15? Est-ce qu'il y a quelqu'un qui se lève avant sept heures? Qui aime dormir tard le matin? Qui aime dormir jusqu'à dix heures? onze heures?** Continue to introduce the drawings one by one, reviewing previous ones. As you introduce each one, write the infinitives or the entire sentences on the board (students copy them in their vocabulary notebooks).

There are many options from which to choose when students begin to do the activity. For example, partners can brainstorm statements that fit each frame, or they can ask each other questions: **Qu'est-ce que Clarisse va faire à une heure? Où est-ce que Clarisse va déjeuner? Avec qui... ?** Note that during most **Récits,** there may be a need for new vocabulary. We provide some words as **Vocabulaire utile,** but classes will generate their own words as well. These should be added to students' vocabulary notebooks as new class vocabulary. For a culminating activity, after you and the class have worked with all the frames, you might help students write a class composition based on the drawings or have the class tell you the story as you write it on the board.

Récits allow students to receive a great deal of input and to practice thinking through an extended narrative, a story, in French. Keep in mind that these activities are not grammar exercises and that students will gain much by being allowed to speak freely, even though they make errors. The **Récits** are flexible and can be used in other chapters simply by changing the context. **«Qu'est-ce que Clarisse va faire vendredi prochain?»** can easily become **«Si Clarisse était libre la semaine prochaine, qu'est-ce qu'elle ferait?»** or **«Qu'est-ce que Clarisse a fait vendredi dernier?»** Récits can also be used for writing activities, which the instructor collects for grading and correction of grammatical errors.

Situations

These Stage 3 activities involve three or more students. The goal is to allow students to engage in free conversation within the "reality" of the fictional context of a particular situation. They consist of a description of the particular situation, followed by a few introductory lines that begin a possible dialogue arising from the situation. Most **Situations** in the book allow students to apply what they have learned in a simulation of a typical life situation. For example, **Activité 10, Chapitre 12,** asks students to play a typical scene with a doctor hearing a patient's symptoms. The **Situation (Act. 5, Ch. 14),** however, is a cultural awareness activity. Students are asked to use their work in a previous activity to play the roles of immigrants who are discussing the hardships of leaving their homeland.

A **Situation** can be successful and entertaining. Make sure that everyone understands the roles they are to perform and that they know enough language to accomplish the assigned task. We suggest that you ask the class to imagine a few things each character might say before assigning the **Situation,** perhaps writing at least some of the suggestions for each role on the chalkboard for reference. Encourage students to expand the role imaginatively as much as they can. As a follow-up, we suggest that you ask for volunteers to perform the role-play for the class. You might also assign students to repeat the same **Situation** with new partners, so that they can experience new language and points of view while still working within a familiar framework. The more often students play a role, the more they know about it, and the more they can uphold it. You may also wish to assign skits based on these activities.

Sondage

Sondages are input activities that take an opinion survey on nonpersonal topics such as an environmental or political question, or test one's knowledge about a topic or an issue. The instructor introduces the activity and reads the items aloud, explaining as needed. You may then opt to have students read the items silently and write their answers, or simply have them answer while you're reading the items aloud.

- **Activité 8** in **Chapitre 8** is an example of a self-test based on factual information, and it has fixed answers. Read the answers aloud after students have completed the survey, taking a count of how many got them right. Alternatively, students might be paired to discuss their responses together before you read the answers to the class. Such activities do not lend themselves to much discussion.

- **Activité 8** in **Chapitre 11** asks students to make a value judgment about what should not be shown on television. It is followed with vocabulary suggestions and a conversational model. This is an excellent topic for discussion and students now have enough linguistic ability to enjoy it. The instructor will need only to introduce the activity and facilitate the follow-up.

Other Communicative Activities in *Deux mondes*

Activités Supplémentaires (AS)

The **Activités Supplémentaires (AS)** are optional activities that are found only in the margin notes of the Instructor's Edition. They are intended to enhance class discussion of a topic or to suggest activities for additional practice of particular vocabulary and structures, as in **AS 6,** placed with **Activités 5** and **6** in **Chapitre 1.** Students are asked to say more about what they like to do, giving additional practice in a conversational setting. **AS** suggestions can also be for Stage 3 activities that extend the communicative nature of a particular activity. Later in **Chapitre 1,** for instance, **AS 14** extends **Activité 16** by asking students to create original ads using those in the realia as models. It then proposes that the student-produced ads be distributed for use in open discussions by small groups or partners.

Allons plus loin!

The **Allons plus loin!** activities are also optional "trailers" to other activities. They differ from **À vous la parole!** in that they usually propose slightly more complex projects and conversations among students. They usually add enrichment or at least a new approach to the subject of the activity that they follow. At early levels, they may ask students to venture into giving a simple explanation that calls for more linguistic creativity than usual (see **Act. 14, Ch. 1**). As students grow more advanced, there are projects to be done in small groups. The **Allons plus loin!** following **Activité 5, Chapitre 8,** for example, is a group writing project, and the exercise that follows **Activité 1, Chapitre 10,** calls for situational role-play. Techniques and methodology for these activities vary depending on the activity and are accompanied by margin notes in the Instructor's Edition.

À vous d'écrire

The functional writing task at the end of every chapter in *Deux mondes* is thematically related to the chapter. It is planned to encourage students to draw on the primary vocabulary and most prominent structures of that chapter. In **Chapitre 11,** for example, students are asked to apply what they have been discussing in the chapter in order to hypothesize, using the present conditional tense, what they would do to help market some proposed new products. The focus is on meaning in the **À vous d'écrire** writing activities, although the instructor should correct (or have students correct) grammar errors.

For this particular task, the instructor might introduce the activity and read the example aloud, then assign it in class for partners to discuss. At the end of the discussion time, students could then be given a few minutes to jot down the products they intend to write about and some ideas from the discussion. The composition should be prepared at home, and class notes should be used only to prepare the content.

Some instructors prefer to correct errors themselves. Many report success by simply marking them for students to look up and correct. Still others allow class time for correction of an early draft by a fellow student (peer), before the writer prepares a final copy to hand in. How one approaches the teaching of writing in French depends on both program and instructor goals. Our own wish is to present a writing task that "works," that can elicit a clear piece of expository writing focused on communicating a message, and that requires students to use language that is going to be useful to them as they move toward proficiency. The resulting composition can be used to call attention to areas of linguistic or orthographic weakness. However, language errors that do not interfere with message, in our opinion, need to be noted and corrected but should count less than those important to the message, such as the correct formation of conditional tense forms to communicate hypotheses.

À vous la parole!

This feature occurs from time to time as an extension of the main activities. It is optional and encourages students to approach the topic of an activity in a more personal manner or to see its content in a different light. Some **À vous la parole!** suggestions merely turn an input activity into a partner activity, as in **Activité 13, Chapitre 1,** which asks students to compare their responses to a survey in the main activity to their partner's. Other **À vous la parole!** activities propose projects. For instance in **Chapitre 5,** students are asked to prepare a persuasive argument in a class competition (see **Act. 11, Ch. 5**). The **À vous la parole!** feature also appears after most **Lectures.** In such cases, it may encourage partner or group discussions (**Chapitre 6**), creative language activities such as restating prose in dialogue form (**Chapitre 5**), and so on. There is no one particular method for this type of activity. The Instructor's Edition margin notes include teaching suggestions. As a rule, **À vous la parole!** generates both output (student-talk) and input, the latter usually occurring during follow-up activities when the instructor leads a discussion to survey what students have done during the activity.

Ça fait penser

These boxes contain facts taken from the public domain—from printed materials and the Web. The information is chosen to add an extra dimension to the content of the **Activités,** readings, or other features in the book. They enter the book in **Chapitre 7** because they are taken directly from the sources and contain unfamiliar language that students at earlier levels might find too difficult to read for pleasure. The instructor should read these pieces of information aloud and explain them if needed, in conjunction with doing the related activity. Extend the discussion by asking if students agree, if the same statistics apply to their home country, if this is how they would do things, and so forth. (See **Ça fait penser, Ch. 7,** near **Act. 10** and **Ch. 8,** near **Act. 12** for typical examples.)

Cliquez là!

The first **Cliquez là!** box appears with **Activité 13** in the **Deuxième étape** and reappears frequently throughout the remainder of the book. This feature proposes an interesting topic that is related to an activity, **Info,** or other feature for students to look up on the Internet by using a Francophone search engine. **Cliquez là!** is optional, but we hope that you will use it regularly. The instructor should work with the class from the beginning to learn to use the Web on their own. Some students have reported that looking at Francophone websites has greatly facilitated their acquisition of French and stimulated their interest in both French and the Francophone world. We suggest that the instructor exhibit home pages in class (onscreen if possible) or use handouts of photocopies of Web pages from *Voilà, Nomade,* and other Francophone engines. Work with students to recognize the many cognate words and to come to recognize important terms like **Bienvenue, page d'accueil,** and **retour.** Ask students to bring Web terms to class, share interesting URLs, and so on. (See **Act. 9, Ch. 7,** for another example.)

Espace vidéo

Espace vidéo occurs at the end of each chapter and refers to the *Deux mondes* functional video, which contains scenarios that relate thematically to the chapter and functionally to its goals as stated on the opening page.

Exprime-toi!

This small, colored heading is placed near designated activities to indicate supplementary vocabulary that can be used when doing these activities. This feature provides idioms and current expressions that students enjoy using to express their feelings while talking. The instructor decides if the **Exprime-toi!** words become a part of the chapter vocabulary for which students are responsible. (See **Act. 5, Ch. 1,** and **Act. 15, Ch. 4,** for examples.)

Info

Infos are titled according to the thrust of the content. **Info: Société** refers to issues related to how people function in society; **Info: Arts et lettres** includes articles about artists and their arts; and **Info: Vie quotidienne** contains interesting information about everyday life. For a fuller discussion on teaching reading, see "Teaching Reading and Writing" in Chapter 4 of the Instructor's Manual.

La langue en mouvement

La langue en mouvement begins in **Chapitre 3,** after students have had time to acquire enough language to begin to appreciate the fact that French is and has always been a dynamic and changing language. These pieces often intend to show how French is changing, but they also provide a source of information that can help students appreciate the origins of the English language and the many cognates and borrowed words that English shares with French. For teaching suggestions, see "Teaching Reading and Writing" in Chapter 4.

Les francophones sur le vif

These short articles are primarily composed of the answers made by various Francophone respondents to a question posed by the authors. They demonstrate a more idiomatic language, since they are direct quotes, as well as fresh and varied points of view. Each article is accompanied by a photograph of the speaker. See "Teaching Reading and Writing" in Chapter 4 for a specific discussion on teaching materials like **Les francophones sur le vif.**

Lecture

The **Lecture** is a longer reading at the end of each chapter. **Lectures** are very different; some are pieces of literature (see **Ch. 7**); others retell fiction or historical fact (see **Chs. 5** and **6**); some are author-written fiction (see **Ch. 2**); and so forth. All are followed by comprehension activities and, frequently, by **Allons plus loin!** or **À vous la parole!** For a complete description of teaching **Lectures,** see "Teaching Reading and Writing," Chapter 4.

Maintenant, c'est à vous!

Maintenant, c'est à vous! follows some input activities and indicates that an optional second part can be added for partner talk. At times this feature includes optional supplementary vocabulary and a **Modèle** (see **Act. 1, Ch. 4**).

Vocabulaire utile

This small feature reminds students of the low-frequency vocabulary they have encountered or supplies them with new terms that are needed to do the activity. In the **Récit (Act. 15, Ch. 10),** the words **aquarium, marché,** and **poisson** are not essential to doing the activity but enhance it and make what students say feel more natural to them. Usually, **Vocabulaire utile** appears with **Récits** and other art-based activities.

World Wide Web Icon

At the end of every chapter, students are reminded of the McGraw-Hill *Deux mondes* website (**www.mhhe.com/deuxmondes5**). At the site, you will find additional grammar exercises and many exciting acitivites that require the use of current websites. Many of the activities at the site are tasks that students may need to perform for themselves, such as getting sightseeing information, finding their way around Paris, and using public transportation.

Chapter 8
Videoscripts for the Video to accompany *Deux mondes*

This chapter provides the scripts for the **Espace vidéo** segments that accompany each chapter, as well as the scripts and cultural notes for the new **Escales francophones** video segments that are featured in the text after **Chapitres 4, 6, 8, 10,** and **12.** Note that the **Escales francophones** scripts follow the **Espace vidéo** section.

Videoscripts for *Espace vidéo*

CHAPITRE 1   Ma famille et moi

Décrire quelqu'un

CLAIRE:	Salut, Aimée!
AIMÉE:	Salut!
CLAIRE:	C'est bien la sieste en plein air?
AIMÉE:	Je médite. J'aime méditer surtout en plein air.
JACQUES:	Peut-être que je peux méditer avec toi. D'habitude, à cette heure-ci, j'aide Marc avec la philosophie, mais, je ne sais pas où il est.
AIMÉE:	Il est comment, ce Marc?
JACQUES:	Il est grand avec les cheveux noirs et les yeux marron. Il est sportif. Il est sociable, mais pas très intéressant. Et il est toujours avec une fille.
AIMÉE:	Comme toi, n'est-ce pas?
JACQUES:	Ah, non! Moi, je suis plus individualiste! Marc est plus BCBG. Par exemple, j'ai une classe avec lui. Et aujourd'hui il porte un pull-over jaune—très BCBG.
CLAIRE:	Oh, là là! J'ai un rendez-vous avec M. Depétri, le prof de commerce international! Vous savez, le professeur avec un veston vert. Il porte toujours un veston vert! Salut!
JACQUES:	Salut!
AIMÉE:	Salut, Claire! Moi, je cherche une personne pour m'aider en maths. Je suis artiste, je ne suis pas mathématicienne!
JACQUES:	Je connais quelqu'un. Elle s'appelle Anne. Elle est dans mon cours de philosophie. Elle est petite, mignonne, avec les cheveux longs et roux. Et aujourd'hui, elle...
AIMÉE:	...elle porte une robe marron, un gilet blanc, des sandales et des boucles d'oreille.
JACQUES:	Ben, ouais, mais comment tu...
AIMÉE:	Elle est là-bas avec...
JACQUES:	...Marc! Et voilà! Ça c'est Marc, beau, sociable et toujours avec une fille. Mais, il n'est pas très sérieux avec ses études.
AIMÉE:	À mon avis, il étudie avec Anne.
JACQUES:	Écoute, je suis assez bon en maths. Je veux bien t'aider.
AIMÉE:	Ah, ça. C'est une bonne idée!

CHAPITRE 2   La vie quotidienne et les loisirs

Parler de la température

LE PROF:	Faites attention!
AIMÉE:	Oh, excusez-moi, monsieur.

LE PROF:	Ça va, ça va. Pas de problème. Alors, on a besoin de parler. J'ai votre examen... Dites-moi, est-ce que vous étudiez?
AIMÉE:	D'habitude, je regarde où je vais, mais aujourd'hui, il fait beau—le soleil, le ciel bleu, la lumière est parfaite.
LE PROF:	Toujours l'artiste, n'est-ce pas? Mais est-ce que vous étudiez?
AIMÉE:	Mais quand il fait froid et qu'il pleut, je préfère dessiner avec des crayons. Je vais au café et là, je prends un chocolat chaud et je dessine.
LE PROF:	L'art est très important, mais les études, mademoiselle, sont importantes aussi. Et, vous savez, vos notes dans ma classe ne sont pas très...
AIMÉE:	C'est clair, j'ai besoin d'étudier, et je...
LE PROF:	J'ai une idée. Il y a un groupe d'étude aujourd'hui à 17 h. Je vous invite.
AIMÉE:	Merci, monsieur. Mais je ne peux pas. J'ai déjà quelque chose de prévu le mardi soir...
LE PROF:	Alors, vous n'êtes pas libre. C'est dommage. Mais n'oubliez pas... vous pouvez nous rencontrer à la bibliothèque le mardi à 17 h.
AIMÉE:	Excusez-moi, mais quelle heure est-il, s'il vous plaît?
LE PROF:	Il est 14 h 15.
AIMÉE:	Je suis presque en retard. Je vais retrouver mes amis à l'Hacienda. On va... faire nos devoirs et... euh... étudier, bien sûr! Au revoir!

CHAPITRE 3   En ville

Acheter des timbres et poster un colis

CLIENT:	Merci, madame. Au revoir.
EMPLOYÉE:	Au revoir. Monsieur?
JACQUES:	Bonjour, madame. Je voudrais envoyer ce colis à Paris. Est-ce que je devrais l'envoyer par courrier recommandé ou l'assurer?
EMPLOYÉE:	Ça dépend si c'est un colis de valeur ou un colis fragile. Pour l'envoyer recommandé ou pour l'assurer, il faut que vous remplissiez ce formulaire.
JACQUES:	En fait, non, ce n'est pas vraiment un colis de valeur et le contenu n'est pas particulièrement fragile. Mais merci quand même!
EMPLOYÉE:	Quel est le code postal? Je ne peux pas le lire.
JACQUES:	Oh, excusez-moi. C'est le 75006, Paris.
EMPLOYÉE:	Bon. Votre colis pèse 2 kilos.
JACQUES:	Et ça coûte?
EMPLOYÉE:	Ça coûte 5,33 euros.
JACQUES:	J'ai aussi une carte postale. C'est combien une carte postale pour le Canada?
EMPLOYÉE:	Ça coûte 0,67 euro.
JACQUES:	D'accord. Je vais prendre un timbre pour la carte postale.
EMPLOYÉE:	Autre chose?
JACQUES:	Non, c'est tout.
EMPLOYÉE:	Pour le colis et la carte postale, ça fait 6 euros.
JACQUES:	Voilà. Merci, madame. Au revoir.
EMPLOYÉE:	Au revoir, monsieur.

CHAPITRE 4   La maison et le quartier

Chercher un appartement

AIMÉE:	«Une salle de séjour, une cuisine, une chambre, une salle de bains: idéale pour les étudiants. 600 euros.» «Appartement pour étudiant... pas très grand, rez-de-chaussée: 600 euros.» «Chambre à louer: 300 euros.»
CLAIRE:	Salut!
AIMÉE:	Salut, Claire!

CLAIRE:	Ça va?
AIMÉE:	Bof, comme ci, comme ça. Je n'ai pas d'énergie, et j'ai sommeil.
CLAIRE:	Ouais, tu as l'air fatiguée.
AIMÉE:	Ouais, ma colocataire est folle. Elle joue de la trompette tout le temps. Et la chambre est toujours en désordre à cause d'elle. En plus, il n'y a pas de fenêtre et la chambre est très moderne, très stérile.
CLAIRE:	Oh, là là!
AIMÉE:	Donc, je cherche un appartement tranquille. Mais, maintenant le problème c'est que tous les appartements sont trop chers. Quoi? Qu'est-ce qu'il y a?
CLAIRE:	J'ai une solution, une bonne solution! Pourquoi ne pas chercher une colocataire, une personne pour aider à payer le loyer?
AIMÉE:	Non, j'ai besoin de trouver une autre solution. Je n'ai pas beaucoup de chance avec les colocataires.
CLAIRE:	Tu as tort. Regarde. «Je cherche une colocataire pour partager un joli studio, une grande pièce avec une petite cuisine équipée. 400 euros par mois. Téléphoner: 04.55.31.03.45.» Ça fait 200 euros par mois. C'est idéal.
AIMÉE:	Oui, mais une colocataire? Je ne sais pas.
CLAIRE:	Écoute, moi. Je connais cette personne et ce studio. Le studio n'est pas très grand, mais il y a une grande fenêtre et beaucoup, beaucoup de lumière. Il est en ordre, le studio, avec une ambiance très tranquille. Et cette personne, elle a le même âge que toi. Elle est dynamique, aimable, intelligente, belle et professionnelle.
AIMÉE:	Et tu connais cette personne professionnelle?
CLAIRE:	Ouais! Et toi aussi!
AIMÉE:	Ah, bon? C'est qui?
CLAIRE:	C'est moi!
AIMÉE:	C'est toi, l'annonce?
CLAIRE:	Uh, huh.
AIMÉE:	Bon.
CLAIRE:	Alors?
AIMÉE:	C'est pas mal.

CHAPITRE 5   Dans le passé

Raconter des événements

JACQUES:	Merci à vous deux d'avoir gardé mon chien, le week-end passé.
CLAIRE:	Oui, mais attends: samedi matin, notre appart était tellement en désordre! Je me suis réveillée et il y avait des vêtements, des déchets partout, et nos belles plantes, et les tableaux d'Aimée, par terre! Une vraie tragédie, n'est-ce pas Aimée?
AIMÉE:	Ben, Jacques, qu'est-ce que tu as fait pendant ce week-end?
JACQUES:	Écoute, mon petit chien est toujours tranquille. Je n'ai jamais eu de problème avec lui.
AIMÉE:	Moi, j'ai exposé quelques tableaux au parc samedi, une exposition pour aider les sans-abri. On a vendu des peintures, des sculptures, des textiles, et on a donné tout l'argent à l'Association des sans-abri.
CLAIRE:	Oui, et j'espère que tu as passé un bon week-end.
JACQUES:	Non, j'ai...
CLAIRE:	Parce que, moi, j'ai rangé le studio, j'ai nettoyé les tapis et j'ai balayé la cuisine. Puis, j'ai remis les plantes dans leurs pots. Alors, tu vois, je me suis bien amusée! Je t'assure!
AIMÉE:	Jacques, et ton week-end? Jacques, est-ce que tu es allé à la montagne ce week-end?
JACQUES:	Euh... Oui, c'est vrai. Je suis allé à la montagne pour faire un peu d'escalade. Mais pas grand-chose. En réalité, il a plu tout le temps et je suis resté dans ma tente. J'ai lu un nouveau livre pour ma classe de philosophie. Donc, vous voyez, je ne me suis pas vraiment amusé ce week-end.

CLAIRE: Oh, là là! Quel dommage! Bon, à propos de ton chien...

AIMÉE: Non, non. Son chien n'a rien fait. C'est moi qui suis responsable pour le... désordre. Je suis désolée. Mais samedi matin, je me suis réveillée en retard. Alors, je me suis dépêchée. J'ai cherché des vêtements propres partout, sans beaucoup de succès. Puis, j'ai pris mon petit déjeuner et j'ai fait tomber la poubelle dans la cuisine. Puis, j'ai couru choisir quelques tableaux. En me retournant, j'ai fait tomber la plante sur le tapis. J'avais l'intention de tout ranger à mon retour, mais tu l'avais déjà fait et... désolée, vraiment.

CHAPITRE 6   L'enfance et la jeunesse

Décrire des événements au passé

CLAIRE: Aimée, qu'est-ce qui s'est passé? Je suis en retard, un peu, mais on se rencontre toujours à l'Hacienda?

AIMÉE: Oui, moi aussi, je suis en retard. Mais, regarde ma mobylette. Le pneu est crevé.

CLAIRE: Mais, comment?

AIMÉE: Comme d'habitude, je suis partie pour aller te rejoindre à l'Hacienda. Mais cette fois-ci, j'ai tourné à gauche dans la rue Entrecasteaux, j'ai entendu mon nom, je me suis retournée et...

CLAIRE: Arrête! Je peux voir la fin de cette histoire. Moi, je connais cette rue. Elle est trop dangereuse, surtout pour les mobylettes. Tu es entrée en collision avec une voiture! C'est horrible!

AIMÉE: Non. Ce qui s'est passé c'est que, pendant que je tournais la tête, je n'ai pas vu les clous dans la rue. Alors, évidemment, je suis passée sur les clous et...

CLAIRE: Oh, là là! Je comprends maintenant. Tu es passée sur les clous; tu as eu une crevaison; à ce moment-là, la voiture derrière toi qui allait trop vite t'a frappée. Tu sais les mobylettes sont trop dangereuses. Quand j'étais gamine, j'avais une mobylette. Et ma mère s'inquiétait toujours. Et elle avait raison. J'ai eu de la chance: aucun accident.

AIMÉE: Ah bon?

CLAIRE: En fait, ma mère prenait toujours ma mobylette en cachette et elle me disait que les promenades à pied étaient meilleures pour les jeunes! Mais, Aimée, ton casque? Il est éraflé! Est-ce que tu es tombée? Est-ce que tu t'es fait mal?

AIMÉE: Mon pneu était dégonflé. Alors, je me suis arrêtée juste au carrefour, à côté du parc. Puis...

CLAIRE: Puis, une autre mobylette t'a frappée. Tu es tombée; tu t'es frappé la tête au sol! C'est sérieux. Il faut aller chez un médecin...

AIMÉE: Non, mais Claire, calme-toi, calme-toi.

CLAIRE: Je suis calme. Mais je suis aussi raisonnable et après un accident comme celui-là, il faut consulter un médecin.

AIMÉE: Tu as raison. Mais, mon accident n'était pas vraiment dramatique. J'étais simplement fâchée, j'ai enlevé mon casque et puis je l'ai jeté par terre! Voilà pourquoi il est éraflé.

CLAIRE: En effet, ce n'est pas très dramatique!

CHAPITRE 7   À table!

Commander au restaurant

AIMÉE: Jacques, tourne un peu à ta droite. Non, un peu! Voilà!

CLAIRE: Qu'est-ce que tu vas prendre, Aimée?

AIMÉE: Je n'ai pas très faim. Je vais prendre un citron pressé.

CLAIRE: C'est noté. Et pour toi, Jacques...

JACQUES: Pour moi...

AIMÉE: Non, Jacques, attends une seconde. Ne bouge pas! Surtout la bouche.

CLAIRE: Vite, Aimée. Voilà le serveur.

SERVEUR: Bonjour. Que désirez-vous?

CLAIRE: Elle voudrait un citron pressé et...

SERVEUR: Excusez-moi, mais vous êtes artiste?

AIMÉE:	Oui, et je veux quelque chose à manger aussi. Qu'est-ce que vous me recommandez?
SERVEUR:	On a...
AIMÉE:	Attendez une minute. Jacques, ne bouge pas, surtout la bouche. Je la dessine.
SERVEUR:	Bon, pas de problème. Prenez votre temps. C'est fascinant.
CLAIRE:	Bon. Pour moi, je prends un café crème. Et toi, Jacques?
AIMÉE:	Jacques! Tes lèvres, je les dessine!
SERVEUR:	Je vous recommande le croque-monsieur ou la quiche ou bien...
AIMÉE:	Est-ce que vous avez des salades?
SERVEUR:	Oui, on a une très bonne salade de tomates.
AIMÉE:	Alors, une salade de tomates, s'il vous plaît.
SERVEUR:	Très bien. C'est tout?
JACQUES:	Ummmmmh!
AIMÉE:	Ah! Jacques! Excuse-nous! Tu veux quelque chose?
JACQUES:	Du vin rouge!
AIMÉE:	Ne bouge pas. Remets-toi à droite un peu, un peu.

CHAPITRE 8   Parlons de la Terre!

Échanger une marchandise

VENDEUR:	Monsieur, bonjour.
JACQUES:	Bonjour. J'ai un petit problème.
VENDEUR:	Désolé. Je ne peux pas vous aider.
JACQUES:	Mais...
VENDEUR:	Jeune homme, je vous ai déjà dit: je ne peux pas vous aider! Non, je rigole! Qu'est-ce que je peux faire pour vous?
JACQUES:	La semaine dernière, j'ai acheté ce papier à lettres et j'avais l'impression que c'était du papier recyclé et malheureusement ce n'était pas le cas. Vous voyez, j'aimerais contribuer à sauver des arbres. Est-ce que je pourrais...
VENDEUR:	Non, jeune homme, je suis désolé, mais je ne peux pas vous rembourser. Mais, vous pouvez l'échanger contre autre chose, si vous voulez.
JACQUES:	Et vous rigolez là?
VENDEUR:	Non, cette fois, je suis sérieux!
JACQUES:	Bon, d'accord, est-ce que vous avez quelque chose à me suggérer? Quelque chose qui respecte l'environnement?
VENDEUR:	Bien sûr! Pourquoi pas ce paquet de cartes faites à la main? Il est bien évident qu'elles sont fabriquées avec du papier recyclé. Et c'est le même prix aussi.
JACQUES:	Bon, d'accord. Je les prends.
VENDEUR:	Et vous dites que vous avez pris la décision d'utiliser seulement des produits qui respectent l'environnement?
JACQUES:	Euh oui!
VENDEUR:	Intéressant ça!
JACQUES:	Quoi?

CHAPITRE 9   L'enseignement, les carrières et l'avenir

Passer une entrevue

PATRONNE:	Notre société n'est pas la plus grande, mais vous acquerrez beaucoup d'expérience en marketing. C'est un poste idéal pour une étudiante comme vous.
CLAIRE:	Cette année, à l'université, j'étudie le commerce et le marketing. L'été dernier, j'ai travaillé dans une société de fabrication de produits chimiques.
PATRONNE:	Des produits chimiques? Ce n'était pas un peu dangereux?

CLAIRE:	Ah non! Pas du tout! La société prend beaucoup de précautions. En fait, c'est une société allemande. L'usine se trouve en Allemagne, mais les bureaux de vente se trouvent ici.
PATRONNE:	Donc, vous avez de l'expérience en commerce international?
CLAIRE:	Oui. J'étais responsable, en partie, de trouver de nouveaux marchés.
PATRONNE:	C'est-à-dire?
CLAIRE:	En fait, j'aidais la directrice de marketing. Ensemble, on a rédigé un nouveau plan de commercialisation.
PATRONNE:	Alors, c'était très spécialisé...
CLAIRE:	Oui. Mes connaissances en chimie et en marketing m'ont été très utiles. J'ai également appris beaucoup sur ce type d'industries et...
PATRONNE:	...et vous me dites que vous possédez une telle expérience?
CLAIRE:	Mon père est chimiste et pendant toute mon enfance et pendant toute ma vie, il m'a donné, et il continue à me donner, une bonne base en sciences. Mes études m'ont également bien préparée à ce type de travail. Donc, le travail n'était pas trop difficile, mais quand même un bon défi que j'ai su relever.
PATRONNE:	Très bien, mademoiselle. Écoutez, nous devons rencontrer d'autres candidats. Nous vous recontacterons très bientôt.
CLAIRE:	Merci, madame. Si vous désirez des informations supplémentaires, n'hésitez pas à me contacter.
PATRONNE:	Merci à vous. Et bonne journée, mademoiselle.

CHAPITRE 10   Les voyages

Réserver une chambre d'hôtel

RÉCEPTIONNISTE:	Hôtel Central, bonjour.
AIMÉE:	Bonjour, madame. Je voudrais faire des réservations, s'il vous plaît.
RÉCEPTIONNISTE:	Avec plaisir, madame. Combien de chambres?
AIMÉE:	Il me faudra deux chambres pour trois personnes. Une chambre simple et une chambre à deux lits, s'il vous plaît.
RÉCEPTIONNISTE:	Avec bains ou douche? Une chambre avec douche coûte 9 euros supplémentaires.
AIMÉE:	Alors, deux chambres avec douche, s'il vous plaît.
RÉCEPTIONNISTE:	Ce serait pour quand?
AIMÉE:	À partir du 22 juin jusqu'au 27 juin. Mes amis et moi, on va visiter des châteaux. Je suis artiste et je voudrais les peindre, surtout Azay-le-Rideau et Chenonceau.
RÉCEPTIONNISTE:	Excellent! Moi aussi, je fais de la peinture et j'ai fait une étude de tous les châteaux de la région. Vous savez, c'est la saison des spectacles «son et lumière» aussi. Il faudra que vous visitiez quelques-uns de ces châteaux la nuit. Vous verrez, c'est une expérience très magique.
AIMÉE:	Vous êtes très gentille, madame. Merci de votre suggestion.
RÉCEPTIONNISTE:	Il n'y a pas de quoi. Voyons voir, pour les chambres. Un instant, s'il vous plaît.
CLAIRE:	Le petit déjeuner?
AIMÉE:	Oui, oui.
RÉCEPTIONNISTE:	D'accord, madame. Je peux vous proposer la chambre à deux lits pour 55 euros et la chambre simple pour 50 euros.
AIMÉE:	Et le petit déjeuner est compris?
RÉCEPTIONNISTE:	Non, madame. Le petit déjeuner n'est pas compris. D'habitude, le petit déjeuner coûte 9 euros.
CLAIRE:	Il faut que tu marchandes.
AIMÉE:	Et vous n'avez pas...
RÉCEPTIONNISTE:	Mais, aujourd'hui, uniquement pour les artistes, ce tarif comprend le petit déjeuner.
AIMÉE:	Merci, madame. Vous êtes adorable. Bon.

CHAPITRE 11　Les moyens de communication

Exprimer son désaccord

CLAIRE: Aaarrrgh! Cette dissertation, c'est pénible!

AIMÉE: Quoi? Qu'est-ce qu'il y a?

CLAIRE: J'ai un cours de cinéma, de la théorie. Je dois écrire une dissertation sur le film «Les Nuits fauves». Je l'ai vu trois fois.

AIMÉE: Oui, j'ai vu la cassette vidéo sur la table. C'est un film par Cyril Collard. Je suis folle de lui.

CLAIRE: Il est mort, Aimée.

AIMÉE: Oui, ça. Je le sais. Je veux dire que je l'aime comme acteur et réalisateur. Il avait beaucoup de talent. Il a écrit le roman et puis il l'a adapté pour le cinéma aussi.

CLAIRE: En fait, je n'aime pas tellement le cinéma français. C'est trop sérieux.

AIMÉE: Mais, Claire, «Les Nuits fauves» a gagné le prix du meilleur film aux Césars 1993.

CLAIRE: Voilà. En France, si un film est sinistre, il gagne des prix!

AIMÉE: De toute façon, je veux toujours le voir. Est-ce que je peux le visionner?

CLAIRE: Et sa copine dans le film, Laura, j'avais envie de lui tordre le cou! Elle était cinglée, mais il n'y a aucune motivation à sa folie! Et lui aussi, Cyril, il était fou. Dans son monde, il n'y a pas de santé d'esprit!

AIMÉE: Écoute, je ne l'ai pas encore vu.

CLAIRE: Oui, il aime Laura, il aime les autres. Elle devient folle.

AIMÉE: Eh, je te dis que je ne l'ai pas encore vu.

CLAIRE: Il devient fou et... Je le déteste comme je déteste tout le cinéma français. Ce n'est pas Hollywood!

AIMÉE: Bon, merci de ne pas...

CLAIRE: À la fin, il meurt!

AIMÉE: ...me raconter la fin du film! Merci! Merci! Vraiment!

CHAPITRE 12　La santé et les urgences

Décrire ses symptômes

PHARMACIENNE: Vous avez de la fièvre?

JACQUES: Non, je crois que je suis enrhumé.

PHARMACIENNE: Est-ce que vous avez consulté un médecin?

JACQUES: Non. Je suis sûr que j'ai attrapé un rhume. Je tousse sans arrêt, j'ai mal à la tête et j'ai le nez bouché.

PHARMACIENNE: Est-ce que vous avez mal à la gorge?

JACQUES: Atchoum! Non, mais j'éternue et il faut que je me mouche de temps en temps. Est-ce que vous pourriez me recommander des médicaments?

PHARMACIENNE: Mais, bien sûr! Mais pour guérir, le sommeil est la chose la plus importante... Faites des siestes, dormez au moins huit heures par nuit. Aussi, pour soulager la toux, prenez ce sirop. Pour aider votre corps à combattre ce rhume, prenez beaucoup de vitamine C. Voilà des comprimés.

JACQUES: Et pour le mal de tête?

PHARMACIENNE: Oui, oui, je ne l'ai pas oublié! Je suggère que vous preniez de l'aspirine.

JACQUES: C'est tout?

PHARMACIENNE: Oui. Et ne consommez pas d'alcool.

JACQUES: Ah oui, à cause du sirop, j'aurai sommeil, encore plus sommeil que maintenant. Atchoum!

PHARMACIENNE: Mon pauvre! Tenez, pour vous, les plus doux que je vende.

JACQUES: Des mouchoirs en papier. Merci.

CHAPITRE 13   La famille et les valeurs en société

Exprimer ses opinions

AIMÉE: La cérémonie sera très belle.

CLAIRE: J'en suis sûre. Sandrine a des goûts de luxe.

AIMÉE: Mais elle est si jeune, je peux pas croire qu'elle se marie déjà.

CLAIRE: Jeune? Elle a le même âge que nous.

AIMÉE: Ouais! Précisément! Elle est trop jeune, à mon avis.

CLAIRE: Ma grand-mère ne dirait pas ça. Elle s'inquiète parce que je ne me suis pas encore mariée. Lorsqu'elle avait mon âge, elle était déjà mère de famille!

AIMÉE: Tu parles! Ma grand-mère aussi! Mais, c'est exactement pourquoi je trouve le mariage de Sandrine un peu bizarre. Je veux dire qu'ils sont trop jeunes. D'habitude aujourd'hui, les gens de notre âge attendent un peu.

CLAIRE: C'est-à-dire?

AIMÉE: Je ne sais pas. Il semble qu'ils viennent de se rencontrer il y a six mois?

CLAIRE: C'était le coup de foudre! C'est romantique.

AIMÉE: Claire, c'est ma réplique, ça! Non mais, je me demande simplement pourquoi elle ne pense pas d'abord à sa carrière.

CLAIRE: T'en fais pas! Elle est comme moi, très rationnelle, très...

AIMÉE: ...oui, comme toi.

CLAIRE: Et Jacques fera un beau garçon d'honneur, n'est-ce pas?

AIMÉE: Et son frère sera un très beau marié aussi.

CLAIRE: Et les deux petites cousines de Sandrine seront les deux demoiselles d'honneur.

AIMÉE: C'est mignon.

CLAIRE: Alors, il faudra être à l'église à midi. Donc, on partira vers 11 heures et demie? On prendra ma voiture.

AIMÉE: Oui, ça marche. On ne voudrait pas salir nos robes. Mais, de toute façon, si on change d'idée, on pourrait toujours prendre ma mobylette.

CHAPITRE 14   Les enjeux du présent et de l'avenir

Suggérer et conseiller

AIMÉE: Salut!

CLAIRE: Ah, te voilà. Je voulais te parler.

AIMÉE: Alors, qu'est-ce que tu fais? Tu prépares un pique-nique?

CLAIRE: Écoute. Cet après-midi, j'ai vu un clochard ou plutôt un sans-abri. Il m'a demandé de l'argent. J'avais peur et en même temps, j'étais furieuse contre lui. J'ai continué à marcher, sans lui dire un mot et sans lui donner un sou. Je me suis dit qu'il était paresseux, qu'il n'avait aucune ambition. Moi, j'ai un job, il pourrait trouver un job, lui aussi.

AIMÉE: Peut-être, mais la vie n'est pas la même pour tout le monde. Il y a toujours des circonstances...

CLAIRE: Oui, tu as raison. J'aurais dû l'aider. Et juste après avoir vu ce sans-abri, j'ai pensé à toi et à ton travail avec l'Association des sans-abri. Tu n'hésites jamais à aider quelqu'un qui en a besoin.

AIMÉE: Oui, c'est vrai. Mais, il faut que tu sois prudente. Il y a des types dangereux.

CLAIRE: Je sais. Tu me connais, je suis très logique. Je ne veux pas réinventer la roue. Lorsque j'ai une idée, je préfère en parler d'abord avec quelqu'un qui a de l'expérience. C'est pourquoi je voulais te parler.

AIMÉE: À mon avis, c'est bien que tu donnes un carton de nourriture à l'Association des sans-abri.

CLAIRE: Je voudrais aussi aider ce sans-abri que j'ai vu cet après-midi. Qu'est-ce que tu en penses?

AIMÉE: On pourrait appeler Gérard, le directeur de l'Association. Peut-être qu'il le connaît. Au moins, il pourra te donner des conseils.

CLAIRE: Ça, c'est une bonne idée. Je lui parlerai quand j'irai porter le carton.

Videoscripts and Cultural Notes for *Escales francophones*

Please note that the numbers in parentheses in the scripts refer to cultural notes that are linked to images seen in the segments. These notes can be found following each script.

Web links related to these videos and cultural notes can be found on the *Deux mondes* website at **www.mhhe.com/deuxmondes5**.

Escales francophones—La France (après Chapitre 4)

Introduction: Montage (1)

Paris est la capitale de la France et du monde francophone. Avec ses vastes espaces, ses nombreux monuments et ses petits cafés, Paris est un mélange fascinant d'ancien et de moderne.

Le matin, beaucoup de Parisiens prennent le métro pour aller au travail ou à l'université. (2) On circule aussi à moto ou à vélo. C'est pratique parce qu'il y a beaucoup de trafic à Paris! (3-5) On se promène au jardin du Luxembourg. (6) Il y a de beaux parcs à Paris. C'est idéal quand on fait du jogging.

Le roller a beaucoup de succès. Le skate-board aussi. (7)

Le matin, on achète du pain ou des croissants à la boulangerie. Et puis on peut prendre un café et regarder les gens qui passent. On peut aussi aller au marché. On trouve de tout au marché: fromage, olives, poissons, fruits et fleurs.

L'après-midi, nous allons explorer les musées et regarder les monuments. La cathédrale de Notre-Dame se trouve en plein centre de Paris. (8) Dans le quartier historique du Marais, on peut voir le centre Pompidou. (9) C'est un musée d'art moderne. Son architecture futuriste est beaucoup critiquée. À côté du centre Pompidou, il y a souvent des musiciens et des artistes. La fontaine Stravinsky (10) est un hommage au grand musicien du vingtième siècle, Igor Stravinsky. Elle offre un spectacle très coloré.

Après le centre Pompidou, on peut visiter un endroit historique: le musée du Louvre. (11) Ancienne résidence de Louis XIV et d'autres rois de France, le Louvre est aujourd'hui un musée d'art avec une collection extraordinaire. Construite pour le Bicentenaire de la Révolution française, la pyramide en verre d'IM Pei est le point d'entrée du musée. Après une visite au Louvre, il est agréable de faire une promenade. Il y a beaucoup de choses à voir: la place de la Concorde avec son obélisque, l'Arc de triomphe et les célèbres Champs-Élysées.

En soirée, on va à Montmartre. (12) Avec son atmosphère de petit village et sa vue extraordinaire sur la ville, ce quartier de Paris est bien agréable. Sur la place du Tertre, près du Sacré-Cœur, les artistes font le portrait des touristes. Il est maintenant l'heure de dîner. Dans certains cafés, on peut écouter de la musique pendant le repas. Après, on peut aller voir un spectacle dans un des petits théâtres du quartier.

À la fin de la journée, on prend le métro ou le bus pour rentrer chez soi. C'est la nuit, mais Paris ne dort pas. Elle est maintenant la ville-lumière. Tous les monuments sont éclairés: l'Opéra, Notre-Dame, le Sacré-Cœur et, bien sûr, la tour Eiffel, majestueux symbole de Paris.

Notes culturelles

(1) Montage (selected shots)

- **Le pont au Change** is one of Paris' thirty-five bridges. Money-changers and goldsmiths used to have their shops on this bridge. The bridge was later destroyed in a fire. The bridge we see today dates from the reign of Napoléon III, emperor of France in the mid-19th century.
- The numerous visitors who go down the Seine on a **bateau-mouche** get a guided tour of Paris and see many of the city's famous monuments such as the Eiffel Tower, the Louvre, and the Conciergie.
- **Crêpe** stands are scattered throughout Paris. They are a popular stop for children on their way home from school. **Crêpes** and **galettes** are very similar. **La galette,** traditionally from the Bretagne region of France, is a buckwheat **crêpe.** Its batter is salty. Both **crêpes** and **galettes** can be served with many different fillings.
- The uniforms of the Parisian meter maids are dark purple, very similar to the color of an eggplant. As a result, these officers are often referred to as "eggplants": **les aubergines.**

- About 250 **bouquiniste** stalls are found on the Right and Left Banks of the Seine. **Bouquinistes** sell old books, etchings, photos, records, and postcards. The first **bouquinistes** were seen in Paris in the 17th century. At the time, they were thought of as an undesirable group and were regularly chased away by the authorities. Today, the **bouquinistes** are one of Paris' beloved traditions.

(2) In the heart of the Latin Quarter, the Jussieu campus includes the Pierre and Marie Curie University (also known as **l'Université Paris VI**), the Denis Diderot University (also known as **l'Université Paris VII**) and **l'Institut de Physique du Globe de Paris.** There are about 45,000 students at Jussieu, which is but one of Paris' campuses; there are thirteen universities located throughout Paris.

(3) French cars are generally smaller than American cars. The "Smart," a tiny (just over 8 feet long) two-seater built by Daimler Chrysler is not an unusual sight on French roads. Not only is it economical, but it is easy to drive and park.

(4) Note the sign warning pedestrians that, in this lane, buses go against the flow of traffic. Although reserved for buses (and sometimes bicycles), these special lanes are often used by pedestrians, joggers, and in-line skaters.

(5) French street sweepers wear colorful yellow and green uniforms. They are part of the team of some 7,800 people (**les agents de la propreté**) employed by the city for the purpose of keeping Paris clean. Streets are swept on a daily basis and washed at least once a week. There are about 200,000 dogs in Paris, responsible for a daily 32,000 pounds of waste. In 2002, Paris introduced a campaign called **"La propreté, c'est l'affaire de tous"** (Cleanliness is everybody's business). This campaign included an increased budget for sanitation as well as the implementation of fines for individuals who do not follow the rules. Dog owners beware!

(6) **Le jardin du Luxembourg** is close to the lively student district called **le Quartier latin.** This garden surrounds the Luxembourg Palace. Originally built for Marie de Médici (mother of King Louis XIII) in the 17th century, the palace has served many purposes over the years: During the Revolution it was a prison; today it houses the Senate. The garden has pleasant paths with numerous flowers and trees. It contains about eighty statues, three fountains, and is one of Paris' most beautiful public parks. Children can rent small remote-controlled boats to play with on the ponds. They can also watch a puppet show, ride the merry-go-round, or go for a pony ride. Older gentlemen are often seen playing chess. The park is an oasis of peace in the center of Paris.

(7) This fountain, **la fontaine des Innocents,** was built in the 13th century. Since the 18th century, it has marked the location of an old cemetery that had to be closed for structural and sanitary reasons. The bones of almost two million people were moved to an underground location: the catacombs. Today, the fountain square (**la place Joachim Du Bellay**) is a very popular meeting place.

(8) Around 200 BC, Celtic fishermen, from the tribe of the Parisii, settled on the largest island of the Seine (**l'île de la Cité**) and founded a town. This marked the birth of Paris. It was on this same island, in 1163, that construction of Notre Dame began. It lasted until 1345. **La cathédrale Notre-Dame,** situated in the heart of Paris, surrounded by the Seine, is a masterpiece of Gothic architecture.

(9) The Pompidou Center (**le centre Pompidou,** also known as **le centre Beaubourg**) was named after a French President, Georges Pompidou. Pompidou wanted the center to be devoted to the arts of the 20th century—architecture, sculpture, literature, and music.

The center was designed inside out. The frame and pipes were put on the outside to provide more interior room for the numerous visitors. Colors indicate the purpose of the different sections on this building: Blue is for air flow, green for water pipes, yellow for electricity, and red is for elevators and escalators. The center houses the Museum of Modern Art on two levels, an enormous library, and the Institute of Acoustical Music Research (IRCAM—**l'Institut de recherche et de coordination acoustique/musique**), which is partially located below the **fontaine Stravinsky.**

(10) Situated just outside the Pompidou Center, **la fontaine Stravinsky** was created in 1983 by two sculptors—Jean Tingueli and his wife, Niki de Saint Phalle—as an homage to the 20th-century musician, Igor Stravinsky. It is a colorful fountain with moving statues and water spouts. The whimsical figures that populate the fountain represent the composer's works.

(11) Originally a 12th-century fortress, the **Louvre** was rebuilt in the 16th and 17th centuries and became the residence of the Kings of France. During his reign in the first half of the 16th century, François 1er began a collection of art. One of the paintings he acquired was the famous *Mona Lisa* (*La Joconde*) by Leonardo da Vinci. Each subsequent king enlarged the collection, which was reserved strictly for the pleasure of the Court. In 1793, after the French Revolution, the **Louvre** became a public museum. The collection continued to grow. In 1989, the impressionist paintings were transferred across the Seine to **le musée d'Orsay.** Today there are 300,000 works at the **Louvre.**

In the early 1980's, President Mitterrand commissioned Ieoh Ming Pei to create a new reception area and entrance to the museum. The Pyramid was completed in 1989. It was then, and still is, the subject of much criticism, but it never affected the popularity of the museum. In 2002, the Louvre welcomed 5.7 million visitors.

(12) Set on one of the six hills (**collines** or **buttes**) that surround the center of Paris, **Montmartre,** with its small paved streets, has the feel of a village. Until 1860, it actually was an independent municipality. In the 19th century, **Montmartre** became a popular place of residence for artists, who were attracted by the cheap rents. Today, **Montmartre** attracts tourists trying to recapture the flavor of those days. Today's artists gather on **la place du Tertre.** There, tourists can have their portrait drawn or sit on the terrace of one of the numerous cafés surrounding the square.

The beautiful white **basilique du Sacré-Cœur** is not far from this square. Construction of the basilica began after the Franco-Prussian War, and was ongoing between 1876 and 1912. The basilica contains one of the heaviest bells in the world. From the terrace in front of the church, one has a breathtaking, panoramic view of Paris.

Escales francophones—Le Québec (après Chapitre 6)

Introduction: Montage (1)

Bienvenue à Québec, (2) capitale de la province de Québec. C'est l'explorateur français Samuel de Champlain (3) qui fonde Québec au début du dix-septième siècle. La ville conserve de nombreuses marques de son riche passé et évoque plus l'Europe (4) que l'Amérique, par son atmosphère et son architecture.

Québec est une ville pleine de charme, mais elle est particulièrement belle sous la neige. De novembre à mars, il fait très, très froid, surtout le matin. (5)

Le matin, les passagers prennent le ferry pour traverser le Saint-Laurent. Du bateau, on a une vue superbe du Château Frontenac qui domine la ville. (6) Construit au dix-neuvième siècle pour les voyageurs de la compagnie de chemins de fer Canadien Pacifique, le château est aujourd'hui un hôtel de luxe. Quand on descend du ferry, on arrive dans la Basse-Ville. Il y a là beaucoup de bâtiments anciens comme Notre-Dame-des-Victoires (7) et la Maison Chevalier. (8)

Aujourd'hui, dans ce quartier, il y a beaucoup de cafés et de petits restaurants. On y va pour déjeuner ou pour prendre un bol de café au lait.

Après le déjeuner, on prend le funiculaire pour monter dans la Haute-Ville. (9) Dans ses rues pittoresques, on peut faire du shopping, une promenade en calèche ou visiter des musées (10) ou des endroits historiques (11) ou culturels. (12) On peut même faire du patin à glace en plein air! Ne manquez pas de visiter la Basilique-Notre-Dame, (13) une vieille église à la façade classique et à l'intérieur splendide.

L'après-midi, à l'extérieur des fortifications de la vieille ville, des gens qui ont du courage font une promenade sur les plaines d'Abraham (14) ou s'amusent dans la neige.

«Vive le Carnaval!» En février, au moment du Carnaval, (15) la ville est transformée: les visiteurs admirent le grand palais de glace et des artistes du monde entier participent à la compétition de sculpture sur neige. C'est un spectacle magnifique! La mascotte du Carnaval, c'est le bonhomme Carnaval, un bonhomme de neige qui vit et qui bouge. Chaque année pendant le Carnaval, de nombreuses personnes mettent leur maillot de bain et prennent un bain de neige! (16) On s'amuse bien au Carnaval, le jour comme la nuit.

À Noël, les illuminations sont magnifiques. Toutes les petites rues sont décorées et il est bien agréable de s'y promener. Si on a faim, on peut prendre un steak-frites délicieux dans un des nombreux restaurants de la ville.

Le soir, on rentre à la maison. C'est beau, la nuit à Québec!

Notes culturelles

(1) Montage

Among the opening shots is one of the Parliament building, **l'hôtel du Parlement,** home to the National Assembly. The four wings of this large, square-shaped "château" were built between 1877 and 1886 in the Second Empire style.

(2) Two different flags can be seen flying in Quebec. The national Canadian flag—red and white with a maple leaf in its center—was inaugurated on February 15, 1965. The blue and white flag with fleurs-de-lis (named **le fleurdelisé**) dates from January 21, 1948. On that date, it replaced the Union Jack at the top of the tower of the Parliament building and became the official flag of the province of Quebec.

(3) In 1608, Samuel de Champlain landed on the north bank of the Saint Lawrence River in a place the Indians called *Kebec,* meaning "where the river narrows." There, he established a fur-trading post and built a fort where Notre-Dame-des-Victoires can be seen today. A second fort was built in 1664. Soon after, the first colonists began settling in Quebec City. Craftsmen and merchants settled in **la Basse-Ville,** which became the commercial and residential section of town. For protection, administrative buildings and religious institutions were built in **la Haute-Ville** inside the fortifications. Quebec City became the administrative, political, and military center of New France.

The statue of Champlain on **la terrasse Dufferin** across from **le château Frontenac** was created by Paul-Romain Chevré, a French sculptor. It was inaugurated in September 1898.

(4) **Le Manège militaire,** or Armory, was built in 1888 by architect Eugène-Étienne Taché who also designed the **l'hôtel du Parlement.** With its turrets, the building looks like a medieval castle. It belongs to the ministry of International Defense.

(5) Quebec City, Canada's oldest city, was a site of great strategic importance. Built during the French and British regimes, the fortifications reflect the evolution of Quebec City's defense system from the 17th to the 19th century. Today, Quebec City is the only walled city north of Mexico.

(6) Opened in 1893, **le château Frontenac** owes its name to Louis de Buade, Comte de Frontenac, a 17th-century governor of New France. Architect Bruce Price, father of Emily Post, designed this castle, which was built as a stopover for railroad passengers in order to promote tourism. Construction of the chateau continued until 1924, with a final wing being added in the 1990's. Today **le château Frontenac** is a luxury hotel, and its position on the bluff overlooking the Saint Lawrence River makes it the symbol of Quebec City.

(7) Built in 1688, **Notre-Dame-des-Victoires** church is located on the site Champlain chose in 1608 for his first residence. Originally named **Notre-Dame-de-la-Victoire** after the French victory over the British in 1690, it was renamed **Notre-Dame-des-Victoires** after the 1711 victory. The church has been destroyed and repaired several times over the centuries. The present building was remodeled in the mid-1800's. It contains several paintings from the 17th, 18th, and 19th centuries.

(8) Built in 1752 as the home of a wealthy merchant named Jean-Baptiste Chevalier, **la maison Chevalier** was converted into an inn at the beginning of the 19th century. The "London Coffee House," as it was then called, was a popular place with sailors and travelers for almost a century. In 1950, the government decided to restore the house, which later became a museum. Today, in addition to admiring the original fireplaces, wood floors, and authentic furnishings, one can also enjoy exhibits on Quebec history and civilization.

(9) Lower Quebec (often called **le quartier Petit Champlain**) and Upper Quebec are connected by stairways built in the face of a cliff—one of these stairways is named **l'escalier casse-cou** (Breakneck Staircase)—and a funicular that travels at a 45-degree angle for more than 200 feet. Originally steam-powered, **le funiculaire** was completely rebuilt in 1997. It offers a beautiful panoramic view of the city and the Saint Lawrence River.

(10) **Le musée du Québec,** now known as **le musée national des Beaux-Arts du Québec,** has more than 20,000 works of art (paintings, sculptures, drawings, prints, photographs, and decorative art) produced mostly in Quebec between the end of the 17th century and today.

(11) Inspired by a vision, Sister Marie de l'Incarnation of the Order of Saint Ursula wanted to come to America to evangelize and educate young native women. In 1639, she arrived in Quebec with Madame de La Peltrie. The first Ursuline school in New France was soon established. By 1642, a convent was built. Today, **l'école des Ursulines de Québec** is still an all-girls' school. Located on the same property as the school are **le musée des Ursulines**—where one can find out more about the educational work of the Ursuline Sisters in the 17th century—and **la chapelle des Ursulines.**

(12) **Le Grand Théâtre de Québec** opened in 1971. Classical or popular music concerts, dance performances, as well as plays are presented here. The theater is at the heart of Quebec's artistic life.

(13) **La basilique cathédrale Notre-Dame-de-Québec** has known destruction through storms, fires, and bombardments over the years. It was even reduced to rubble after British bombing in 1759, but reconstruction efforts have since restored it to its original glory. Parts of today's basilica date to the original structure, built in 1647. Most of the cathedral however, is from the 18th century. Its striking interior was restored at the beginning of the 20th century, after being damaged by a fire. The cathedral contains beautiful paintings and ecclesiastical treasures.

(14) **Le parc des Champs-de-Bataille** (National Battlefields Park), better known as **les plaines d'Abraham** was the scene of the September 13, 1759, battle during the French and Indian War that changed the course of Canadian history. During this battle, the French troops, led by Lieutenant General the Marquis de Montcalm, were defeated by the troops of Major General Wolfe of the British army. Four years later, upon the signing of the treaty of Paris, Quebec was ceded to England.

Today, **les plaines d'Abraham** is a huge and beautiful park where people like to ski, sleigh ride, stroll, bike, inline skate, or picnic.

(15) For more information about **le Carnaval,** you may wish to refer to the cultural readings on the CD-ROM.

(16) **Le bain de neige** is an actual event during Carnaval. Every year, dozens of intrepid snow bathers wearing only swimsuits roll around in the snow for fifteen to twenty minutes, in temperatures of around minus 10 degrees Celsius.

Escales francophones—Le Sénégal (après Chapitre 8)

Introduction: Montage (1)

Le Sénégal est situé en Afrique de l'Ouest. Il est célèbre pour ses plages sur l'océan Atlantique et ses villages de pêcheurs. Mais le Sénégal, c'est aussi la savane, la campagne et les déserts à l'intérieur du continent. (2)

Voici Dakar sur sa péninsule dans la presqu'île du Cap Vert. C'est la capitale et le centre politique et économique du pays. Dakar est une ville multiculturelle et multilingue. Le français est la langue officielle, mais 80 % de la population parle wolof. (3) (4)

Nous voici maintenant dans les rues animées de Dakar le matin. Au centre-ville, les taxis et les autobus contribuent au bruit et à l'agitation de la ville. (5)

Ce sont les marchés qui sont les centres principaux de l'activité de Dakar. (6) Les marchés sont toujours pleins de monde, surtout le matin. On y achète des légumes, des épices et même de la poterie.

(7) Dakar est aussi une ville de culture. On y trouve des arts traditionnels sénégalais, comme la sculpture sur bois. (8) On peut regarder les gens travailler le bois dans des petits ateliers au bord de la rue ou admirer des collections de statues et de masques. (9) Mais Dakar a aussi de nombreux artistes contemporains qui exposent leurs tableaux dans les galeries du centre-ville. Cet artiste fait de la peinture sur verre. (10)

Pas loin du centre se trouve la plage des Almadies, (11) où on peut apprécier la fraîcheur et la beauté de l'océan, surtout à midi. Il est agréable de manger au bord de la mer. Le riz au poisson est une des spécialités du Sénégal. (12) Bon appétit!

En face de la péninsule de Dakar se trouve l'île de Gorée. (13) Cette petite île aux maisons colorées et aux jolies rues calmes a été pendant trois siècles le centre de transit de millions d'esclaves pour les Amériques. À la Maison des Esclaves, un musée que l'on visite avec beaucoup d'émotion, les esclaves attendaient dans des conditions de vie horribles. Une porte de la maison donne sur la mer. Par cette porte partaient des femmes, des hommes et des enfants vendus comme esclaves, victimes de la cruauté d'autres hommes.

En fin d'après-midi, retournons à Dakar pour aller au marché aux poissons de Soumbédioune (14) sur la plage de la corniche ouest. La foule se précipite autour des bateaux et des pirogues qui rentrent de la pêche. On peut y acheter les poissons tout frais que l'on nettoie et que l'on vend sur la plage même.

Le soir, le soleil se couche sur l'océan. Nous sommes sous les tropiques et le soleil descend très vite sur l'horizon!

Notes culturelles

(1) Montage

One of the images seen in the opening montage is of Lake Retba, also known as **le lac rose.** It is a large lagoon situated close to the ocean, which owes its color to micro-organisms and a high concentration of minerals. The proportion of salt in this lake is ten times higher than in the ocean. Locals scrape salt from the bottom of the shallow lake and transport it by boat to the shores where it is piled until it can be sold.

(2) Tea is more than just a beverage in Senegal. It is a ceremony that often takes place after a meal. It is also a great opportunity to talk and visit, as it takes quite a while to prepare. Sweetened green tea mixed with mint leaves is heated over a charcoal fire and poured several times in little glasses until it foams. The teapot is usually held very high above the glasses. The custom is to have three glasses of tea, the first one being extremely strong and the next two progressively lighter as boiling water is added to the original brew. This ritual is called **les trois normaux** and can take several hours.

(3) People from Senegal can often be seen chewing on soft pieces of wood, called chewsticks. These sticks are chewed several times a day to clean teeth. The wood of several different types of trees is used to make these chewsticks. Some of these chewsticks are even used to treat medical ailments.

(4) There are about twenty national languages spoken in Senegal. More than 80% of the population speaks Wolof (**le wolof**), which is the native language of 36% of the population. The other most spoken national languages are **le peul** or **poular, le sérène, le diola, le malinké,** and **le soninké.** In addition, 15 to 20% of the population also speaks French, the official language of Senegal.

(5) There is a lot of traffic in Dakar and small urban buses (**les cars rapides**) are frequently used. The yellow, white, and blue **cars rapides Renault,** such as the one seen on the video, are usually very crowded. Ticket collectors hang from the back door calling out the final destination. Buses do not have determined stops, so stops can be sudden and brutal. Fortunately, the decorations on buses are not only meant to attract customers but also to protect against bad luck.

Note the words **Société musulmane** on the bus: 90% of the population of Senegal is Muslim. About 5% are Christians. Animistic beliefs still exist as well.

(6) For more information on the markets of Dakar, you may wish to refer to the cultural readings on the CD-ROM.

(7) This African xylophone is called **un balafon.** The wooden slats are placed over gourd-like tropical fruits named **callebasses** that act as amplifiers. **Le balafon** is struck with little mallets to produce melodies.

(8) Teak and ebony are local woods used to carve the statuettes and masks that are so popular in Senegal.

(9) There are many colorful, noisy and crowded markets in Dakar since this large city attracts both buyers and sellers from other parts of Senegal. One such market is named Kermel. There, one can find crafts, food, and flowers. The picturesque market building was destroyed in a fire in September 1993 and rebuilt in 1997. One of the Kermel vendors, displaced after the fire, settled in a street near the market square and started displaying his goods on a wall. **Le mur,** as it is now known, is covered with traditional art pieces such as wood carvings and masks from several countries of Africa. It is a striking exhibit.

(10) Reverse glass painting is a popular art in Senegal. Painters first draw an outline in ink and then apply successive layers of paint on the piece of glass. The opposite side of the piece of glass shows the painting as it is supposed to be seen. The style of these paintings is often naïf with bright colors and varied themes such as daily life, portraits, or animals.

(11) **La pointe des Almadies,** just outside of Dakar, is the westernmost tip of the African continent. It has a beach and is a favorite place to watch the sunset over the ocean. One can also sample seafood in the eateries on the beach.

(12) Senegal has the reputation of serving the best food in all of West Africa. The national dish is **tiéboudienne,** a rice dish with fish and vegetables. Another popular dish is chicken served in an onion-lemon sauce called **yassa de poulet.**

(13) For more information about **l'Île de Gorée,** you may wish to refer to the readings in the student textbook (Chapter 8 and in **Bienvenue au Sénégal**).

(14) Many tourists enjoy visiting Soumbédioune in the southwestern end of Dakar. In the 342 little shops of the craftsmen's village located there, one can admire (and buy!) the works of jewelers, basket makers, weavers, potters, and other artisans.

Soumbédioune is also famous for its lively fish market. Every evening, fishermen bring back their catch around 7 pm, at which time prospective clients are already waiting on the beach. The market remains busy until 10 pm.

Escales francophones—La Belgique (après Chapitre 10)

Introduction: Montage (1)

Bruxelles est la capitale du Royaume de Belgique. (2) C'est aussi la capitale de l'Union européenne. (3) Le français est la langue maternelle d'un grand nombre de Bruxellois. L'autre langue officielle du pays est le flamand. (4) Les nombreux fonctionnaires européens donnent à la ville son caractère multilingue.

Il est facile d'apprécier la ville pour ses monuments, bien sûr, mais aussi pour la vie de ses rues et de ses places, pour ses cafés, ses boutiques et ses petits restaurants.

Le matin, la ville s'anime tôt. Les gens se dépêchent pour aller au travail, et les enfants à l'école. Mais si on n'est pas pressé, on peut prendre un café sur la Grand-Place, appelée *Grote Markt* en flamand.

Après avoir mangé, on va vers la galerie royale Saint-Hubert. (5) Inspirée du classicisme italien et construite en 1847, cette jolie galerie couverte est un endroit agréable où on peut passer des heures.

Pas loin de la galerie royale Saint-Hubert, on découvre le personnage le plus célèbre de la ville—le Manneken-Pis. (6) Depuis le dix-septième siècle, cette petite statuette incarne l'esprit bruxellois— indépendant et coquin.

À l'heure du déjeuner, il faut s'arrêter dans un des restaurants de la petite rue des Bouchers (7) et essayer une spécialité de Bruxelles, les fruits de mer, en particulier les huîtres, les moules et les langoustes. Et comme dessert, on peut prendre une gaufre—une autre spécialité culinaire de la ville. On la mange chaude, avec un peu de sucre. C'est délicieux!

L'après-midi, une promenade en ville révèle que Bruxelles est une ville de contrastes. Le moderne et l'ancien se juxtaposent (8) dans l'architecture de Bruxelles. On y trouve aussi bien des églises gothiques comme la cathédrale de Saint-Michel (9) que des gratte-ciel futuristes comme le Parlement européen.

(10) Bruxelles est la ville de la bande dessinée par excellence. Au Centre belge de la bande dessinée, (11) on retrouve des personnages célèbres, comme Lucky Luke (12) et Tintin. (13) Les aventures de Tintin ont tellement de succès qu'elles ont été traduites en plus de vingt langues!

La ville elle-même est un musée de la bande dessinée—des fresques énormes décorent les murs de nombreux bâtiments. (14)

Si on préfère l'art classique, on peut visiter le musée des Beaux-Arts (15) avec ses tableaux de Van Eyck, Brueghel et Rembrandt. Juste à côté, le musée d'Art moderne a une collection de peintures du dix-neuvième siècle et du vingtième siècle. Il ne faut pas manquer les célèbres œuvres du peintre belge Magritte.

Après une longue journée à Bruxelles, on retourne au centre-ville pour dîner au restaurant. Ce soir, on mange à l'Ogenblik, dans la galerie royale Saint-Hubert. (16)

Après le dîner, pourquoi ne pas faire un tour de Bruxelles illuminé? C'est magnifique! (17)

Notes culturelles

(1) Montage (selected shots)

- **La Grand-Place** of Brussels is known for its magnificent architecture. Originally a simple market square with small wooden houses surrounding it, **la Grand-Place** gradually became the center of town. Beginning in the 15th century, powerful families started building stone mansions near the square. In the following centuries, very ornate houses, called guild and corporation houses, were built around **la Grand-Place.** In those days, cities had guilds for different trades (drapers, carpenters, tanners, brewers, millers, boatmen, etc.). The political clout of these guilds was measured by the beauty of their headquarters, which explains the ornamental facades, gilded gables, and numerous statues on these buildings.
- The King's House (**la maison du Roi**) in the Grand-Place was never a king's residence, despite its name. Built on the site of an old bread market, the building was used for the management of what was then a dukedom. Originally named **la maison du Duc,** the house was later renamed **la maison du Roi.** It is today the Museum of the City of Brussels and is devoted to all aspects of the city's history.

(2) Construction of the beautiful City Hall (**l'hôtel de Ville**) began in 1402. Its impressive Gothic tower was built in 1449. After the destruction of Brussels in 1695, only the tower and the outside walls remained. Restoration began immediately and continued over the next centuries. Hundreds of decorative little statues representing the dukes and duchesses who ruled the dukedom between the 6th and 16th centuries now adorn the façade. Today, the town hall is still the seat of the mayor of Brussels.

(3) **Le palais de la Nation** is an 18th-century building that houses the Belgian Parliament (Senate and House of Representatives). Note the two flags in front of the building: the black, yellow, and red flag of Belgium on the left, and, on the right, the blue flag of the European Union with its twelve yellow stars.

Some background information:

In 1970, Belgium became a federal state composed of three regions:

- Wallonia (**la région wallone**) to the South, where French and some German are spoken
- Flanders (**la région flamande**) in the Northern part of the country, where Dutch is spoken
- Brussels-Capital (**la région de Bruxelles-capitale**), where French and Dutch are spoken

Each of these regions has its own House of Representatives and Senate. The Federal government is formed from elected members of the House of Representatives.

Although the king has certain powers, all his political acts must be approved by his ministers. Therefore, the role of the king is mostly symbolic—he represents Belgium and all Belgians and is a symbol of unity. King Albert II has been **le roi des Belges** since 1993.

In 1958, Brussels was selected to become the seat of **la Communauté Économique Européenne,** now known as the European Union. Today, Brussels hosts five administrative branches of the European Union.

- It is the seat of **la Commission européenne,** which defends the general interest of the Union.
- Together with Luxembourg, it is the seat of **Le Conseil de l'Union européenne,** which makes decisions concerning foreign affairs, finances, education, telecommunications, and so on.
- **Le Parlement européen,** which, in cooperation with **le Conseil,** is responsible for decisions about budget and the adoption of European laws meets in Brussels and in Strasbourg, France.
- It is the seat of **le Comité économique et social européen,** which ensures representation of the different economic, social, and professional organizations—employers, workers and various interest groups—in the Union.
- It is also the seat of **le Comité des Régions,** which ensures that local and regional authorities are represented in the European Union.

(4) Belgium has three official languages: French, Dutch, and German.

(5) **La galerie royale Saint-Hubert,** which officially opened in 1847, is divided into three sections: the King's Gallery, the Queen's Gallery, and a smaller Princes' Gallery. The lower level is occupied by shops; the upper floors are apartments. In the 19th century, the concept of a covered shopping gallery for the upper classes was popular, and **la galerie royale Saint-Hubert** became a center of everyday life. Today its luxurious shops and beautiful cafés are still very popular.

(6) For more information about the famous **Manneken-Pis,** you may wish to refer to the cultural readings on the CD-ROM.

(7) Two blocks from **la Grand-Place,** in the center of the former medieval town, the cobblestoned **rue des Bouchers** and the nearby **petite rue des Bouchers** are closed to traffic. Remarkably, virtually every one of the quaint narrow houses in these streets is now a restaurant. Frequented by street musicians, both streets are renowned for their colorful atmosphere.

(8) The first World's Fair after World War II took place in Brussels in 1958. Forty-six countries were represented, and most pavilions looked futuristic. **L'Atomium,** a gigantic structure representing an atom magnified 165 billion times, was one of the most spectacular exhibits. Each sphere of the atom is sixty feet across, and connecting tubes allow visitors to go from sphere to sphere. There are shops, museums, restaurants, and an observation deck inside.

(9) Construction of **la cathédrale Saint-Michel** (also known as **la cathédrale Saint-Michel et Sainte-Gudule**) began in 1226. It lasted three hundred years, which explains the variety of its architectural styles: Roman, Gothic, Renaissance. Its interior is light and airy with stained glass windows that have survived the wars. One of these windows, in particular, dates from 1528.

(10) Gaston Lagaffe and his cat are popular comic book characters. Gaston's creator is the Brussels native André Franquin (1923-1997). Gaston is a lazy and very clumsy young man with a tender heart. He is also very inventive, but most of his creations bring confusion and destruction to the publishing offices where he works. **Gaffe,** in French, means *blunder*.

(11) **Le Centre belge de la bande dessinée,** housed in a beautiful Art Nouveau–style building constructed in 1906, is dedicated to Belgian comic book authors who began their professional careers between 1929 and 1959. The museum has a collection of original drawings, exhibits explaining how cartoons are created, a library, and temporary exhibits focusing on specific artists.

(12) The shadow is that of **Lucky Luke,** the lonesome cowboy who is the hero of a comic book series that parodies the Wild West. Lucky Luke is known to fire a gun faster than his own shadow. He fights crime and injustice, often caused by the four evil, but comical, Dalton brothers. Lucky Luke's creator is Maurice de Bévère, also known as Morris (1923-2001).

(13) **Tintin,** a famous comic book character, is a young reporter by trade, but he is also an adventurer and a detective. He is courageous, reasonable, logical, as well as modest. His adventures have taken him all over the world and even beyond (*Objectif Lune*). Some other **Tintin** characters are:

- the good-hearted and reliable **Capitaine Haddock,** seen just before Lucky Luke's shadow. He is mostly known for enjoying whiskey and swearing a lot.
- two clumsy and unlucky detectives, **Dupond and Dupont,** who are not related but look alike. The bowler hats and canes on display in the museum are part of the official "uniform" of the Dupond and Dupont characters.

Tintin's creator, Georges Remi, is also known as Hergé (1907-1983).

(14) There are 25 murals and statues in the streets of Brussels. The first of the four murals seen on the video shows Ric Hochet, created by the artists Tibet and Duchâteau. It was painted in 1992. The second mural shown in the video was actually the first outdoor cartoon mural painted in Brussels. It was done in 1991 and represents a character named Broussaille, created by artist Frank Pé. The third mural of Bob and Bobette was created in 1995 by artist Willy Vandesteen. The final mural, also created in 1995, shows Néron, who was the creation of Marc Sleen.

(15) The Royal Museums of Fine Arts (**Les musées royaux des Beaux-Arts**) are composed of:

- **le musée d'Art ancien,** which houses paintings, sculptures, and drawings from the 15th to 18th centuries, many of them by Flemish artists
- **le musée d'Art moderne,** which contains art dating from the end of the 18th century to the modern period. This museum has a collection of Belgian and French impressionist paintings, Belgian surrealist and contemporary pieces, as well as an entire room dedicated to the works of Magritte.

(16) **L'Ogenblik,** which means "blink of an eye," is a trendy restaurant located in the Princes' Gallery of **la galerie royale Saint-Hubert.** Its classic French menu can be found on the Web.

(17) **Le parc du Cinquantenaire**, which hosts a large museum complex, was created for the 1880 exhibit, in honor of the 50th anniversary of Belgium's independence from the Netherlands. For the 75th anniversary of Belgium's independence, an **arc de Triomphe,** with a triple arch, was built at the center of this 90-acre park.

Escales francophones—Les Antilles (après Chapitre 12)

Introduction: Montage (1)

Nous voici à la Martinique, découverte pour les Européens par Christophe Colomb (2) en 1502. On l'appelle «l'île aux Fleurs». Cette île tropicale se trouve dans la mer des Caraïbes. Sa végétation est riche et ses paysages variés: montagnes, champs de canne à sucre et plages de sable noir ou de sable blanc. (3)

La capitale de la Martinique est Fort-de-France, une grande ville avec à peu près cent mille habitants. C'est le centre économique et politique de la Martinique.

Depuis 1946, la Martinique est un département français et le drapeau tricolore flotte sur de nombreux bâtiments. (4) Le français est la langue officielle, mais les Martiniquais parlent créole avant de parler français. (5) (6)

Le soleil se lève sur la baie de Fort-de-France. On voit le bateau-navette qui amène en ville les habitants qui vivent de l'autre côté de la baie. (7) C'est le matin et la ville s'anime. (8) Comme dans tous les pays du monde, les enfants vont à l'école. La Martinique a un système scolaire complet qui va de la maternelle à l'université. Presque toutes les écoles publiques et privées imposent un uniforme aux élèves.

Les adultes vont aux marchés du centre-ville: il y a le marché aux épices de la rue Isambert, le marché aux fruits et aux légumes et, près de la rivière Madame, le marché aux poissons où on peut acheter les produits de la mer. (9)

Cette magnifique bibliothèque, qui est proche du marché, porte le nom de Schœlcher, un écrivain abolitionniste français. (10)

La Martinique, c'est aussi les plages avec des sports nautiques comme la planche à voile et le kayak de mer.

À la Martinique, on est toujours entouré des couleurs vives de la vie quotidienne. La mer, les montagnes et les villages pittoresques donnent à la Martinique son caractère tranquille et chaleureux. (11)

Mais une fois par an, les Martiniquais célèbrent la vie et toutes ses couleurs avec le Carnaval. (12) Pendant quatre jours, toute l'île fait la fête! C'est un spectacle pittoresque où tout le monde participe. Des gens et des chars défilent dans les rues au rythme de la musique antillaise. Tout le monde est déguisé et les costumes sont très beaux.

On s'amuse bien jusqu'au mercredi des Cendres qui marque le début du carême catholique.

Après le bruit et le chaos du Carnaval, on peut quitter la ville pour visiter d'anciennes plantations et des monuments historiques, comme la sucrerie-purgerie, au domaine de la Pagerie. (13) C'est dans ce domaine, en 1763, qu'est née Joséphine, l'épouse de l'empereur Napoléon.

Si on préfère se détendre au soleil, on peut aller à la plage pour bronzer et se baigner.

À la fin de la journée, la plage devient plus calme et, juste avant le coucher du soleil, le dernier bateau-navette quitte le quai.

Notes culturelles

(1) Montage (selected shots)

- Note the colorful boats moored along the waterfront. **La rivière Madame,** on the west side of town, is the river on which fishermen arrive when they bring their catch to the fish market, located on **le canal Levassor.**

- The steel drum, called **le steel pan** or **le pan** in the Caribbean Islands, is one of the common instruments used in Calypso, or "Kaiso," music. In Martinique, music and dance are an important part of local culture and traditions. Other favorite styles of music are zouk, reggae, salsa, Caribbean jazz, biguine, mazurka, to name only a few. The music from Martinique has been influenced by European, African, and American music.

(2) The white-domed church, nestled in the mountains just outside Fort-de-France, is **l'église de Balata.** Built in 1923, the church is a scaled-down replica of the Sacré Cœur Basilica in Paris.

(3) Almost all black volcanic sand beaches are situated in the northern part of the island. White sand beaches can be found in the south.

(4) The buildings shown flying the French flag are **l'hôtel de la préfecture** (inspired by **le Petit Trianon** at Versailles), **la mairie,** and **le Fort Saint-Louis,** the first edifice constructed to defend the bay of Fort de France in 1638.

Some background information:

Christopher Columbus landed on the island of Martinique in 1502, but the first settlers, who were French, did not arrive until 1635. They established a settlement that would later become the first capital of Martinique: Saint-Pierre. In 1636, the king of France authorized the use of slaves on the island. These slaves, who came from Africa, worked on the sugar cane plantations. In 1745, Martinique had 80,000 inhabitants; 65,000 of them were slaves. It was thanks to Victor Schœlcher that a proclamation of emancipation was finally signed in 1848, bringing slavery to an end on the island.

In 1902, Saint-Pierre, the capital, was destroyed during the eruption of the volcano *Montagne Pelée*. 30,000 people died. Fort-de-France then became the capital of Martinique. In 1946, the status of Martinique changed: No longer a simple French colony, it became an overseas department of France, and in 1974, its status was further raised to that of region of France. Residents of Martinique are French citizens, they vote in French elections, and they have senators and deputies representing them in the French National Assembly in Paris.

(5) The imposing **Cathédrale Saint-Louis** stands on the site of earlier cathedrals that were destroyed in fires, hurricanes, and earthquakes. This last cathedral, designed by the French architect Henri Picq (also responsible for the Schœlcher Library and the covered market), was built in 1895. Its metal framework and spire are impressive. Special attention was given to the interior of the cathedral, which is luminous. The stained glass windows retrace the history of the island and of the edifice.

(6) Although French is the official language, Creole is widely used on the island. Creole dates back to the days of slavery. Slaves borrowed some of the French words used by their masters, and they mixed them with their own African vocabulary and grammar. Today, Creole is still the native language of many **Martiniquais.**

A Creole proverb: *Tout manjé bon pou manjé, tout pawol pa bon pou di.* (**Toute nourriture est bonne à manger, toute parole n'est pas bonne à dire.**)

(7) "**La Foyalaise**" is the name of one of the boats that tourists and residents take to cross the Fort-de-France Bay or to go on sea excursions. The noun **Foyalais(e)** comes from **Fo'oyalais** which was a term derived from the name of those who lived in Fort-Royal, the original name of Fort-de-France. The inhabitants of Fort-de-France, which is also known as **la cité foyalaise,** are called **les Foyalais** and **Foyalaises.**

(8) Traditional clothing (ample Madras cotton skirts with coordinating head scarves) is still worn by some of the market vendors as well as a few older **Martiniquaises.** European fashion is favored by the younger generation.

(9) There are several markets in Fort-de-France. **Le grand marché** is a covered market where one can purchase a variety of products, including spices, produce, flowers, baskets, and hats, as well as rum and various elixirs. Another is **le marché aux poissons** where fishermen sell their catch every morning. Right next to the fish market is **le marché aux légumes,** where locally grown fruit and vegetables are on display. All are open daily from 6 am to 3 pm and contribute to the charm and animation of the town.

(10) The very ornate **Bibliothèque Schœlcher** (named for Victor Schœlcher, who was instrumental in abolishing slavery in 1848), was originally built for the 1889 World's Fair in Paris. It was then dismantled, shipped, and reassembled at its present site. The library still owns the collection of books donated by Schœlcher, whose wish was for culture to be accessible and free to all.

(11) **Les Anses d'Arlet** are composed of **la Petite Anse d'Arlet,** a fishermen's village, and **la Grande Anse d'Arlet,** whose beautiful beach is popular with vacationers. They are located 39 miles south of Fort-de-France.

(12) For more information about **le Carnaval,** you may wish to refer to the cultural readings provided on the CD-ROM.

(13) **Le domaine de la Pagerie,** the estate where Napoleon's first wife, Empress Josephine, grew up, is located in the town of Les Trois-Îlets, south of Fort-de-France. Josephine's parents owned this large plantation and had 300 slaves. The ruins of the **sucrerie-purgerie** are still visible today. There, sugar was purged of its syrup, and the syrup was used to produce rum.

The museum (**le musée de la Pagerie**), devoted to Josephine, contains memorabilia, furniture, portraits, and a love letter Napoleon wrote to her in 1796. The museum is located in a stone building that was once the estate kitchen.

Index